THE BEGINNINGS OF ANTI-JEWISH LEGISLATION

THE BEGINNINGS OF ANTI-JEWISH LEGISLATION

The 1920 Numerus Clausus Law in Hungary

Mária M. Kovács

CEU PRESS

Central European University Press

Budapest—Vienna—New York

Published in 2023 by
Central European University Press

Nádor utca 9, H-1051 Budapest, Hungary
Tel: +36-1-327-3138 or 327-3000
E-mail: ceupress@press.ceu.edu
Website: www.ceupress.com

Cover and book design by Sebastian Stachowski

ISBN 978-963-386-620-7 (hardback)
ISBN 978-963-386-621-4 (ebook)

Library of Congress Cataloging-in-Publication Data

Names: Kovács, M. Mária, 1953-2020, author.
Title: The beginnings of anti-Jewish legislation : the 1920 numerus clausus law in Hungary / M. Mária Kovács.
Other titles: Törvénytől sújtva. Eng
Description: New York : Central European University Press, 2023. | Includes bibliographical references and index.
Identifiers: LCCN 2023047145 (print) | LCCN 2023047146 (ebook) | ISBN 9789633866207 (hardback) | ISBN 9789633866214 (adobe pdf)
Subjects: LCSH: Jews--Legal status, laws, etc.--Hungary--History--20th c century. | Numerus clausus--Hungary--History--20th century. | Jews--Education--Hungary--History--20th century. | Antisemitism--Hungary--History--20th century. | Race defilement (Nuremberg Laws of 1935) | Civil service--Hungary--History--20th century. | BISAC: HISTORY / Jewish | LAW / Legal History
Classification: LCC KKF3147.3 .K6813 2023 (print) | LCC KKF3147.3 (ebook) | DDC 342.43908/73--dc23/eng/20231012
LC record available at https://lccn.loc.gov/2023047145
LC ebook record available at https://lccn.loc.gov/2023047146

Contents

Acronyms

BME	Budapesti Műszaki és Gazdaságtudományi Egyetem (Budapest University of Technology and Economics)
ELTE	Eötvös Loránd Tudományegyetem (Eötvös Loránd University)
ÉME	Ébredő Magyarok Egyesülete (Association of Awakening Hungarians)
KNEP	Keresztény Nemzeti Egyesülés Pártja (Christian National Union Party)
MEFHOSZ	Magyar Egyetemisták és Főiskolai Hallgatók Országos Szövetsége (National Union of Hungarian University and College Students)
MNL OL	Magyar Nemzeti Levéltár Országos Levéltára (Hungarian National Archives)
MNM	Magyar Nemzeti Múzeum (Hungarian National Museum)
MTI	Magyar Távirati Iroda (Hungarian Telegraph Agency)
PTE	Pécsi Tudományegyetem (University of Pécs)
SOTE	Semmelweis Orvostudományi Egyetem (Semmelweis University of Medicine)

List of Figures

Tables

Foreword to the English Translation

Michael L. Miller

When Mária M. Kovács's groundbreaking book on the *numerus clausus* was first published in 2012, Hungarian intellectuals were in the midst of a heated and rancorous debate about the place of antisemitism in Hungary's twentieth-century history. This debate unfolded not only in the public sphere but also in the town square, as right-wing politicians, activists, and provocateurs clamored to erect statues of problematic historical figures—such as Ottokár Prohászka, Pál Teleki, Bálint Hóman, Kunó Klebelsberg, and Miklós Horthy—who were complicit, in one way or another, in fostering the shrill antisemitic climate that pervaded Hungary in the interwar years. The push for the rehabilitation of such controversial figures—and for their inclusion in a new, right-wing, conservative Hungarian pantheon—does not necessarily translate into a fervent endorsement of their antisemitic beliefs, but it does attest to a willful and worrisome tendency to ignore their antisemitism, downplay its significance, or deny its outright existence.

Mária M. Kovács was deeply disturbed by the attempts to rehabilitate these Horthy-era figures, and she countered the disingenuous and deliberately dissembling arguments of their apologists by dispelling, once and for all, the convenient myth that Law No. XXV of 1920—the so-called "numerus clausus law"—was purely a benign form of positive discrimination devoid of any antisemitic intent (or content). Law No. XXV of 1920, with its rather anodyne title ("On the regulation of enrollment at the universities of arts and sciences, the University of Technology, the Faculty of Economics of the University of Budapest, and law academies") was, in fact, the first antisemitic law in interwar Europe, and its aim was to limit the number of Jews enrolled at Hungarian institutions of higher learning. The drafters of the law did their utmost to hide its true purpose, because they rightly feared that the League of Nations would consider an explicit Jewish quota to be in violation of Paragraph 58 of the

Treaty of Trianon (June 4, 1920), which guaranteed equality before the law to all Hungarian nationals "without distinction as to race, language or religion." Bishop Ottokár Prohászka, the main idealogue of the numerus clausus, proposed a "legal trick" that was intended to offer enough plausible deniability to fend off accusations of anti-Jewish discrimination. He proposed a law that would ostensibly apply equally to all "nationalities and races" without even mentioning the word "Jew."

Mari (as her friends called her) was cautious not to argue that the numerus clausus led inexorably to the Holocaust. Her first book, *Liberal Professions and Illiberal Politics: Hungary from the Habsburgs to the Holocaust* (OUP, 1997) examined the radicalization of professional groups (doctors, lawyers, and engineers) in the interwar period, showing how these supposed bulwarks of liberalism adopted, to varying degrees, exclusionary, antisemitic policies that increasingly demanded the removal of Jews (or people identified as Jews) from Hungary's economic, professional, and intellectual life. Such exclusionary politics were neither a necessary nor a sufficient condition for the eventual extermination of Hungarian Jewry, but Mária M. Kovács understood full well that the successful drive in 1920 to introduce a Jewish quota at institutions of higher learning helped prepare the ground, both legally and psychologically, for the antisemitic laws (the so-called "Jewish Laws") of 1938–1942 that gradually excluded Jews from all sectors of Hungarian public life.

Mária M. Kovács referred to the 1920 numerus clausus law as the first Jewish Law, an appellation usually reserved for the 1938 Law "on the more efficient assurance of equilibrium in social and economic life," the first of Hungary's four "Jewish Laws," which were inspired by the Nuremberg Laws—and in the case of the Second, Third, and Fourth Jewish Laws—directly modeled on them. The numerus clausus law, she argued, prefigured these Jewish Laws, because it "elevated to the plane of government policy the idea that the so-called 'Jewish question' could, and should, only be resolved by extraordinary legal measures applied exclusively to the Jews." It abrogated the principle of equal rights that had been enshrined into law in 1867, and as such, it marked the abrupt reversal of Jewish emancipation in Hungary. Moreover, as Mária M. Kovács has shown, the law's implementation decree deemed "Israelites" to be "a separate nationality," thereby changing their status from members of a religious confession to members of a separate nationality (or race).

Mari's insistence that the numerus clausus law was Hungary's first Jewish Law was not just a question of semantics. By emphasizing the continuity between the 1920 law and the "Jewish Laws" of the late 1930s and early 1940s, she demonstrated that segments of Hungarian society bear moral responsibility for the persecution of its Jews, that Hungary's endemic antisemitism cannot be dismissed as a German import, and that responsibility for Hungary's anti-Jewish laws and policies cannot be blamed solely on political pressure from abroad. In her scholarship and in her activism, she prodded Hungarian society into a reckoning with its difficult past, a reckoning that has, in recent years, given way to a disturbing tendency, especially on the part of the Hungarian government, to whitewash and distort the darker chapters in twentieth-century Hungary.

In July 2014, the Hungarian government unveiled—in the dark of night—the Memorial for Victims of the German Occupation, a controversial monument on Budapest's Freedom Square (*Szabadság tér*), which portrays Hungary as the innocent victim of (Nazi) German aggression, implicitly absolving Hungarian authorities of any responsibility for the persecution and extermination of the country's Jews. In response, a grassroot movement of intellectuals, artists, and citizen activists organized demonstrations, lectures, and even a counter-monument (a so-called "living memorial"), offering a corrective to the official falsification of Hungary's history. Mária M. Kovács took active part in this protest movement, and she fought against more recent efforts to rehabilitate Klebelsberg, Hóman, Teleki, Prohászka, and other Horthy-era Hungarians who supported or defended the numerus clausus, interwar Hungary's first antisemitic law.

This book first appeared in Hungarian in 2012, as *Törvénytől sújtva: A numerus clausus Magyarországon, 1920–1945* (Down by law: The numerus clausus in Hungary, 1920–1945), borrowing its title from Jim Jarmusch's 1986 film classic. Unfortunately, Mária M. Kovács (1953–2020) did not live to see the English edition of her book, but she did have a chance to review the translation, which was carefully and caringly prepared by Mark Baczoni, an alumnus of the Nationalism Studies Program at Central European University, which Prof. Kovács founded in 1998 and chaired for many years. May this book be a "living memorial" to a beloved historian, teacher, and colleague.

Foreword

The numerus clausus law passed in Hungary in 1920 elevated anti-Semitism to an institutional level. Its effects cannot be measured merely by the number of students excluded from higher education. With the coming of the numerus clausus, a new political thinking came to dominate Hungary. According to this thinking, the so-called "Jewish question" in Hungary could only be resolved through special laws applied only to Jews, laws that changed the legal status of Jews and denied their equality before the law. In this sense, the numerus clausus was just as much an (anti-)Jewish law as the so-called "Jewish Laws" of the 1930s. In essence, then, the numerus clausus was the first Jewish Law in Hungary.

This book presents the history of the law from its beginnings in 1920, through its amendment in 1928, the reintroduction of the Jewish quota in 1939, and finally its abolition in 1945. The introduction summarizes the main theses, while chapter one deals with the origins of the law. Chapter two looks at its impact, and chapter three addresses the domestic and international political background of the amendment of 1928, as well as the developments of the 1930s and 1940s.

In writing this history of the numerus clausus, I relied primarily on the work of the following: Andor Ladányi, Lajos Szabolcsi, Katalin N. Szegvári, Victor Karady, Tibor Hajdu, Péter Sipos, Róbert Barta, Csaba Fazekas, Róbert Kerepeszki, Claudia K. Farkas, and Péter Tibor Nagy. In surveying the age in general, the works of the following were of help: István Bibó, Randolph L. Braham, László Karsai, Ignác Romsics, Zsuzsa L. Nagy, Miklós Lackó, Miklós Szabó, Gábor Gyáni, Miklós Zeidler, Krisztián Ungváry, János Gyurgyák, and Balázs Ablonczy. The digitized archives of the National Archives and the Hungarian Telegraph Agency (MTI) became available just at the time of my research. These are searchable not merely around specific dates but also in different ways, bridging the entire period. By doing so, I happened upon numerous links that would have been much slower to find with traditional archival research, had I found them at all.

I would like to thank Vera Pécsi for doing the chronology. Judit Molnár and Katalin Jalsovszky helped choose the illustrations and I could hardly have completed this book without them. I would also like to thank Gábor Sándor, Randolph L. Braham, István Deák, András Kovács, András Gerő, Judit Molnár, László Karsai, Judit Lakner, György Csepeli, Szabolcs Pogonyi, Antal Örkény, Katalin Dezsényi, and Attila Pók for their careful reading of the manuscript, their questions and advice. Further thanks go to Dóra Földes and Péter Kiss, Balázs Martonffy, and Dániel Rapp for their help in preparing the manuscript and my students Júlia Boda and Adrienn Győry for their assistance with my research; also to Márta Schneider, Judit Klopfer, and Anna Egyed for their help with the publishing process.

Budapest, July 2012

Introduction

The rights withdrawn from Jews under the quota system established in September 1920 by the numerus clausus law were ones that had previously been thought to enshrine the unalienable equal rights of Jews in Hungarian society. The law elevated to the plane of government policy the idea that the so-called "Jewish question" could, and should, only be resolved by extraordinary legal measures applied exclusively to Jews, or in other words, by special "Jewish Laws," as Hungary's anti-Jewish laws were called. For this reason, the significance of the numerus clausus went beyond the walls of the universities and signaled the start of a new period for Hungarian Jews, one fraught with danger.

The law establishing the new system of university admissions (Law No. XXV of 1920) did away with the previous system, under which it was sufficient to have a valid secondary school diploma in order to apply for university studies. The law entitled the Minister of Education to determine how many students would be given places at university each year. This in itself would not necessarily have included differences discriminative towards Jews, since it merely meant that the number of undergraduates who could attend university in a given year was predetermined. At around the same time as Hungary, university quotas were introduced in Norway, Finland, and Scotland, without being coupled to any form of discrimination. The Hungarian numerus clausus law defined the concept of a fixed number system thus: "The number of students who may be admitted to each faculty (department) shall be determined by the Minister of Religion and Public Education on the recommendation of the relevant faculty (or, in the case of the University of Technology, the Council)."[1]

1 For the full text of Law No. XXV of 1920, see the Appendix to this volume.

The nationalities quota

The discriminatory mechanism of the numerus clausus law was established in its third clause, which introduced the system of quotas for nationalities. According to this system only as many members of each "nationality" or "racial group" could be admitted to university as was proportionate with their share of the overall population.[2] Since the proportion of Jews among the population as a whole was at 6 percent in 1920, whereas their numbers among university students hovered around 25 percent before World War I and exceeded 30 percent by 1918, it should already be clear that the majority of Jewish students would be shut out of higher education as a result of the law.

An explicit Jewish quota

Clause three, on paper, introduced limits that applied to all nationalities. However, with the exception of the Jews, no other minority was affected, since the youth of no other minority made up a larger proportion of university students than their quota allowed for (see table 1).[3] As a result, the quota system would not have had any ramifications for them, even if the prescribed proportions were enforced.

But the authors of the law were never really serious about the system of nationality quotas. Its sole purpose, stemming from international concerns, was to be able to hide this anti-Jewish action in a law that seemingly applied in equal measure to all nationalities. In reality, however—apart from the anti-Jewish measures—the nationality quota system was never really introduced.

The Council of the University of Budapest[4] established as early as 1922 that the nationality quotas in no way influenced admissions, and that the law was used exclusively against Jewish students. The University Council established that applicants were not obliged to present documents "proving their nationality" and "applicants did not declare verbally whether they are Hungarian, German, Romanian, etc. . . . and the University itself did not look into this."[5]

2 For the full text of the third clause, see page 226 in the Appendix to this volume.

3 Eötvös Loránd Tudományegyetem Levéltára (Eötvös Loránd University Archives, hereafter ELTE Archives), Rector's Office, Minutes of the University Council, 1922/I., ordinary meeting.

4 Founded in 1635 in Nagyszombat (today Trnava, Slovakia), the Royal Hungarian University was moved to Buda and later to Pest in the 1770s and 1780s. After the merging of the two cities in 1873, the institution gained the name University of Budapest. In 1921, it was renamed Royal Hungarian Pázmány Péter University, a name that was changed again in 1950 to Eötvös Loránd University.

5 ELTE Archives, Rector's Office, Minutes of the University Council, 1922/I, ordinary meeting.

Table 1. The quota system included in the implementation decree of the numerus clausus law compared to the overall number of students in higher education, showing figures for native languages and Jewish/non-Jewish students in the academic year 1918-19

	Proportions of the prescribed quota (%)	Number of students by mother tongue*	Proportion of students by mother tongue*	Deviation of the actual rate from the quota rates
Hungarian	79.4	17,753	96.23	+16.83
German	9.4	350	1.89	-7.51
Slovak	2.1	36	0.19	-1.91
Romanian	0.6	140	0.75	+0.15
Ruthenian	0.0	7	0.04	+0.04
Croatian	1.1	26	0.14	-0.96
Serbian	0.3	73	0.39	-0.76
Other	1.1	64	0.34	
Jewish	6.0			
Total	100%	18,449	100%	
	Proportion of the prescribed quota in non-Jewish/Jewish distribution (%)	**Number of non-Jewish/Jewish students in 1918-1919**	**Proportion of non-Jewish/Jewish students in 1918-1919 (%)**	**Deviation of the actual rate from the quota rates**
Non-Jewish	94	11,730	63.58	-30.42
Jewish	6	6,719	36.42	+30.42

* Jews feature among native Hungarian speakers in the data of the Hungarian Central Statistical Office.
Source: *Statisztikai Évkönyv*, 1922.

Or in other words, as the Council itself established, during the admissions process "the proportions of nationalities or racial groups were only applied in so far as made it possible to determine whether the applicant is Jewish, or not."[6] Thus it was the council of one of the most relevant institutions, the university of the nation's capital, which put into words what everyone already knew—namely, that the system of nationality quotas was, in fact, nothing more than a Jewish quota hidden within a nationality quota system.[7]

The drafters of the law proceeded formally in this way at the recommendation of Bishop Ottokár Prohászka, a leading figure of Hungarian Christian Socialism and a prominent anti-Semite, in order to avoid the accusation to be expected from the League of Nations that the numerus clausus was born of

6 ELTE Archives, Rector's Office, Minutes of the University Council, 1922/I, ordinary meeting.

7 This was in fact articulated in the 1920s by critics of the law, such as the former minister of education of the Fejérváry government, who said that the law "conceals its hidden goal under the cloak of nationalities and ethnicity . . . this goal is to restrict Jewish youths from entering higher education." Pál Bethlen, ed., *A magyar zsidóság almanachja* (Budapest: Franklin, 1925), 64.

anti-Semitic purposes. As István Haller, the minister of education in the first Teleki government, expressed it in the spring of 1920, the law reflected an effort to find a solution to the Jewish question that would "achieve the end itself, but which would be unassailable and for which the country and the nation would not face any difficulties anywhere."[8]

It is thus an erroneous belief that has maintained itself in the publicist literature on this subject for almost a century that the expression "Jewish" does not appear anywhere in the text of the numerus clausus law. Enactment of the law was determined by the corresponding implementation decree. And in this, not only does the expression "Jewish" feature, but it is also specified that Jews—in contrast with the constitutional rules then in force—should be regarded not as a religion, but as a nationality. In other words, the explicitly Jewish quota was not brought into being by the main text of the law itself, but by the accompanying ministerial decree which clarified how to implement the law.[9] This included a table where the eight nationalities affected by the quota were presented (see figure 1 and table 2). The provision that "Israelites are [to be] treated as a separate nationality," revealed the true intention of the law: the creation of a Jewish quota.

Thus, according to the implementation decree, "Israelites" had to be treated as a separate nationality. This indicated rather alarmingly that the law had selected a group of citizens for whom the same rules did not apply as to all the others. So, despite language being the basis of the nationality quota system, when it came to Jews, their native language made no difference whatsoever. They had to be considered—irrespective of their native tongue—a "separate nationality," even if their native language was Hungarian. Thus, with these few simple words, the clause changed the previous legal status of Jews and—without any specific explanation—declared them to be a nationality rather than a religious group.

The process was, in both form and content, illegal. As to the question of who was to be considered Jewish from the point of view of the implementation of this law, neither the law nor the accompanying implementation decree provided an answer. This error of omission led to a perpetual state of scandal for the universities, since even different faculties of the same university inter-

8 Parliamentary session of April 29, 1920, in *Az 1920. évi február hó 16-ára összehívott nemzetgyűlés naplója* (Budapest: Athenaeum Irodalmi és Nyomdai Részvénytársulat, 1920), vol. 2: 395.

9 Decree no. 123.033 of 1920 of the Royal Hungarian Minister of Religion and Public Education, in *Magyarországi rendeletek tára, 1920* (Budapest: Pesti Könyvnyomda Részvénytársaság, 1920), 1455–60.

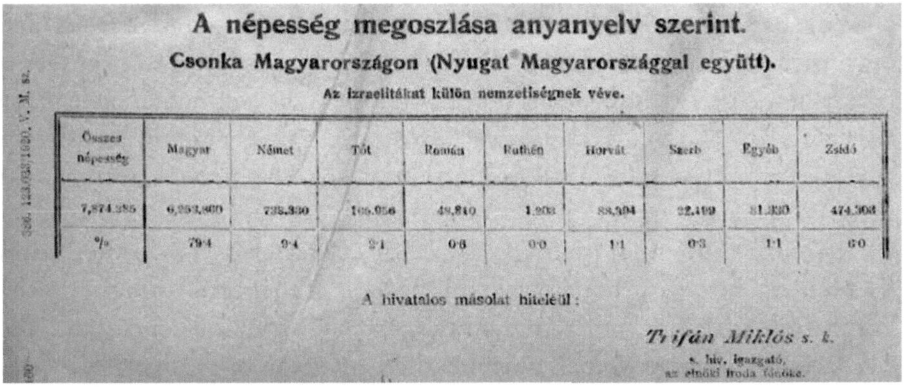

A népesség megoszlása anyanyelv szerint.

Csonka Magyarországon (Nyugat Magyarországgal együtt).

Az izraelitákat külön nemzetiségnek véve.

Összes népesség	Magyar	Német	Tót	Román	Ruthén	Horvát	Szerb	Egyéb	Zsidó
7,874.385	6,253,860	738,330	165,956	48,810	1,203	88,394	22,199	81,330	474,303
%	79·4	9·4	2·1	0·6	0·0	1·1	0·3	1·1	6·0

A hivatalos másolat hiteléül:

Trifán Miklós s. k.

h. hiv. igazgató,
az elnöki iroda főnöke.

Figure 1./Table 2. Appendix to the implementation decree of the numerus clausus law: "Distribution of the population by mother tongue in post-Trianon Hungary (including Western Hungary),"* with the note "Israelites treated as a separate nationality." Source: Decree no. 123.033 of 1920 of the Royal Hungarian Minister of Religion and Public Education, in Magyarországi rendeletek tára, 1920 (Budapest: Pesti Könyvnyomda Részvénytársaság, 1920), 1460.

Total Population	Hungarian	German	Slovak	Romanian	Ruthenian	Croatian	Serbian	Other	Jewish
7,874,385	6,253,860	738,330	165,956	48,810	1,203	88,394	22,199	81,330	474,303
percent	79.4	9.4	2.1	0.6	0.0	1.1	0.3	1.1	6.0

* Western Hungary refers here to regions disputed between Hungary and Austria, at that point under occupation by Hungarian paramilitary forces.

preted the law differently. Some faculties, for example the Faculty of Law of the Budapest University, only applied the quota to those professing the Jewish faith, while other faculties, such as the Faculty of Medicine, considered applicants who had converted to Christianity but had Jewish "origins" to be "Jewish," family origin trumping religious belonging.

The university was unable to settle the debate within its own walls. The reason for this was not, of course, that there were not enough competent professors of law, but rather that the arguments about the interpretation of the Jewish quota were political, not legal. In 1922, the Council of the University of Budapest called the clause ordering the establishment of the Jewish quota a makeshift "scrap of paper" (*cédula*), stating that it was "obvious that both the parliament and the government wanted to transfer all the difficulties and unpleasantness of this affair onto the academic faculties."[10] The Council showed that the Jewish quota was in itself inconsistent since the legislators had created

10 ELTE Archives, Rector's Office, Minutes of the University Council, 1922/I, ordinary meeting.

it on the basis of the religious data in the census, but the "scrap of paper" left open the possibility that the universities could nevertheless count converted Jews as Jewish. This, however, cast doubt on the 6 percent quota, since if the legislators "were to count those of the Christian religion but of the Jewish race as Jewish too, then the overall proportion of Jews in the population would exceed 6 percent as well."[11]

The most influential politician in cultural matters at that time, Kunó Klebelsberg, however, thought that on the basis of the law of 1920, it was the Faculty of Medicine that had drawn the correct and logical conclusion. The legislature—declared Klebelsberg in parliament seven years after the law was passed—had the "explicit intention" in creating the numerus clausus law "to declare Jews a race. . . . For once Jews have been classified as a race, one cannot escape from race as one does, say, from a religious denomination by converting, or from a nationality by declaring oneself to be of another nationality."[12] In other words, Jews had to be classified according to their origins in order to prevent them from using religious or linguistic justifications for "escaping" the restrictions imposed upon them. Prime Minister István Bethlen also thought that the 1920 law classified Jews as a race or nationality. Nonetheless it is a fact that by the mid-1920s he had carefully distanced himself from this position and declared that "patriotic" Jews should be considered Hungarians of the Jewish religion. But even in 1925, he confirmed that the 1920 numerus clausus law changed the legal status of Jewry, regarding it not as a religion but as a race or nationality: "The law establishing the numerus clausus declared the Jews to be a racial group or a nationality, respectively. Of this there can be no doubt."[13]

Therefore, we can say that contrary to the frequently held interpretation in Hungarian historiography, discrimination on the basis of one's origins in Hungary did not start in 1939 with the so-called Second Jewish Law, but in 1920 with the explicit Jewish quota of the numerus clausus. This, with its chaotic legal background, created an opportunity for the Jewish quota to exclude not only those of the Jewish religion, but also those who had converted but had Jewish ancestors.

---

11 ELTE Archives, Rector's Office, Minutes of the University Council, 1922/I, ordinary meeting.

12 Minutes of the parliamentary session of February 23, 1928, in *Az 1927. évi január hó 25-ére hirdetett országgyűlés képviselőházának naplója* (Budapest: Athenaeum Irodalmi és Nyomdai Részvénytársulat, 1928), vol. 9: 198.

13 István Bethlen's speech at the parliamentary session of December 7, 1925, in *Az 1922. évi junius hó 16-ára hirdetett nemzetgyűlés naplója*, vol. 38: 223.

The risks and the double-talk

For a Hungary struggling with the heavy losses of World War I, the Jewish quota was a risky move, both domestically and abroad. In the aftermath of defeat, the goodwill of the Western Powers was needed in order to achieve Hungary's diplomatic goals, but state-level anti-Semitism damaged Hungary's reputation abroad and made it somewhat more difficult to raise the international loans necessary for Hungary's economic consolidation. This explains the unusual phenomenon that while in parliament and in the press the subject of the numerus clausus was accompanied by explicit and vicious anti-Semitic rhetoric, in government circles the topic was surrounded by a less than frank dissimulation and double-talk. For, on the one hand, no one in Hungary could—or did—have any doubt that the numerus clausus was clearly an anti-Jewish measure. As Lajos Méhely, a biology professor known for his anti-Semitic views put it, the quota system based on the proportions of the nationalities within the population overall was "too cautious, in that it goes out of its way not to shed light on the origin of the numerus clausus. . . . Even if I didn't come out and say it, you would all still know that one of the main, if not the only, goal and purpose of the numerus clausus is to prevent the unrestricted influx of Jewish students."[14]

On the other hand, the political leaders of the country—from international considerations—thought that these anti-Jewish intentions could not be discussed quite so openly, since the country had to maintain its respectability within the Western diplomatic scene. According to this way of thinking, the limits of anti-Semitic legislation were not defined by constitutional, legal, or humanitarian considerations, but rather by tactical considerations connected to the country's foreign policy. In other words, it was a matter of determining how far the Hungarian government could go with these anti-Semitic measures without the European Great Powers withdrawing their cooperation from the country. Alajos Kovács, ministerial advisor to the Statistical Office (and its president from 1929), described the need for this careful camouflage: "Those statesmen who today hold in their hands the future of the country . . . will have a difficult time resolving the Jewish question without making the philosemitic West angry at us."[15] In other words, these anti-Semitic measures had to be hidden within a legal framework that neither the international community nor the League of Nations could take exception to.

14 Ladányi, *Az egyetemi ifjúság*, 147.

15 Alajos Kovács, *A zsidóság térfoglalása Magyarországon* (Budapest: n.d., 1922), 53.

The tactical consideration of how best to camouflage the Jewish quota turned out not to be in vain after all. It made it possible for the Hungarian government to deny the discriminatory intention of the Jewish quota for a total of five years (until 1925) in international fora. It also allowed the Great Powers, who had an interest in Hungary's postwar recovery under the Bethlen government, to turn a blind eye to the matter. As late as the 1925 League of Nations meeting in Geneva, Klebelsberg, the minister of religion and education, tried to present the numerus clausus as a measure designed to protect the Jews, arguing that it guaranteed them at least a 6 percent level of participation.[16] The League—revising its former, milder, opinion—did not accept Klebelsberg's argument. The story does, however, illustrate that there were all sorts of tactical considerations behind the camouflaging of the Jewish quota.

Yet, the introduction of the law had risks not only in the international sphere, but also in domestic politics: it shook the feeling of security of the Jewish bourgeoisie, which played an important role in the Hungarian economy, and thus endangered the postwar economic recovery. As Lóránt Hegedűs, the minister of finance for the Teleki government stated: "Patriotic [Hungarian] Jews cannot effectively cooperate in attracting foreign investment to Hungary until we Christians have destroyed this law."[17] Apart from his moral objections, Lóránt Hegedűs's position was also determined by the fact that on October 10, 1920, his daughter Ilona (who had curly black hair and was then in the third year of her humanities degree) was physically assaulted in a corridor of the university by a group of students affiliated with the Association of Awakening Hungarians shouting "Jew! Jew!"[18]

The law adversely affected the position of the Hungarians in Transylvania who had become a minority. Romania closed a string of Hungarian schools in Transylvania, pointing to the numerus clausus law and saying that the posi-

---

16 Magyar Távirati Iroda (Hungarian Telegraph Agency, hereafter MTI) report on Klebelsberg's speech in Geneva, MTI News Release, December 10, 1925.

17 *Pester Lloyd*, Aug 1, 1926. Quoted in István Haller, *Harc a numerus clausus körül* (Budapest: n.d., 1926), 248.

18 MTI Confidential Notifications, October 28, 1920, 1. The Association of Awakening Hungarians (Ébredő Magyarok Egyesülete, ÉME) was a racist, anti-Semitic, far-right association founded in November 1918. Its leadership included prominent figures of the far right as Gyula Gömbös, Tibor Eckhardt, Pál Prónay, and Iván Héjjas. The goals of the association included the restoration of the historical borders of the Kingdom of Hungary, the preservation of the "purity of the Hungarian race" through anti-Jewish discrimination, among others. With a membership of several hundreds of thousands in the early 1920s, ÉME became a major political force that enjoyed significant popular support. Members of the association also carried out a number of atrocities, including deadly terror attacks, against Jews.

tion of the Hungarians in Romania was just like that of the Jews in Hungary. Therefore, they reasoned, it was possible to withdraw from the Hungarians in Transylvania the "disproportionately" favorable educational opportunities inherited from the previous system. The Romanian argument was based on the fact that barely a few years previously, before the break-up of historical Hungary, Hungarians comprised 95 percent of the students at the universities, although the proportion of Hungarians in the country was only 54.5 percent. They therefore felt that as long as the educational opportunities for the Romanian population were not in line with the proportion of the population overall, they were justified in restricting the educational opportunities of the Hungarians. The bishops of the Hungarian churches in Transylvania asked the Hungarian government as early as 1922 to repeal the numerus clausus law and thereby help the position of the now minority Hungarian population.[19]

This prejudicial effect of the law was also emphasized towards the end of the 1920s by Minister of Religion and Public Education Kunó Klebelsberg, who had spent the previous seven years defending the law and keeping it alive, together with István Bethlen. Nonetheless, when the task fell to him after seven years to satisfy the demands of the League of Nations by removing the Jewish quota from the law, he acknowledged that with the law on the Jewish quota "the conviction had been planted among a majority of international opinion that we are dealing with the minority in Hungary unfairly, which can serve as an excuse for unfair treatment of Hungarian minorities in foreign countries."[20]

Hungary's leading politicians were aware of the international and domestic political risks of the Jewish quota right from the start. A good indication of this is that three successive governments—from the autumn of 1919 to the autumn of 1920—were unwilling to put the Jewish quota into law, resisting the demands of the extreme anti-Semitic forces. When the law was finally accepted by parliament in the autumn of 1920, the majority of government ministers did not attend the vote. Of the thirteen ministers in the government, nine were absent in addition to the prime minister himself, while two of the ministers present

19 Minutes of the parliamentary session of July 20, 1922, in *Az 1922. évi junius hó 16-ára hirdetett nemzetgyűlés naplója* (Budapest: Athenaeum Irodalmi és Nyomdai Részvénytársulat, 1922), vol. 2: 224.

20 Kunó Klebelsberg, "Explanatory memorandum to the bill amending Law No. XXV of 1920 on the regulation of enrollment at the universities of arts and sciences, the University of Technology, the Faculty of Economics of the University of Budapest, and law academies," November 18, 1927, in *Az 1927. évi január hó 25-ére összehívott országgyűlés felsőházának irományai* (Budapest: Athenaeum Irodalmi és Nyomdai Részvénytársulat, 1928), vol. 4: 398.

voted against the law. Only one minister, István Szabó de Sokorópátka voted in favor. A total of 71 percent of parliamentary deputies were absent from the vote. All this would suggest that the political leadership of the country had serious doubts about introducing this law. Presumably, they were trying to preserve their international reputations when they decided not to take any public part in the creation of the law.

In this work, then, I will also try to answer the question of how—despite these serious doubts—the numerus clausus could have ended up becoming one of the defining measures of the age.

Ideology and apologia

The Jewish quota introduced by the law was in force in an unchanged form until 1928, and during that time, the Hungarian government faced repeated criticism both at home and abroad on account of the quota. In the end, the League of Nations ordered an investigation in 1925 as to whether the Jewish quota contravened international law as it then stood. It was in response to these strictures that the Hungarian government developed a system of ideological apologia to deflect foreign criticism. The Jewish quota was finally formally abolished in 1928. However, the professional quota that replaced it also served to exclude the Jews, just like its predecessor. Then, from 1934 onwards, the euphemistically named professional quota was once more called what it really was: a Jewish quota. Five years later, the 1939 anti-Jewish law formally reestablished the racial quota of the numerus clausus.

The ideology behind, and the apologia for, the Jewish quota which emerged in the early 1920s nonetheless survived these developments. So much so that to this day, more than a hundred years later, certain elements of the contemporary apologia for the law continue to pop up from time to time in the historiography of the period.

One of the goals of the present work is to reconstruct this system of ideological apologia and show that this apologia for the law does not explain the real reasons behind the legislation, or does so only to a very small degree. Although when the law was passed there was much talk of the very real effects of the crisis of the time, including the difficulties facing the intellectual middle class and the problem of securing employment for Hungarian refugees coming from territories lost after the war, the law itself did not present a solution for these problems. The Jewish quota was not a well-thought-through policy for tackling this crisis, but rather—as Kunó Klebelsberg, the minister of religion and education responsible for keeping the quota alive for years, acknowledged—the product of "desultory legislation," which—in an exceptional historical moment—was improvised in an ad-hoc way and translated ideas based on false premises into the language of the law. It was precisely for this reason that the law could not fulfill the expectations attached to it. Indeed, it was nonsensical from the point of view of the majority of society.[21]

As Victor Karady, a researcher on the history of Hungarian Jewry, wrote: "It is extremely hard to consider rationally this mass of obvious gobbledygook that is the hallmark of anti-Semitic speeches, which often therefore remind one of the emotional product of delirium tremens. . . . The causal connection between the justifications produced [for their views] by modern Jew-haters and the consequences of the hatred of Jews is either entirely non-existent or remarkably vague."[22]

My intention in this work is not to look for these vague causal connections. Rather, I would like to direct attention to those rhetorical and logical traps which contemporary justifications for the numerus clausus have set for subsequent historiography. For it is thanks to these that the idea that the racial clause represented a well thought-out contemporary response to the crisis caused by the war, the revolutions, and the loss of territory remains current to this day.

---

21 When doing away with the racial clause in 1927, Kunó Klebelsberg argued that it gave rise to "misunderstandings" and did not even strictly belong with the numerus clausus law. As he wrote in the appendix to the draft amendment, "Though Law No. XXV of 1920 intended to deal with each nationality and racial group in fair proportion, since it allows each such group into higher education according to its overall proportion of the population, clause three of the law has given rise to misunderstandings on the part of international opinion on the one hand and domestic Jewry on the other. . . . Moreover, Hungarian Jews have complained that they feel stigmatized by clause three. For these reasons, the government considers it to be in the national interest to subject Law No. XXV of 1920 to revision, in such a way as to maintain the socio-political part of the measure but to ensure that clause three, which has given rise to numerous misunderstandings, is suitably amended. This is all the more unobjectionable since clause three does not even feature in the original draft law introduced by István Haller (then minister of religion and education) on July 22, 1920 (publication no. 89). It was only mooted during the detailed debate of the law at the suggestion of then-deputy Nándor Bernolák and colleagues on September 21, 1920. As can be seen, it belongs more to the category of improvised law making and does not belong to the structure of the law." Kunó Klebelsberg, "Explanatory memorandum to the bill amending Law No. XXV of 1920 on the regulation of enrollment at the universities of arts and sciences, the University of Technology, the Faculty of Economics of the University of Budapest, and law academies," November 18, 1927, in *Az 1927. évi január hó 25-ére összehívott országgyűlés felsőházának irományai*, vol. 4: 398–400.

22 Viktor Karády, *Zsidóság Európában a modern korban* (Budapest: Új Mandátum Könyvkiadó, 2000), 333–34.

The refugee question and the war years

During the political debates on the Jewish quota in 1920, arguments of a socio-political nature were frequently espoused. The primary argument was that the law could be used to address the refugee question and the problem of graduate unemployment.

This is one of many justifications for the numerus clausus put forward by Ignác Romsics, a researcher of this period:

> The appearance of four hundred thousand Hungarian state employees expelled from neighboring countries after Trianon led to a surplus of intelligentsia, which is why this social stratum came to regard the Jewish intelligentsia as a source of competition. It was this tense situation that the Hungarian government attempted to alleviate with the introduction of the numerus clausus, but this measure was rejected by Western Europe.[23]

It is, of course, debatable how much a law that served to exclude five thousand Jews from higher education over the course of ten years (from 1920 to 1930) could have alleviated the crisis situation brought on by the appearance of four hundred thousand refugees. There were no other Jewish quotas in the 1920s in any other fields.[24]

Shortly after the introduction of the Jewish quota, it became clear that as far as the universities were concerned, the linking of the Jewish quota with the problems facing the refugees was not really sustainable. Neither the refugees nor the Christian middle class of post-Trianon Hungary applied to the universities in such alarming numbers that might have justified continuing this entire process. This was especially so since the problem of overcrowding due to the large number of applicants was a temporary problem, which was resolved within two to three years. In Hungary, as in many other European countries, many people postponed or did not complete their studies during the war years. Due to the chaotic circumstances, there were also students who had just finished secondary school and had not enrolled at university, yet had not given

23 As reported in Ferenc Kósa, "Diktatúra, vagy demokrácia? Harag és elfogultság nélkül a Horthy-korszakról," *Gyulai Hírlap*, October 29, 2009, https://www.gyulaihirlap.hu/936-diktatura-vagy-demokracia.

24 If the quota had been applied more strictly, which is to say if the proportion of Jews had been forced beneath 6 percent and not 10 percent, the number of Jews excluded would not have been so great as to make the refugee problem easier to handle.

up on the idea of higher education altogether. This problem could also have been resolved through temporary measures, such as summer semesters. This is what happened in many other European countries where there was a backlog of students due to the war, just as in Hungary.[25] Within two or three years, it also became obvious that the large number of refugee students did not justify excluding Jewish students from the universities either. At the start of the 1920s, there were around 4,500 students registered in Budapest who had been born in the lost territories, a good part of whom had refugee status.[26] But in the same period, two universities were relocated to Hungary from territories that had become part of Romania and Czechoslovakia, thereby increasing the number of universities in post-Trianon Hungary; the universities of Kolozsvár (Cluj) and Pozsony (Bratislava) were moved to Szeged and Pécs, respectively. Those students, therefore, who had studied at these universities and then fled to post-Trianon Hungary, could well have continued their studies at the same institutions where they began them. The University of Kolozsvár, which moved to Szeged,[27] could have accommodated 2,000 students, while the University of Pozsony, which moved to Pécs,[28] could have offered places for around 700 students at first and 1500 later on. Very few people took advantage of these opportunities, however. The majority of the refugee students insisted on going to university in Budapest rather than at their transferred alma maters. Meanwhile, the University of Szeged, which had been moved from Transylvania, did not have enough students; in 1922, there were about a thousand fewer students studying at the institution than had studied at its predecessor in Kolozsvár in 1914. The reason for this was not only that the university in the capital was more attractive than the provincial universities, but also that there was in fact a reduced demand for university education since the poor economic circum-

25 Minister of Education István Haller put the number of students unable to graduate during the six years of war and revolution at nine to ten thousand. Haller, *Harc a numerus clausus körül*, 132.

26 Zoltán Pálfy, "Nemzetállam és felsőoktatási piac," *Erdélyi Társadalom* 2, no. 2 (2004): 151. Among the students born in the lost territories there were those who came to Budapest before the territories were lost and there were some whose families had also moved to the capital before the territorial losses.

27 The University of Kolozsvár was founded in 1872 in Kolozsvár (today Cluj-Napoca) under the name Franz Joseph University as the second modern university in Hungary. In 1919, the university was temporarily relocated to Budapest, before being moved to Szeged in 1921. Following the Second Vienna Award that returned Northern Transylvania to Hungary, the Franz Joseph University moved back to Kolozsvár, while the institution that remained in Szeged was turned into a new university named Miklós Horthy University.

28 The University of Pozsony was founded in 1912 in Pozsony (today Bratislava, Slovakia) under the name Royal Hungarian Elizabeth University. In 1919, it first moved temporarily to Budapest, then in 1921 it was officially relocated to Pécs, where it began to function in 1923.

stances meant that new post-graduate employment could not be counted on (although the enrollment backlog caused by the postponements of the war years concealed this for a while).

Lack of students during the numerus clausus

The universities of Pécs and Szeged could only fill their official place allocations at the start of the 1920s by having Jewish students filling empty positions in the higher academic years where the Jewish quota did not apply, thus making up for the lack of Christian applicants.[29] This solution, however, outraged the "racial defense" organizations.[30] Paradoxically, there were a good number of refugees among the Jewish students at the provincial universities during this period. This, however, was not taken into consideration by the politicians of the time for ideological reasons. According to the official philosophy of the Jewish quota, someone was either Jewish or a refugee. The conjunction of these two labels would have caused confusion in the simplistic view that held that "Jews" had to be restricted in their studies in order to provide more spaces for "refugees."

The fanaticism of the race defenders surpassed all other reasoning. Those professors at the University of Budapest who endorsed the ideology of racial defense even employed the anti-Hungarian measures instituted by the Romanian state in their arsenal of ideas. Romania considered the establishment of the University in Szeged a breach of the Treaty of Trianon, and therefore refused to recognize its degrees. The Faculty of Medicine of the Budapest University, led by Károly Hoór (professor of ophthalmology) determined, with reference to the

---

29 There were 2,119 students at the University of Kolozsvár in 1913–14 and 971 in 1921–22—of whom 240 were Jewish. In the following year, the number of students grew to 1,291 and the number of Jews to 407. Haller, *Harc a numerus clausus körül*, 134. Károly Hoór was among others who objected to this, complaining about that "the universities of Pécs and Szeged accept Jewish students from the occupied territories [by registering them] as 'foreign nationals.'" Károly Hoór, *A numerus clausus a szegedi és a pécsi egyetemen* (Budapest: Centrum, 1923), 16.

30 The so called "racial defense" (*fajvédő*) movement emerged after World War I as one of the most influential political and ideological movements in Hungary. Combining racialist ideas—primarily anti-Semitism—with a strong opposition to leftwing progressivism and the rejection of traditional conservative liberalism, race defenders sought to achieve a social and political transformation that would bring about a political and cultural "changing of the guard" and national revival. Subscribing to the myth of "Jewish takeover" and blaming Jews for the postwar revolutions and territorial losses, race defenders were the main proponents of anti-Jewish discriminative legislation, including the numerus clausus. Although parties endorsing the racial defense ideology remained on the sideline of parliamentary politics, the movement had a profound and lasting impact on the political thinking of interwar Hungary.

Romanian decision, that students from Szeged could not take their degrees in Budapest, because this would "drag down" the value of the University of Budapest's degrees.[31]

The government did not wish to hinder students of the academic years disrupted by the war from finishing university. For this reason, they set the official allocation of university places between 1920 and 1923 so high (except for Jewish students) it was as if the law made no limitation on enrollment theoretically possible. This is how it came to pass that 1920–21 was the only year when it was possible to fill the entire official allocation with students. Even by 1921–22, there were about a thousand too few Christian applicants to fill the official allocation, and this number had risen to around two thousand by the following academic year. According to parliamentary deputy Károly Schandl, this rendered the "impact of the numerus clausus" almost "illusory."[32]

The delayed academic year groups exited the higher education system within two or three years, and then a new situation presented itself: the problem was no longer that there were too many applicants, but that the number of non-Jewish applicants began to decrease significantly.[33] From the mid-1920s, the universities themselves began asking the minister of education to reduce the official allocation of places, because it was impossible to fill them with Christian students. This was not surprising, given that to achieve the prewar level of students, 20–25 percent more Christian students had to be admitted than before the war, thanks to the strictures of the Jewish quota. The number of Christian students with secondary school diplomas did not, however, grow to this extent, and hence the resupply of the entire system began to falter. When, therefore, the Bethlen government continued to proffer the refugee crisis as the explanation for maintaining the Jewish quota in the mid-twenties, the reason given was more of a rationalization than a genuine rationale for maintaining the quota.

---

31 Hoór, *A numerus clausus a szegedi és a pécsi egyetemen*, 17; and Károly Hoór's contribution, Semmelweis Orvostudományi Egyetem Levéltára (Archives of the Semmelweis University of Medicine, hereafter SOTE Archives), I/a, volume 48, 320 (ordinary meeting of the faculty, January 17, 1922).

32 For data on the number of applicants and allocated places, see note 47 in chapter 2 in this volume. For Károly Schandl's observation, see the minutes of the parliamentary session of September 16, 1920, in *Az 1920. évi február hó 16-ára összehívott nemzetgyűlés naplója*, vol. 5: 339.

33 In 1910, of every hundred Jews with secondary school diplomas, 85 went on to higher education, while the number was 67 for non-Jews. By 1923, this proportion had sunk to 45 among Jews and had risen to 90 among non-Jews, which is to say that of a hundred non-Jews with secondary school diplomas, 90 went on to university. This number, however, soon began to decrease among the non-Jewish youth and by 1933 barely more than half (57 percent) enrolled for university. Viktor Karády, *Iskolarendszer és felekezeti egyenlőtlenségek Magyarországon (1867–1945)* (Budapest: Replika, 1997), 251.

By 1926, it had become obvious that the number of Christian applicants could not even satisfy the admissions targets, even though these decreased year after year.[34] Even the anti-Semitic statistician Alajos Kovács, a fiery proponent of the numerus clausus, professed that "life . . . itself is now regulating the question," because the number of students at the university was "constantly decreasing" on its own.[35] Kunó Klebelsberg admitted in 1925 that despite the exclusion of Jews, "the children of the Christian professional class did not apply to university in greater numbers."[36] The University of Szeged in 1927 simply asked the government to reduce the official allocation of places because it turned out that they did not have enough Christian applicants.

The socio-political reasoning

The other important element of numerus clausus discourse, also inherited from the 1920s, is the theory that the anti-Semitic law was primarily necessary from a socio-political standpoint, in order to slow the frightening (as it seemed) overburgeoning of people with university degrees, or—as Kunó Klebelsberg, the minister of education, put it at the 1925 meeting of the League of Nations—to protect "against the development of an intellectual proletariat."[37] This rationale featured in the official justification of the law as well, according to which the "gravest enemy of the social order is the intellectual proletariat," the spread of which had to be prevented.[38] The numerus clausus, then, according to this way of thinking, primarily had to do with the overcrowding of the graduate labor market that shrank significantly as a result of Trianon and only contained anti-Jewish restrictions because in Hungary a disproportionate number of potential future graduates were Jews.[39]

---

34 For more on this issue, see pages 135–36 in this volume.

35 Haller, *Harc a numerus clausus körül*, 233.

36 Magyar Nemzeti Levéltár Országos Levéltára (Hungarian National Archives, hereafter MNL OL), K 305, VKM Töredékiratok, Count Kunó Klebelsberg's address to the League of Nations concerning the *numerus clausus*, November 30, 1925. "It is dangerous to ask," wrote Klebelsberg, "why it is that the children of the Christian professional class do not apply to university in greater numbers." Klebelsberg explained this phenomenon with the differing material circumstances of Jewish and non-Jewish parents.

37 MNL OL, K 305, VKM Töredékiratok, Count Kunó Klebelsberg's address to the League of Nations concerning the *numerus clausus*, November 30, 1925.

38 Bethlen, *A magyar zsidóság almanachja*, 103.

39 Andor Ladányi, "A numerus clausus-törvény 1928. évi módosításáról," *Századok* 128, no. 6 (1994): 1119.

Figure 2. Minister of Religion and Public Education Kunó Klebelsberg (in center). Source: Fortepan, 77086, László Rosta.

Despite using this apologia in international fora for diplomatic ends, not even Klebelsberg himself believed it. "I never associated myself with this law," he told the press in 1927. "I merely inherited it." This led to the accusation that he changed his opinions to suit his audience.[40] As for the theory about the surplus of graduates, he considered it simple demagoguery. As he said in parliament: "Unfortunately in Hungary, one can achieve absolutely anything with catchy phrases. The talk of a surplus of intellectual proletarians is just such a phrase, which may have dangerous consequences. . . . School is school, you can't make a socio-political or economic question out of it."[41] In reality, Klebelsberg thought that preventing a surplus of university graduates through state intervention was a downright "impossibility," which in the long run could have the decidedly harmful effect of excluding the children of the Christian middle class from the universities. "They've whined so much to me about the rampant intellectual proletariat that in the end I had to show them the impossibility of these demands."[42] Klebelsberg viewed state intervention to suppress the expan-

40 MTI News Release, October 21, 1927.

41 *Pesti Napló*, September 4, 1928, 5.

42 *Pesti Napló*, September 4, 1928, 5. See also *Pesti Napló*, September 2, 1928, 9. In 1928, Klebelsberg reduced the official allocation of places from the 550 of the previous year to 290 in order, as he said, to take the matter "*ad absurdum*" and to prove that those who were asking for a reduction of the of-

sion of an intellectual proletariat as a "cacophony of statements" that pointed to an "impassable path" leading to unnecessary political conflict.[43]

But there was an aspect of the numerus clausus law that Klebelsberg seems to have supported, and this was that Jews should be forced out of the universities. This is shown by his private letter to István Bethlen in 1926 in which he identified the "core of the institution of numerus clausus" as making it possible to exclude "thousands of Jewish students" from the universities. "As a lawyer," he wrote,

> I can see quite clearly that the way our law is currently phrased, we cannot approach the *Cour Permanent* in The Hague with any hope of success. . . . We will, therefore, have to revise the law, not in order to unleash thousands of Jewish university students on the nation once again, but rather in order to conserve the meaning of the enterprise by taking certain rational actions. In this regard, I have my ideas (autonomous admission committees at the universities, stressing, alongside intellectual ability or talent shown in one or two subjects, the rating of comportment and physical education, etc.). . . . I would consider the complete opening of the floodgates a catastrophe, and therefore I think it is necessary to construct, with the cooperation of discreet Christian politicians, a text that will give no pretext for interference from Geneva or The Hague.[44]

All of Klebelsberg's suggestions had to do with how the anti-Jewish restrictions deleted from the letter of the law for reasons of international policy could continue to be maintained in practice by the state, skirting the law in a more authoritarian way.

In this work, therefore, I intend to examine whether the true purpose of the numerus clausus was to address a general socio-political problem (the overabundance of the intelligentsia) or whether it was a form of targeted discrimination against Jews. I will show that the political powers that fought for the introduction of the racial clause did not merely wish to slow the growth of a

---

ficial allocations were "demanding something impossible." He made reference to the political conflict the reduction of the allocations was going to cause: "If anyone brings this question up again, I will personally send round to their house those parents whose children did not get into university because of these sorts of demands."

43 *Pesti Napló*, September 2, 1928, 9.

44 Miklós Szinai and László Szücs, eds., *Bethlen István titkos iratai* (Budapest: Kossuth Könyvkiadó, 1972), 256–57.

Jewish graduate class, but wanted to introduce a Jewish law that was far wider in scope and would extend to all fields of the economy.[45]

This idea was supported not merely by politically inexperienced demagogues, but also by politicians in important positions of power, extending even to ministers. For example, Károly Ereky[46] came out and said in parliament in April 1920 in black and white that the goal of such a measure would be to use the political power "to take away from the Jews their billions in income within the framework of the law."[47] The Christian National Union Party (*Keresztény Nemzeti Egyesülés Pártja*, KNEP) entrusted a five-member committee in the spring of 1920 (consisting of Elek Avarffy, Albin Lingauer, Károly Hencz, János Nagy, and József Vass) to study the legislative and executive resources available for the solution of the Jewish question.[48] Alajos Kovács, who worked out the statistical background for the Jewish quota, was also in favor of such a more general and widespread measure. Kovács's aim was for the state to put an end to the perceived advantages enjoyed by Jews in various sectors of the economy and introduce employment policy measures that would change the imbalances manifest in the "social stratification" of Jews and non-Jews. The goal was to reduce the proportion of Jews among the bourgeoisie and graduates, and thereby increase the proportion of non-Jews.

But the legislation of the 1920s must have left Kovács's expectations largely unfulfilled. The result of Kovács's "proportionality" program would have been the exclusion of Jews in the branches of the economy where they were present in the greatest proportion, principally banking and commerce. Compared to the proportion of Jews in these two sectors in 1920, their proportion of 13.4 percent among graduate professionals as a whole was not so high: in bank-

---

45 This topic is not frequently discussed in Hungarian historiography, most writers confining themselves to the field of higher education when discussing the efforts at a numerus clausus. An exception is Róbert Kerepeszki's work dealing with the history of the Turul Alliance. According to him, the primary goal of the Alliance's "racial defense" was a numerus clausus for Jews, which is to say that "that social group should be present in the public, economic, financial, and intellectual-graduate fields only in proportion to its overall proportion within the population." Róbert Kerepeszki, "A Turul Szövetség," in *A magyar jobboldali hagyomány, 1900–1948*, ed. Ignác Romsics (Budapest: Osiris, 2009), 364.

46 Károly Ereky was minister for food under the Friedrich government from August 29 until November 24, 1919. He later entered parliament under the banner of the Christian National Union Party (KNEP) but quickly crossed the floor to Andrássy-Friedrich's Christian National Party (KNP), for which he ran unsuccessfully for election in 1922 and then retired from political life.

47 Parliamentary session of August 18, 1920, in *Az 1920. évi február hó 16-ára összehívott nemzetgyűlés naplója*, vol. 4: 542.

48 Bethlen, *A magyar zsidóság almanachja*, 101. In 1907, Károly Hencz introduced a motion recommending that a numerus clausus be instituted in the universities. Founded in October 1919, the Christian National Union Party became part of the governing coalition under the premiership of István Bethlen.

ing, 80.6 percent of directors and 43.7 percent of white collar employees were Jewish, while in commerce, 53.6 percent of self-employed merchants and 48.2 percent of clerks were Jewish.[49] At the beginning of the 1920s, though, there was no realistic expectation that the Hungarian state—while trying to court the goodwill of the European Powers—would regulate the workings of an economy based on the principle of private property with a racial quota system enforced by the state. It was inconceivable that the law could dictate to firms the religion or race from which they could—and could not—hire employees; this historic change would not come to pass until 1938. In the international political climate of the 1920s, anti-Jewish employment regulations could only be introduced in areas where the state itself was the employer, principally in the civil service, from which—by means of compulsory retirements—they got rid of most Jewish employees.

According to Alajos Kovács's account, the process of differentiating between private property in Jewish and non-Jewish hands had nonetheless begun in the 1920s in that the basic principles of the 1920 land reform were deliberately formulated in order "to transfer estates from the Jews, who had become rich and bought property during the war, into the hands of Christian Hungarians."[50] Indirectly, the Jewish quota in higher education also contained this form of differentiation in the use made of Jewish and non-Jewish taxpayers' money. For while the quota restricted the participation of Jews in university education, it did not give Jewish taxpayers a proportional relief from the state taxes that covered almost half of the budgets of the universities. "I would ask the right honorable minister," the liberal Ernő Bródy said to Klebelsberg in parliament, "to imagine the feeling with which our Jewish citizens should pay their contributions to institutions from which they are excluded and shut out? . . . In this, you are throwing away the seed, the kernel of equality, when rights are

---

49 Alajos Kovács, *A csonkamagyarországi zsidóság a statisztika tükrében* (Budapest: Egyesült Nemzeti Keresztény Liga, 1938), 64.

50 Kovács, *A csonkamagyarországi zsidóság*, 42. The appendix of the 1942 law that restricted the right of Jews to own land referred to Alajos Kovács's results. According to this appendix, the reason why land purchased during the war occupied the largest place among land to be redistributed in 1920 is that this was mostly land bought by Jews. The appendix had this to say on the land reforms of the 1920s: "As a result of the land reform, the amount of land in circulation fell by 925 acres (625,000 *holds*) and of this decrease, almost half affected Jewish landowners. The result of the combined land reform and the inspection of real estate transactions was that in 1933 only 11.7 percent of medium and large estates were in the hands of persons belonging to the Jewish religion, while in 1916, this number had been 16.5 percent. *Az 1939. évi június hó 10-ére összehívott országgyűlés felsőházának irományai* (Budapest: Athenaeum Irodalmi és Nyomdai Részvénytársulat, 1942), vol. 5: 471.

accorded only to certain classes and certain professions, while everyone must bear responsibilities equally."[51]

The overrepresentation of Jews among graduate professionals

In this work, I will also look at the concept of "the Jewish takeover" which was often repeated in connection with the socio-political justifications for the numerus clausus law at the time. According to this notion, after emancipation, Jews took over more and more of the privileged social and economic positions in the country and squeezed out the non-Jewish population. The purpose of the numerus clausus in higher education was—so the thinking went—to stop this process, slow down the growth in the number of Jewish graduates, and thereby offer the children of the Christian middle class institutional protection.

However, a few years after the introduction of the numerus clausus, what could have been already known in principle in 1920 became evident in practice, namely, that this way of thinking was based on a sort of optical illusion. It turned out that despite forcing the Jewish students out of the universities, non-Jewish families could not or did not want to send their children to university in significantly larger numbers. As it was, it had not been the Jewish students who had kept non-Jews out of the universities, even when the universities had complained of overcrowding. The numerus clausus introduced anti-Jewish restrictions in an area where prior to the law there had been no restrictions of any kind. Everyone with a valid secondary school diploma had the right to enroll at university. The proportion of Jewish students was indeed high, but this was not the result of "too many" Jewish students in a system with a limited number of places, since there had been no such restrictions prior to the introduction of the numerus clausus. The high proportion of Jews among university students was not caused by the disproportionate exploitation of some previously established limit on places, but because the number of "Christian" applicants did not live up to expectations. A similar situation occurred towards the end of the war when the government ran so-called "military catch-up semesters" for university students in the military, in which the academic demands on students were relaxed. Christian students made less use of this opportunity than Jewish students: this serves to explain why the percentage of Jewish students in

51 Ernő Bródy's address at the parliamentary session of February 28, 1928, in *Az 1927. évi január hó 25-ére hirdetett országgyűlés képviselőházának naplója*, vol. 9: 232.

the last year of the war rose above 30 percent.[52] However, the phenomenon of "takeover" (*térfoglalás*) at the universities of which the Jews were accused was not the result of an exclusionary rivalry between Jewish and non-Jewish university students, but rather that, proportionally speaking, a greater number of Jewish youths went to secondary school than their non-Jewish counterparts, and a greater proportion of Jewish secondary school graduates enrolled at university than non-Jewish ones.[53]

In the first chapter, I will show that the politicized statistical literature of the 1920s tended, for campaign purposes, to deliberately exaggerate the overrepresentation of Jews in the graduate professional class. With its exclusive focus on ethno-religious issues, it also served to skew the matter. The reasoning at the time was based on the statistical fact that in 1920 Jews constituted 13.4 percent of graduates in the liberal professions and civil service, which exceeded their proportion (5.9 percent) in the overall population of the country.[54] Even if the facts were correct, the interpretations placed on them were used in a misleading and biased manner.

Three quarters of the Jewish population was urban, while the majority of the non-Jewish population lived in rural communities, that is to say, in villages.[55] It is obvious that if we compare a mostly urban population with a mostly rural population (whether in terms of education or occupation) in a purely mechanical way, the results will show that the majority urban population has a higher degree of education and as a result will have a higher proportion of members engaged in the professions, since there is easier access to educational institutions in the towns than in the villages. This was particularly so among the poorer classes of that time, who—although they could afford to have their children educated in their own town—could not bear the cost of sending their children somewhere else to continue their studies. It is not surprising then that the exclusion of the Jews after 1920 did not bring about changes in the educational tendencies of the rural population. In 1914, the children of agricultural laborers (and maids and day laborers, who made up the majority of the

52 Kovács, *A zsidóság térfoglalása Magyarországon*, 34.

53 Karády, *Iskolarendszer és felekezeti egyenlőtlenségek Magyarországon*, 251.

54 Kovács, *A csonkamagyarországi zsidóság*, 67.

55 The agrarian proletariat comprised more than two million people, while the overall numbers of the social classes holding up to seven acres (five *holds*) of land was around 3 million. Approximately 56 percent of the country's population lived from agrarian occupations. Gábor Gyáni and György Kövér, *Magyarország társadalomtörténete a reformkortól a második világháborúig* (Budapest: Osiris, 2006), 215. In 1920, 344,234 Jews lived in towns while 129,121 lived in the countryside. Kovács, *A csonkamagyarországi zsidóság*, 61.

rural population) comprised 0.6 percent of all university students. Their absolute numbers remained under 50, and this number did not rise even after the introduction of the Jewish quota: only 49 of the 16,930 students at university in 1930 came from such families.[56] The children of smallholders made up a total of 6.3 percent of all university students in 1914, and after the introduction of the numerus clausus, this number remained similar right up until the middle of the 1930s.[57] Given, however, that within the social pyramid, these rural classes made up the majority of the population, it was an irrational and politically biased act to compare the overrepresentation of the Jewish population, which was three-quarters urban, with the mostly rural agrarian population.

In order to assess the degree of Jewish overrepresentation, without resorting to demagoguery, we have to compare Jewish percentages within the general urban population, rather than within the overall population of the country, which was mostly rural. In the capital, for instance, where nearly a quarter of the population was Jewish, the 25–28 percent of university students who were Jews was high, but not nearly as disproportionate as the statistical literature of the day (which was anti-Semitic in spirit) made out. Indeed, compared to some Central European capitals, such as Berlin and Vienna, the Jews were "overrepresented" to a relatively smaller extent at the University of Budapest. The percentage of Jews in the overall population of Vienna was 9 percent, but their proportion of university students hovered around 25 percent, while in Berlin the proportion of Jews was 5 percent but among university students they made up around 30 percent. Given that 85 percent of university students in Hungary were in Budapest, the proportions in the capital largely determined the national proportions as well. And since about 90 percent of graduates came from urban families, it is hardly surprising that the percentage of Jews among graduate professionals was roughly the same as their percentage in the overall urban population.[58]

Contemporary observers had noted the spread of biased and exaggerated data and interpretations on the "takeover" of Jews in the graduate professional

56 Rudolf Andorka, "Az egyetemi és főiskolai hallgatók társadalmi összetétele, 1898–1942," *Statisztikai Szemle*, 57, no. 2 (1979): 178. The number of students comprising the children of agricultural workers began to increase somewhat from the middle of the 1930s thanks to the establishment of various scholarships.

57 Andorka, "Az egyetemi és főiskolai hallgatók," 183. The children of smallholders made up 6.3 percent of university students between 1914 and 1919, 7.7 percent between 1920 and 1925, 7.2 percent from 1925 to 1929, and 6.7 percent in 1930.

58 In 1920, the 21 percent proportion of Jews among university graduates exceeded their proportion of the urban population (13 percent). It did not, however, exceed their proportion among those in the public sector and liberal professions. The number of female graduates was relatively high among Jews, but not all of them went on to work.

class years before the introduction of the numerus clausus law. The Christian Socialist politician, Sándor Giesswein, warned in 1917 that it was misleading to attribute the high proportion of Jews in the graduate professions to ethnic or religious causes. Since Jews and non-Jews take part in the process of urbanization to different extents, wrote Giesswein, it is natural that the participation of Jews and non-Jews in education should develop differently too:

> First of all, a much higher percentage of Jewish children live in the cities than Christian children, and they have concomitantly greater access to the means of education and learning than Christian children. Second, the Jewish child is allowed to learn, whether he be a rag-picker's son or a banker's son. Among Christians, however, it is mostly only the sons of the upper classes, the gentry, and the intelligentsia who make it to the halls of learning. . . . Very few of the children of people who work on the land make it to secondary schools, and those who do mostly go on to be priests or teachers. As far as I know there are hardly any children from the working class who attend secondary schools or polytechnics. This is the reason why the opportunity for academic selection is much smaller for Christian children.[59]

The participation of Jews in all levels of education was also higher than that of non-Jews; so much so that the anti-Semitic statistician Alajos Kovács called the difference simply "horrifying."[60] In 1910, 18.2 percent of Jewish men aged 19 or older had secondary school diplomas (which was the requirement for applying to university), while for Catholics the figure was 4.2 percent, and for Protestants, 3.9 percent.[61]

---

59 *A zsidókérdés Magyarországon: A Huszadik Század körkérdése* (Budapest: Társadalomtudományi Társaság, 1917), 86–87.

60 Kovács, *A zsidóság térfoglalása Magyarországon*, 29. There was hardly any illiteracy among Jews, since Jewish children mostly mastered numbers and perhaps Hebrew letters—if not always Hungarian—at an early age. By comparison, 31 percent of Hungarians over the age of six were illiterate in 1910. True, the census of 1910 only considered 87 percent of Jews able to read and write, but the reason for this was that the census takers listed anyone who could only read and write Hebrew as illiterate. Miklós Szabó, "A modernizáció kiválasztott népe," *Mozgó Világ* 26, no. 9 (2000): 106–9; and Karády, *Iskolarendszer és felekezeti egyenlőtlenségek*, 17.

61 The proportion of Jewish men who had completed four years of secondary school was 21.8 percent, while it was 4.6 percent in the population overall. The proportion of Jewish men with six years of secondary education was 12.9 percent as opposed to the overall average of 2.9 percent, while the proportion of Jewish men having completed eight years of secondary education was 10.1 percent compared to the national average of 2.3 percent. There were similar differences in the Jews' favor in the figures for women. Among Jewish women 14.7 percent completed four years of secondary education, compared to 2.8 percent of the overall female population, 3.7 percent of Jewish women had six years of secondary education compared to 0.8 percent overall, and 1.1 percent of Jewish women had eight

The link between education, urbanization, and the professional structure was obvious to contemporary observers too. Sándor Giesswein put it the following way during the 1920 debate on the numerus clausus law:

> The supremacy of the Jews is in direct correlation with illiteracy [of the Christian population]. The lower the rate of illiteracy, the less the Jews were able to settle in. The statistics say that the lowest rate of illiteracy is in Germany and the Germans can take care of their own commerce. There are more illiterates among the Hungarians, so Jews get more of a toe-hold, more still among the Slovaks, and even more among the Rumanians. Among the Ruthenes, the Jews are unquestionably ruling the roost. . . . Illiteracy is the bridge across which the Jews, the Galicians, come. . . . I bring this up because this disproportionality is not to be cured with a numerus clausus, but by bringing more and more Christian children into further education. . . . I, then, do not subscribe to the view, which several people have expressed, that Jews have greater talent or have talent in greater proportion, but I say that Jews have more opportunities to educate themselves. Therefore, we must give the children of the Hungarian nation an opportunity, so that as many of them can make use of these selfsame tools as possible.[62]

If we measure the "overrepresentation of the Jews" within the urban population (13 percent), rather than the overall population, including the rural population (5.9 percent), then we can conclude that the 13.4 percent proportion of Jews in the graduate professions (the civil service and liberal professions) was not so disproportionate after all, or that this overrepresentation was present in merely a few of the smaller professions.[63] In some of the graduate liberal professions, primarily among doctors and lawyers, the overrepresentation of Jews was pronounced by any standard: 49.4 percent of lawyers and trainee lawyers were Jewish, along with 46.3 percent of doctors. These were small professions, however, and their members constituted less than one fifth of all Hungarian graduate professionals. The proportion of Jewish graduates was lowest in the civil service (at 4.9 percent), the sector that employed the most graduate professionals (roughly 30,000), but public opinion was little interested in this fact. The

years of secondary education compared to 0.4 percent overall. See Kovács, *A zsidóság térfoglalása Magyarországon*, 29–31.

62 Parliamentary session of September 18, 1920, in *Az 1920. évi február hó 16-ára összehívott nemzetgyűlés naplója*, vol. 5: 389.

63 Kovács, *A csonkamagyarországi zsidóság*, 67.

presence of Jews was much more obvious in certain liberal professions where their real numbers were far smaller (a few thousand people), but their proportion of the whole was unusually high, for example among doctors, pharmacists, lawyers, or in the urban press and entertainment industry (an increasing part of mass culture).[64]

Nonetheless, many people considered the Jewish "takeover" since the turn of the century to be a grave issue, and not necessarily out of anti-Semitic motives. The journal *Huszadik Század* (Twentieth Century) conducted a survey in 1917 on the "Jewish question," with several contributors addressing the issue. Ede Alföldy, a judge, raised the question of what lay behind the exaggerations that magnify the extent of this overrepresentation. He argued that Jews had been excluded for so long from the liberal professions, that when this prohibition was lifted following emancipation, Hungarian society could not come to terms with the new situation. "First and foremost, when considering the accusation that the better social positions are awash with Jews, let us not forget our traditional prejudice that deems it natural for Jews to be excluded from any significant position in public life, which makes even insignificant gains on their part look like the gathering of untrammeled power. Even the appearance of Jews in fields where we are not used to their presence gives the impression that some unscrupulous intrusion has taken place."[65]

The perception of the "takeover" of the intellectual job market by Jewish professionals was also magnified by the fact that in everyday language, "intelligentsia" referred not only to university graduates, but to all those who were engaged in white collar work. Though the debate over the numerus clausus theoretically affected only graduates of the universities and polytechnics, the anti-Semitic politicians fighting for the law frequently and at will complained of the "judaization" of professions that did not even require a university degree. Such was the case with employees in banking, commerce, and manufacturing, which had almost twice as many Jews (32,194) as the civil service and liberal professions (16,091). Among white collar employees in the economic field, both the proportion of overrepresentation of Jews (at 40–50 percent) as well as their absolute numbers were significantly higher than in the graduate professions generally.[66] When, therefore, the anti-Semitic politicians who were cam-

64 Contemporary statistics counted journalists and actors among the category of "public servants and the liberal professions," but these professions did not require a university degree.

65 *A zsidókérdés Magyarországon: A Huszadik Század körkérdése*, 42.

66 About ten percent of white collar employees in the economic field were graduates. In 1920, the total number of white collar employees in trade was 28,000, of whom 13,640 were Jewish. White collar em-

Figure 3. Caricature in the satirical *Borsszem Jankó* entitled "Numerus clausus in the elementary school." Caption reads: "Do all the children belong to Madame? — No, please, just this one, I brought the rest so that the percentage would work out." *Borsszem Jankó*, no. 29 (1920): 12.

paigning for the numerus clausus referred to the everyday perception that Jews were disproportionately well-represented in white collar jobs, their arguments would more often have led logically to a call for a numerus clausus not in the universities, but in the secondary schools.

But the numerus clausus law did not apply to secondary schools. The anti-Jewish quota was only extended to secondary schools nineteen years later with the passage of the Second Jewish Law.[67] True, there were attempts to introduce

---

ployees in the banking sector numbered 19,335, of whom 8,457 were Jewish. In industry, there were 25,850 employees, of whom 10,097 were Jewish. The total number of employees in the trade, industry, and banking sectors of the economy was 73,185, of whom 32,194 were Jewish and 40,991 non-Jewish. Kovács, *A csonkamagyarországi zsidóság*, 64–67. The overall numbers of the "professional classes" consisted of employees in the public sector and the liberal professions, once assistants and other support staff had been subtracted. This number in 1920 was 121,085—of whom 16,091 were Jewish and 104,967 non-Jewish.

67 A numerus clausus for secondary schools was not contained in either the numerus clausus law or in the Jewish Laws or in their respective implementing decrees. This restriction was brought into being in 1939 after the passage of the Second Jewish Law with a secret directive of the Ministry of Religion and Public Education. Under the terms of this directive, the 6 percent quota had to be applied to admissions to secondary schools as well. Moreover, segregated Jewish classes, so-called "B classes," had to be established. Jewish secondary school students performed labor instead of religious education (e.g., weeding), and could not become scouts. Claudia K. Farkas, "Az elkülönítés látható falai," *Kutatási füzetek* 11 (2005): 86–96.

a numerus clausus in secondary schools as early as 1920. István Haller, the minister of education, known as "the father of the numerus clausus," issued a decree in the summer of 1920 which stated that entrance exams had to be introduced for secondary schools at the age of ten.[68] According to Haller, they "managed" to reduce the proportion of Jewish students in secondary schools in the capital from 41 percent to 32 percent in the very first year.[69] The decree was in force for four years, and during that time, it was commonly called the "secondary school numerus clausus" since the decree, in the words of the President of the Union of Protestant Teachers, Imre Dóczi, "wants to close off the secondary schools from Jews and other undesirable social elements."[70] Because of the introduction of entrance exams in 1920, around 2,000 Jewish schoolchildren were excluded from secondary schools.[71] The majority of the Protestant Church's schools did not consider the statute lawful from the start and did not enforce the entrance exams, while other schools abandoned them in 1924 when István Bethlen did away with the decree.[72] But in the end, the 1920 law created anti-Jewish restrictions only for university students. It did not include the idea espoused in 1919 by the Budapest Faculty of Medicine that would have excluded all women from higher education, but it did reestablish the restrictions on women's rights to education that had been in force prior to 1918. Nonetheless, the Faculty of Medicine excluded women from higher education for years with no legal basis, proving that certain groups of students could be excluded without requiring a separate law.

68 Decree No. 113.240/1920 of the Ministry of Religion and Public Education. The text of the directive and its impact was discussed by deputy Béla Fábián at the July 2, 1924 session of the parliament, see *Az 1922. évi junius hó 16-ára hirdetett nemzetgyűlés naplója*, vol. 25: 332.

69 For Haller's data, see the minutes of the parliamentary session of September 4, 1920, in *Az 1920. évi február hó 16-ára összehívott nemzetgyűlés naplója*, vol. 5: 204. The directive was criticized in parliament by Győző Drózdy: "[I would like to say to the] Honorable House that the Minister of Religion and Public Education published a directive at the end of the past academic year, which said that from that moment on students could only be accepted to secondary school with admissions exams. The results of this directive were horrible. Secondary schools observed the admissions exams, but students with only 'satisfactory' grades from the four years of primary school were not even examined, but summarily sent away. Those students who came with better grades were submitted to tests where sometimes even students with absolutely perfect grades failed. . . . The law on public education and secondary schools clearly states that any student who satisfactorily completes the four years of primary school has the right to enroll in secondary school. The Hon. Minister's directive says, however, that they do not have the right to enroll, but must complete an admission exam first." Parliamentary session of September 1, 1920, in *Az 1920. évi február hó 16-ára összehívott nemzetgyűlés naplója*, vol. 10: 596.

70 Bethlen, *A magyar zsidóság almanachja*, 130.

71 "Report on the Győr meeting of the Christian Socialist Party," MTI News Release, October 11, 1920, 8.

72 Bethlen, *A magyar zsidóság almanachja*, 130. For the Protestant schools, the Protestant diocese should have ordered admissions exams to take place, but since the Transtisza diocese did not do so, no admissions exams were instituted.

Due to the Jewish quota, the proportion of Jewish university students fell from its previous level of 25–30 percent to below 10 percent by the mid-1920s. The racial clause of the numerus clausus therefore had a significant impact on the number of Jewish students. According to estimates, the law excluded almost five thousand Jewish students seeking higher education during the 1920s, and there were many who did not even try to enter higher education because of the law.

At the same time, the numerus clausus law did not bring about significant changes among non-Jewish university students, although the official allocation of places theoretically served to maximize the number of Christian students. But in the course of time, it turned out that there was no need for such crisis measures in the case of non-Jewish students. Indeed, the numerus clausus law, which was passed in the hysterical atmosphere of 1920 excluded Jews from university on the basis of false premises. The exclusion of the Jews from the universities did not lead Christian youth to apply in greater numbers.

Anti-Semitism and the "provocative law"

Considering the above, I intend to examine why the first anti-Jewish law was aimed at university students. The supply of future Jewish university students could have been restricted more effectively with a numerus clausus in the secondary schools, since Jewish youth would therefore have been unable not only to apply to university, but even to get their secondary school diplomas. If, therefore, this was the socio-political background to the law, why did it aim to exclude the Jews only and specifically from the ranks of university students?

The answer is not obvious. Numerous historical works argue that the purpose of the measure was in fact to diffuse the anti-Semitic "mood of the masses." But the law against Jewish university students was in itself hardly enough to influence the "mood of the masses," since the "masses" were little interested in the composition of the student body at the universities. In their eyes, the numerus clausus had at most symbolic importance, since of the almost half a million Hungarian Jews, only five or six thousand went to university.[73] The extreme right mobilized the masses, not with the numerus clausus, but with general demands for the confiscation and redistribution of Jewish property. The

73 According to Tibor Hajdu's calculations, the 3,500 Jewish students at university in 1910 came from roughly 6–7 percent of Jewish families. Tibor Hajdu, "A diplomások létszámnövekedésének szerepe az antiszemitizmus alakulásában," in *A Holokauszt Magyarországon európai perspektívában*, ed. Judit Molnár (Budapest: Balassi Kiadó, 2005), 58.

broad base thus developed was then used by the political forces, among them the anti-Semitic student associations, who were fighting for the introduction of the anti-Jewish quota at the universities.[74]

But neither the masses nor the Christian middle class could expect quick improvements from the Jewish quota at the universities. The most they could expect is that it would reduce the number of Jewish graduate professionals in the long run, over a number of decades. Directly palpable benefits could only have been expected if the Jewish quota was extended to the professional occupations which required a graduate degree—medicine, law, engineering, teaching, etc. "The main goal," wrote the race defender organizations in their petition to parliament "is the national protection of breadwinning occupations."[75] But the legislative extension of the numerus clausus to the breadwinning occupations was unthinkable in the Europe of the 1920s.

It was therefore obvious to contemporary observers that the numerus clausus in the universities was not an instrument for dealing with any kind of social problem. This is what Rezső Rupert, deputy of the Smallholders' Party, expressed when he called the numerus clausus a "provocative law," a "pinprick law" which, although it "put bayonets" at the gates of the universities, could not alleviate the economic woes of the professional classes, and was only good for "provoking Jewry, and with it the world."[76] Károly Grecsák, Minister of Justice in the Wekerle government (1917–1918), was of a similar opinion. He noted that the university numerus clausus did not solve any social problem, because it was no more than "a hate law conceived in hysteria."[77] Grecsák, of course, did not use the expression "hate law" in the modern colloquial sense, whereby the point of such laws is to protect people from attacks incited by hatred, but in the sense that the law itself was born of hatred. His point was that its goal was precisely to maintain, render permanent, and elevate into a norm the anti-Jewish feeling which had been whipped up throughout the country during the

74 Tibor Zinner, *Az ébredők fénykora, 1919–1933* (Budapest: Akadémiai Kiadó, 1989), 35–39.

75 MNL OL, K636, item 257/10. Submission of the Unified Christian National League, the Turul Alliance and the Association of Awakening Hungarians to parliament, September 1, 1920.

76 Minutes of the parliamentary session of September 4, 1920, in *Az 1920. évi február hó 16-ára összehívott nemzetgyűlés naplója*, vol. 5: 421. Founded by peasant politician István Szabó de Nagyatád in January 1919, the National Smallholders and Agrarian Workers Party (*Országos Kisgazda- és Földműves Párt*) became one of the most popular parties in the early 1920s. Although it largely won the elections in 1920, it joined the government coalition and in 1922 merged with István Bethel's Christian National Union Party to form the Christian Peasant, Smallholder and Civic Party, known as the Unity Party.

77 Bethlen, *A magyar zsidóság almanachja*, 29. Grecsák did not accept that the law was effective against overproduction in general and believed that it came into being purely to exclude the Jews.

war, the revolutions of 1918 and 1919, and the White Terror that followed.[78] The provision of the numerus clausus law which gave the university admissions boards the right to judge an applicant's "loyalty to the nation" (*nemzethűség*) and make recommendations against applicants who had taken part in the revolutions or had belonged to left-wing organizations, served a similar purpose.[79]

Primarily a Jewish Law

Nonetheless, the numerus clausus was primarily a Jewish law, a "barbarian" measure, in Grecsák's phrase, that aimed to punish the Jews for the sins for which influential political powers made them the scapegoats. This sort of politics of scapegoating was familiar to Grecsák from the war years, since as minister of justice from 1916 to 1918 in the wartime government he experienced the flaring up and intensification of political anti-Semitism firsthand. He witnessed how the fortunes made by speculators, suppliers of wartime materials, and black marketeers became tools of religious/racial scapegoating in the hands of anti-Semites. He also witnessed the appearance of sharply anti-Semitic rhetoric in parliament and how the capital of the banks which financed the suppliers of war materials came to be called "Jew-money" and trade deals to be called "Jewish

78 Following widespread protests by soldiers and civilians about the prolongation of an already lost war in the last days of October 1918 that included street demonstrations, marches and strikes, Emperor Charles I was compelled to appoint opposition leader Mihály Károlyi as head of government. The events known as the October or Aster Revolution led to the proclamation on November 16 of the First Hungarian People's Republic, the declaration of the country's independence and consequently the dissolution of Austria-Hungary. However, the economic and social crisis that followed the war and the territorial demands of the neighboring successor states greatly undermined the First Republic and its effort to stabilize the country. It was ultimately a note by the Entente on March 20 demanding the withdrawal of Hungarian forces beyond the lines established in the armistice that led to the fall of the Károlyi government and to the establishment on March 21 of the Hungarian Soviet Republic (sometimes known as the Republic of Councils), led by a coalition of Social Democrats and Communists. Exposed to internal discontent and external military intervention, the Soviet Republic lasted until August 1919. Partly in response for the Red Terror that targeted those who resisted the Soviet Republic, the next period (1919–1923) witnessed a wave of murderous anti-Leftist and anti-Semitic attacks committed by armed military detachments. This White Terror, as it was known, targeted officials of the Soviet Republic, but more often it targeted anyone accused of sympathizing with the revolutions, especially Jews. Moreover, in the counter-revolutionary interwar period, the "revolutions" were blamed for all of postwar-Hungary's misfortunes, most of all for the territorial losses codified in the Trianon Peace Treaty.

79 The action merely codified events: the majority of left-wing students had been removed from the universities through disciplinary actions by the time the law was passed in the autumn of 1920. Many of them emigrated, some were jailed. Nonetheless, the admissions councils made their decisions working from various lists (Galileo Circle members, members of university student union groups, etc.). In the case of the Galileo Circle (see note 2 on page 213 in this volume), it was enough to have been a member of the group, there was no need for proof of individual actions. See Ladányi, *Az egyetemi ifjúság*, 161.

usury." He saw lists of merchants with Jewish names read out in parliament, clearly with a political edge; in other words, he saw how religious incitement became an everyday event in the Hungarian parliament, which (in the words of a deputy of the governing National Party of Work) "seeks to deal with the entire burden and odium of the war on a denominational basis."[80]

The flaring up of anti-Semitism in Hungary generally followed the events taking place in Germany. One sign of the intensification of anti-Semitism in Berlin during the war was when, in the autumn of 1916, the Ministry of War undertook a focused investigation to show how the Jews were shirking their wartime duties. The final results of the investigation were never published, but in the court of public opinion—as was the intention—the mere fact of the investigation cast suspicion on the Jews (especially since the investigation was undertaken by a government agency). The spiritual father of the investigation, General Erich Ludendorff, deputy to the chief of staff of the German army, would later become an associate of Hitler's and demand that Jews be stripped of their citizenship and expelled from Germany. Bishop Prohászka mentioned the German investigation during the parliamentary debate on the numerus clausus and presented a number of false claims—taken from an anti-Semitic pamphlet—about the Jews' shirking their duty, and then presented similarly false claims about Hungarian Jews' shirking their own wartime duties.[81]

A day later, deputy Pál Sándor exposed Prohászka's falsehoods in parliament backed up by the relevant documentation. In 1921, the Central Statistical Office published evidence denying the accusations.[82] But Prohászka never withdrew these false claims. With his made-up accusations concerning the paltri-

80 Pál Farkas's speech quoted in Péter Bihari, *Lövészárkok a hátországban: Középosztály, zsidókérdés, antiszemitizmus az első világháború Magyarországán* (Budapest: Napvilág Kiadó, 2008), 235. The National Party of Work (*Nemzeti Munkapárt*) was a liberal political party in Hungary between 1910 and 1918, successor of the former Liberal Party (*Szabadelvű Párt*), which was in government from 1875 to 1906.

81 For Prohászka's statement, see the minutes of the parliamentary session of September 16, 1920, in *Az 1920. évi február hó 16-ára összehívott nemzetgyűlés naplója*, vol. 5: 350. For a summary of the case, see Lajos Szabolcsi, *Két emberöltő: Az Egyenlőség évtizedei* (1881–1931) (Budapest: MTA, 1993), 312–13.

82 Minutes of the parliamentary session of September 16, 1920, in *Az 1920. évi február hó 16-ára összehívott nemzetgyűlés naplója*, vol. 5: 350. In 1921, deputy Elek Avarffy took up Prohászka's allegations, alleging that only 500 Jewish soldiers died out of the 50,000 who were enlisted and that therefore the death rate among Jewish soldiers was much lower than for non-Jews. The journal *Egyenlőség* (Equality) sued Avarffy and even the noted anti-Semitic statistician Alajos Kovács took its side against Avarffy. The Central Statistical Office issued an official declaration stating that the number of dead Jewish soldiers was 10,000, meaning that the death rate for Jewish soldiers was the same as for non-Jews. See Szabolcsi, *Két emberöltő*, 318.

ness of the Jews' contribution to the war effort, the bishop created a tradition that was later made use of by Hungarian anti-Semites.

This sort of anti-Semitism was alien to the key figures of the pre-1918 Hungarian political elite. The political generation of István Tisza determinedly rejected anti-Semitic scapegoating as a dangerous phenomenon.[83] When, in August 1918, a parliamentary debate on the war economy and food supplies degenerated into an anti-Semitic protest, István Tisza warned that the false generalizations of the anti-Semites were incendiary towards those hundreds of thousands of Jews who had nothing to do with these scandals. "Fundamentally, the problem here," said Tisza "is that a significant proportion of those social or professional classes where these wartime scandals most commonly occur is drawn from the ranks of the Jews. Therefore, a good deal of the revolting things that happen are done by Jews. As a result, we are undeniably faced with the danger that the justified anger and bitterness that develops towards these acts and those who commit them will take on a denominational aspect."[84]

Prior to 1918, the Hungarian governing elite saw it as their task to put the brakes on anti-Semitic propaganda and prevent a lynch mob mood from developing. "I believe we must all take a stand and fight against this danger," Tisza said. "We must all do our bit to help the people understand so that they won't see this in denominational or racial terms and that the justified anger that develops against these crimes and against these shameful and cowardly acts should not be directed at a religion or a race."[85]

The majority of the political leaders who came to power after 1920 no longer shared Tisza's conservative liberal way of thinking and did not resist political scapegoating. They gave in to the temptation of blaming all of Hungary's losses and revolutions on the actions of the Jews, ignoring the problems arising from economic difficulties and the dissatisfaction of the nationalities that the war had brought to a boiling point.

In the summer of 1920, Pál Teleki, a politician who—being in agreement with the anti-Semitic camp—made a promise to address the Jewish question "institutionally," assumed leadership in the country.[86] Teleki considered the whole of Hungary's development during the liberal age to have been erroneous.

83 Miklós Szabó, *Politikai kultúra Magyarországon 1896–1986* (Budapest: ELTE-MKKE, Medvetánc Könyvek, 1989), 191.

84 Minutes of the parliamentary session of August 7, 1920, in *Az 1910. évi június hó 21-ére hirdetett országgyűlés képviselőházának naplója* (Budapest: Athenaeum Irodalmi és Nyomdai Részvénytársulat, 1918), vol. 41: 172–73.

85 *Az 1910. évi június hó 21-ére hirdetett országgyűlés képviselőházának naplója*, vol. 41: 173.

86 In his speech introducing his program as prime minister, Teleki promised to take steps to "defend the

He regarded the emancipation of the Jews as a historical error, which "had to be corrected" even "at the price of the removal of rights." Bishop Prohászka, president of the governing Christian National Union Party, was of a similar opinion. He acknowledged that the entirety of "post-1867 development had been created by the Jews" and that, from the Austro-Hungarian Compromise onwards, "the Hungarian economy and Hungarian trade had taken off" thanks "to the Jews, not the Hungarians," but he believed the Hungarian state had nonetheless committed a "historical crime" in letting in the Jews, in the first place. It was necessary to recognize that this situation had to be put to an end because "Hungary only needs a certain percentage of Jews."[87]

A year later, when István Bethlen took Teleki's place at the country's helm, explicit anti-Semitism was forced out of government-level politics. Bethlen, unlike Teleki, did not reject the tradition of liberal politics. But despite the fact that anti-Jewish sentiment disappeared from Bethlen's political statements in the 1920s, and his enemies frequently accused him of being "friendly to the Jews," Bethlen himself was not free from anti-Semitic feelings and preconceptions. Bethlen also used the false generalizations of a "Jewish conspiracy" to explain the turn of historical events; thus, he viewed the actions of the Jews as the root cause of the left-wing revolutions of 1918–19. It is typical of his prejudiced thinking that he thought that a "large part" of the Jews took part in the left-wing revolutions, whereas barely two or three thousand of the nearly half a million Hungarian Jews participated in them.[88] True, Bethlen was not exaggerating when talking about the markedly high number of Jewish leaders in the Hungarian Soviet Republic, a short-lived communist state that lasted from March 21 to August 1, 1919. According to Gusztáv Gratz's calculations, 71 percent of the 45 commissars were Jewish (32 people). Tibor Hajdu puts this percentage closer to 60 percent, which is nonetheless still high.[89] Bethlen did not take into account that non-Jews also took part in the leadership of the Soviet Republic. He also failed to acknowledge that only a small fraction of Hungary's several hundred thousand Jews took part in the revolutions, as opposed to the vast majority of Hungarian Jewry who either opposed or were uninterested in

interests of Christian society institutionally." Minutes of the parliamentary session of July 22, 1920, in *Az 1920. évi február hó 16-ára összehívott nemzetgyűlés naplója*, vol. 4: 15.

87 Minutes of the parliamentary session of September 16, 1920, in *Az 1920. évi február hó 16-ára összehívott nemzetgyűlés naplója*, vol. 5: 350.

88 *Az 1920. évi február hó 16-ára összehívott nemzetgyűlés naplója*, vol. 5: 350.

89 Tibor Hajdu, "Kun Béla mint zsidó," *Élet és Irodalom* 54, no. 27 (July 9, 2010), 20; and Gusztáv Gratz, *A forradalmak kora: Magyarország története, 1918–1920* (Budapest: Magyar Szemle Társaság, 1935), 102.

the communist enterprise. It was to this that the Liberal deputy Sándor Pető referred when he said that "you are bringing in such general laws, statutes, and rules that will be to the detriment of all Jews, including those leading a respectable, Hungarian, middle-class existence."[90]

The leading politicians of the 1920s, being themselves prejudiced when it came to Jews, reacted ambiguously when it came to the politics of anti-Semitic scapegoating. Though they opposed the anti-Semitic acts of violence that severely threatened foreign opinion of Hungary, they nonetheless sympathized with those who presented the Hungarian Soviet Republic as a Jewish revolution, and accordingly blamed "the Jews" for the revolution, and demanded that they be held to account.

The "Jewish conspiracy" even pertained to the post-Trianon borders. István Haller, minister of education when the numerus clausus was introduced, perpetuated this view. In his memoirs, in a chapter entitled "As long as there's Trianon, there'll be a numerus clausus," he accused the Jews of "using nine tenths of [their] economic means for the benefit of the Entente powers. There are grave documents showing the extent of the participation of world Jewry both morally and economically in the fight against the Central powers."[91] "The Jews" now had to "balance" this account by using their influence "to restore Hungary's historic borders and regain the territories unlawfully stolen from us."[92] Hungarian Jewry became hostage to the Trianon treaty and the object of any bargain to be struck with the Great Powers. This was a thought shared by the political leadership of the country from the radical right through to the moderates. The difference was primarily in tone. One of the leaders of the moderate camp, Kunó Klebelsberg, announced directly in parliament that the fate of the Jews in Hungary depended on what concessions the European Great Powers were willing to make in the question of Hungary's borders. "Let them give us back the old Greater Hungary," he said in parliament in 1924, "and we will be able to repeal the numerus clausus."[93]

In this mentality, foreign and Hungarian, rich and poor, communist or non-communist Jews were conflated: the Jews bore the burden of collective responsibility. According to Smallholder deputy Rezső Rupert, the principle

---

90 Minutes of the parliamentary session of September 3, 1920, in *Az 1920. évi február hó 16-ára összehívott nemzetgyűlés naplója*, vol. 5: 191.

91 Haller, *Harc a numerus clausus körül*, 244 and 253.

92 Haller, *Harc a numerus clausus körül*, 253.

93 Minutes of the parliamentary session of June 4, 1924, in *Az 1922. évi junius hó 16-ára hirdetett nemzetgyűlés naplója*, vol. 24: 320.

of collective responsibility was the populist mechanism that made it possible to "generalize—even by law—the 'guilt' of a few to hundreds of thousands, even millions."[94] In line with this mentality, there was no contradiction in simultaneously applying racial, political, and even gender-based arguments: university applicants were to be judged not only on the basis of their origins, but also from the point of view of what political "behavior" they had demonstrated prior to 1920; in other words, if they were sufficiently "loyal to the nation." The combination of racial and political criteria cast suspicion on leftists as being "Jews," and Jews as being automatically left-wing, which in turn reinforced the conviction that the left-wing revolutions served some kind of special "Jewish" interest.

Nándor Bernolák, the law professor who introduced an amendment to the numerus clausus draft which included the racial clause, openly spoke in parliament about how in his opinion the political and racial aspects of the numerus clausus law had to be in strict conformity with one another.

> One of the fundamental characteristics of Jewry . . . is an excessive intellectualism which pushes considerations of emotion and mercy far more into the background and places utilitarian considerations into the forefront. . . . It is no coincidence that, for example, a professor of utilitarian philosophy at the University of Budapest and thus the founder of a great school was a Jewish professor who made quite a serious, significant, and respected name for himself in the philosophical field. However, by founding such a school and gathering around himself not only similar thinking people, but also a similar sort as himself, he became to a very significant extent the one who prepared the way for—as he himself acknowledged—and was, to a certain extent, the father of the revolution that turned this country upside down.[95]

The way Bernolák created the link between "similar thinking" and "similar sort" is typical of the numerus clausus law itself, which punished the left-wing students while at the same time restricted the admission of Jewish students. "Under the circumstances," said Bernolák,

94 Rezső Rupert's minority opinion on the second Jewish law, February 3, 1939, in *Az 1935. évi április hó 27-ére összehívott országgyűlés irományai* (Budapest: Athenaeum Irodalmi és Nyomdai Részvénytársulat, 1939), vol. 12: 514.

95 Minutes of the parliamentary session of September 3, 1920, in *Az 1920. évi február hó 16-ára összehívott nemzetgyűlés naplója*, vol. 5: 187.

> I cannot deny that the proposition I place before you entails the wish that the Jews should not take part in such overwhelming numbers in the graduate professional fields. Yes, it is my wish, and I say it quite openly that it is as much in the interest of the Jews living in Hungary as it is of the Hungarian nation that the proportion of Jews in higher education should decrease. I find this very necessary in the interests of social stability and the peaceful functioning of the university, but most of all to ensure that it should once more be the spirit of the Hungarian people that guides this country.[96]

Figure 4. Nándor Bernolák in the 1920s. Source: Magyar Nemzeti Múzeum Történeti Fényképtára (Historical Photo Department of the Hungarian National Museum, hereafter MNM.

In saying this, Bernolák not only viewed the racial clause as a means to punish the Jews, but also as a means to legitimize punishing the Jews for the loss of the war, the revolutions, and the post-Trianon borders.

The numerus clausus was above all a product of this mentality. It was an anti-Jewish law, which—after 1920—punished Hungarian Jewry as a group, without individual considerations, for the losses which Hungary had suffered as a result of the war, the revolutions, and the peace treaty. The racial quota of the numerus clausus was thus linked with the post-revolutionary anti-leftist political cleanup: the same clause that institutionalized the racial quota tied university admissions to the demands for "loyalty to the nation and moral uprightness," thereby conflating the political cleanup with the exclusion of the Jews. The requirement of the "loyalty to the nation" was maintained by the Hungarian government even after the amendment of the Jewish quota in 1928. This meant that according to the letter of the law, university admissions were made theoretically conditional on the behavior of young people who at the time of the war and the revolutionary "chaos" were barely ten years old.

96 *Az 1920. évi február hó 16-ára összehívott nemzetgyűlés naplója*, vol. 5: 187.

Most of the major proponents of the numerus clausus—Ottokár Prohászka, Pál Teleki, and Alajos Kovács—did not merely want to punish the Jews for their perceived negative traits, but wanted to exclude them from Hungarian society, insofar as possible, precisely because of their perceived positive traits. Hungarian anti-Semites did not consider Jews inferior—quite the opposite. They held them to be in many ways superior and therefore dangerous to Hungarians. It was, of course, not only the radical anti-Semites who held this opinion among the Hungarian political elite. Even István Bethlen, who was usually less forthright, had a distinct opinion on the competitive advantage of Jews: "[The Jews] with their economic inventiveness, skill, and talents which exceed—I say this with absolute objectivity—the economic capabilities of the Hungarian race as well as those of other people living here (the ethnic Germans, for example) have netted themselves great successes in the economic field."[97] Prohászka, for example, spoke of the Jews' "massive" intelligence and industry, while he described Hungarians as "incapable of handling life," exhibiting "gentry arrogance" (*úrhatnámság*), and laziness.[98] Prohászka said that the Hungarian trading sector was simply "created by the Jews" because "with their immense business sense and agile intelligence, attuned to contemporary events, with their great industriousness, they were perfectly placed to thoroughly supplant this generation, with its apathy, indolence, refusal to work, and spirit of gentry arrogance, [a generation] unaccustomed to struggle and totally incapable of handling life."[99]

Alajos Kovács was of a similar opinion, saying that Jews were generally "more receptive" to culture than Hungarians and were therefore more successful in modern business. In this way of thinking, the "struggle of the races" overruled every other—economic, cultural, professional, or human—consideration. This struggle of the races, in the description given by professor of ophthalmology Károly Hoór (one of the chief propagandists of the Jewish quota), began to take on the aspect of fully-fledged National Socialism: "If the Hungarian nation ever reached the point where it had or could have only Jewish doctors,

97 Minutes of the parliamentary session of May 11, 1937, in *Az 1935. évi április hó 27-ére hirdetett országgyűlés képviselőházának naplója* (Budapest: Athenaeum Irodalmi és Nyomdai Részvénytársulat, 1937), vol. 13: 64.

98 Minutes of the parliamentary session of September 18, 1920, in *Az 1920. évi február hó 16-ára összehívott nemzetgyűlés naplója*, vol. 5: 347.

99 *Az 1920. évi február hó 16-ára összehívott nemzetgyűlés naplója*, vol. 5: 347. "We do not have a problem," Prohászka said "with the fact that the Jews created Hungarian commerce. We don't even deny it. And the Hungarian people were never anti-Semitic because their merchants were Jewish. I can well remember when we were trying to establish that big coal cooperative and someone said that if we do this, then this, that, and the other Jew will all leave. The response from one of the Hungarians was 'but then where will we get ourselves new Jews? The Hungarian people cannot prosper without them.'"

then it will be completely ripe to be decimated by epidemics and wiped from the face of the earth, because it will then have ceased to be a nation worthy of life anyway."[100] The leading exponents of the numerus clausus, then, let it be known completely openly that the sole goal of the measure was to exclude the more competitive for the sake of the weaker. When, therefore, people argued against the numerus clausus by saying it was dangerous and detrimental for the progress of Hungarian science and culture, these arguments fell on deaf ears because the supporters of the numerus clausus had already weighed these dangers before the law had been introduced in the first place and made the decision to support it in the light of their conclusions.

The "idea" of a racial clause

What was new in the historical circumstances leading to the legislation of the Jewish quota was not the appearance of political anti-Semitism in Hungarian public life itself, as this sentiment had already a long tradition in the country. Even the idea of an anti-Jewish numerus clausus was not new in Hungarian political writing in 1918; it appeared much earlier, in the last decades of the nineteenth century, following the introduction of an anti-Jewish numerus clausus in Russia in 1887. There had been occasional calls in the Austrian and Hungarian parliaments for an anti-Jewish numerus clausus as early as the turn of the century. One such proposal came in 1907 when Károly Hencz recommended the introduction of restrictions on the number of Israelite students at university, while Károly Kmety suggested the same in the secondary schools. But despite these signs of political anti-Semitism, it cannot be claimed that these recommendations had any real strength before 1918, nor did they start some sort of inexorable process.

The "idea" of an anti-Jewish numerus clausus really gained ground only during the war and the revolutions. The novelty of the political situation following the revolutions lay not in the appearance of recommendations for a Jewish quota, but rather in the fact that, unlike in the past, the country's political leaders no longer resisted the calls for a Jewish quota. Moreover, by introducing a law to this effect, they raised political anti-Semitism to a governmental level. The real novelty of the law was the introduction of the racial clause, which branded an entire group of people as scapegoats on the basis of collective guilt, rather than targeting specific individuals.

---

100 Károly Hoór, "A numerus clausus." *MONE Orvostársadalmi Szemle* 2, no. 4 (1925): 4.

The introduction of the Jewish quota brought a new facet to Hungarian political life. True, even in the Dual Monarchy, the Hungarian state had not shied away from encouraging the linguistic assimilation of national minorities by introducing educational measures that put non-Hungarians at a distinct disadvantage. State financing for non-Hungarian-language educational institutions was less than for Hungarian ones. But the Hungarian state did not question the equal citizenship rights of national minorities, nor did it foreclose opportunities for individual advancement for the members of these minorities. The events of 1920 were new in that the state now took away the right to higher education for certain individuals (selected on the basis of their origins) with the specific purpose of denying the avenues of advancement that required university degrees.

The rescinding of rights to education on the basis of origin set the Hungarian numerus clausus apart from the other uses of an anti-Jewish numerus clausus in the Western world. In the United States and Canada, numerous universities (for example, Harvard, Yale, Columbia) introduced anti-Jewish quotas at around the same time as the Hungarian numerus clausus, to some degree precisely because of the large number of Jewish immigrants arriving as a result of Eastern European anti-Semitic movements. Many schools of medicine also capped the number of Jewish students. But in these countries, the anti-Jewish quota was never elevated to the level of government action or into law. On the one hand, this meant that students excluded from one university could continue their studies at another university within the same state. On the other hand, the Jewish community was free to establish a university for excluded students. In Eastern Europe, calls for a numerus clausus were on the agenda from the 1920s onwards in Romania, Poland, and Lithuania. And while it did not become law in any of those countries until the 1930s, universities and polytechnics in Romania and Poland instituted "in-house" anti-Jewish quotas, without any legal authority, beginning in the 1920s. It remains uncertain whether it was precisely due to the large number of Jewish students excluded from the Hungarian educational system that demands for a numerus clausus appeared in the Czech parliament as well.[101] In Austria, there were calls for a numerus clausus at a 45,000-strong rally attended by the National Socialists (among others) in January 1923.[102]

101 MTI News Release, November 30 and December 2, 1922. The parliamentary deputies urging the introduction of a numerus clausus wanted a nationalities quota to apply to both the students and the faculty at higher education institutions.

102 MTI News Release, January 22, 1923.

The fate of the racial quota after 1928: The myth of "repeal"

The most misleading myth connected to the history of the numerus clausus is that the law was repealed in 1928. The myth of "repeal" was born at the end of the 1920s, but it remains alive in the historical literature to this day. Its development was made possible by the clever politics of the Bethlen government. The numerus clausus was not really repealed in 1928, but merely renamed. Anti-Jewish discrimination at the universities did not cease. The only element of the myth that is true is that the racial clause of the law underwent some metamorphosis.

In chapter three, I will show that the Bethlen government did indeed formally remove the Jewish quota from the law in 1928 under pressure from the League of Nations. But they added a new quota to the law, a professional quota. The goal of this new quota was exactly the same as that of the old one—namely, to keep the Jews out of the universities. This time, however, it was meant to do so in a way that would not give the League of Nations the grounds to censure Hungary for racial discrimination. For two years prior to the amendment, Klebelsberg had been advising Prime Minister Bethlen to have the law changed in such a way that would still bar "thousands" of Jewish students from enrolling in Hungarian universities. Bethlen, in other words, should concede to demands of the League of Nations, but this concession should be purely formal. In the end, the government substituted the racial quota with a new quota which restricted the number of students to be admitted based on the occupation of the applicant's father.[103] The inner logic of the professional quota was constructed in such a way as to ensure that the proportion of Jews could not rise significantly under the new system either.

The government, for understandable reasons, did not comment on the reasons for the 1928 amendment, since the whole point was to put an end to censureship by the League of Nations for discriminating against the Jews. Ten years later, when Hungarian diplomacy was more interested in currying favor with Germany than with the League of Nations, Alajos Kovács described in detail the inner logic of the 1928 professional quota. According to his account,

> the milder form of the numerus clausus initiated by the late Count Klebelsberg, minister of education, fundamentally served the same purpose . . . though it did not explicitly say that each race was to be admitted to university according

103 For more detail on this amendment, see pages 183–84 in this volume.

> to its proportion within the overall population. . . . Since in the first [professional] category, which accounts for about half the students, there are hardly any Jews, while in the other half of the places . . . it would have been the children of the agrarian workers who were in a majority . . . in the end, the proportion of Jews in the student body would have been roughly equal to their proportion within the overall population.[104]

Bálint Hóman, minister of education from 1932–38 and 1939–42, described the essence of the professional quota in the same way as Kovács: the Jewish quota, removed under international pressure, was replaced by a measure which, without "openly naming the Jews," achieved the same goal as the original Jewish quota of 1920 by "indirect means" through the quota for professional groups.[105]

It was not hard to grasp the motives behind the changes. Lucien Wolf, an Englishman, who wrote the report on the amendment for the League of Nations, clearly saw that the new, professional quota "could be used for anti-Semitic ends"; however, as he wrote, the starting point still has to be that the actions of the Hungarian government were "made in good faith."[106] The League of Nations, therefore, did not concern itself with the hidden motives behind the new quota: it was satisfied that the Jewish quota had been removed from the legislation. It considered the removal of the Jewish quota a symbolic victory, and did not expect anything more. The leaders of the Jewish community in Hungary felt the same, and hoped that the symbolic concessions would be followed by real change in due course. The government increased the number of Jews permitted to attend university (by a suitably minimal number). It raised the number of Jewish students admitted by more than 250 a year and was careful to send the admissions data to the Foreign Ministry as well, where otherwise such data would have had no place.[107] Yet, although the proportion of Jewish students did indeed grow from 8.8 percent in 1928–29 to 12.5 percent in 1933, this by no means implies that Jewish students really enjoyed equal opportunities with their Christian counterparts. Between 1928 and 1932, roughly seven out of ten Jewish applicants to university were rejected, while for Christian students the rejection rate was less than one out of seven. The

---

104 Kovács, *A csonkamagyarországi zsidóság*, 39.

105 Explanatory memorandum to the draft law on the "regulation of university and polytechnic admissions," November 15, 1940, in *Az 1939. évi június hó 10-ére összehívott országgyűlés felsőházának irományai*, vol. 4: 187–88.

106 Ladányi, "A numerus clausus-törvény 1928. évi módosításáról," 1131.

107 MNL OL, K 636, VKM 1928–23-69628, "Kimutatás az elsőéves hallgatókról."

majority of Jewish youth with secondary school diplomas still did not have an opportunity for further study.[108]

Despite the exculpatory arguments of the Bethlen government intended for foreign consumption which stressed that the proportion of Jewish students had risen above the old quota, what was not mentioned was that even so, two thirds of Jewish students wishing to pursue higher education still could not get into university. There was a cynical game of propaganda being played out with the numbers and percentages while thousands of Jewish students hoping to continue their studies remained stranded outside the universities.

The slight easing of discrimination lasted until the 1931–32 admissions cycle. Minister of Education Bálint Hóman instructed the universities in the autumn of 1932 to be "rigorous" in their admissions procedures, while in the autumn of 1933 he spoke in parliament of plans for reforms that would make the 6 percent Jewish quota enforceable once more: "We must make absolutely sure," he said, "that there will be no difference in the ratio of Hungarian Christian youth to Jewish youth in university compared to the national ratio."[109]

In autumn of 1933, following Hitler's accession to power, protests by the Hungarian anti-Semitic student organizations became more forceful. Prime Minister Gyula Gömbös promised in the winter of that year that the universities would, in practice, enforce the original 1920 Jewish quota. But he added that the government was not thinking of removing the 1928 amendment.[110] In that year, the proportion of Jewish students fell back again to 9.7 percent, and the beatings of Jewish students, familiar from the 1920s, started at the universities once again. Minister of the Interior, Ferenc Keresztes-Fischer, declared in a cabinet meeting on January 16, 1934, that "in the coming year, the Jewish quota will be enforced,"[111] and this was five years after the Jewish quota had allegedly been repealed. In reality, however, the Jewish quota continued to exist, since—as Bálint Hóman, minister of religion and education, later openly explained—successive ministers of education "continued to maintain the restriction on the admission of Jews to universities and polytechnics by means of case-by-case measures until the issue was given new and more comprehensive

108 Ladányi, "A numerus clausus-törvény 1928. évi módosításáról," 1140 and MNL OL, K 636, 410-5: "Adatok az egyetemi numerus clausus jövő tanévi meghatározásához" (1929).

109 Bálint Hóman's address at the parliamentary session of November 29, 1933, in *Az 1931. évi július hó 18-ára hirdetett országgyűlés képviselőházának naplója* (Budapest: Athenaeum Irodalmi és Nyomdai Részvénytársulat, 1933), vol. 18: 332.

110 Quoted from the journal of the Turul Alliance in Ladányi, "A numerus clausustól a numerus nullusig," 63.

111 Ladányi, "A numerus clausustól a numerus nullusig," 63.

legal regulation by the creation of Law No. IV of 1939."[112] Thus, the number of Jewish students began to rapidly decline once more after 1934 and sank to under 3 percent by 1940.

The reinstatement of an explicit Jewish quota

The Second Jewish Law formally reinstated the racial clause in 1939. Although the Second Jewish Law did not prescribe a Jewish quota for secondary schools, department V/I of the Ministry of Religion and Public Education extended the aegis of the racial clause to secondary schools as well and capped the number of Jewish students who could be admitted at 6 percent.[113] The seventh clause of the law stated that the proportion of Jewish students among first year admissions could not exceed 6 percent.[114]

The racial clause of the numerus clausus law therefore—despite a temporary and modest relaxation—was in force throughout the entirety of the Horthy period. It was an official law between 1920 and 1928, but the exclusion of Jews continued in the decade (1928–39) when the Jewish quota was replaced with a professional quota. The Jewish quota was again in force between 1939 and 1945. Its history also includes the fact that the first academic year in the 1930s that saw the proportion of Jewish students falling below 8.3 percent—the lowest rate measured in the 1920s—was the 1936–37 academic year, when the Jewish quota of 1920 was officially no longer in place, and the Jewish quota of 1939 was not yet in force. Thus, the widely-held assertion that discrimination had disappeared from the Hungarian institutional system following the amendment of the numerus clausus in 1928 does not stand up.

---

112 Explanatory memorandum to the draft law on the "regulation of university and polytechnic admissions," November 15, 1940, in *Az 1939. évi június hó 10-ére összehívott országgyűlés felsőházának irományai*, vol. 4: 187–88.

113 For more on this, see pages 201–3 in this volume.

114 For the text of the clause, see note 113 in chapter 3 of this volume.

Chapter One

The Genesis of the Law

The numerus clausus law—in contrast to the Jewish Laws of the 1930s—created a Jewish quota, not across the economic sector as a whole, but only in one specific area, namely, higher education. But at least some of the forces fighting for the law were not content with merely changing the face of higher education. They wanted to introduce similar limits more broadly, including in other parts of the economy.

During the parliamentary debate, proposals came thick and fast regarding which other elements of the economy should be regulated by Jewish quotas. The establishment of a professional registry was proposed, which would allow the proportion of Jews to be regulated within the individual professions and fields of economic activity. The proposal was submitted to parliament by the Turul Alliance,[1] the Association of Awakening Hungarians, and the United Christian National League and read: "As for the fields in which the Jews are now present in disproportionate numbers, Jews should be banned from entering them until the proper proportions are restored."[2] Others wanted to impose quotas on the trade in raw materials, granting Jews access to no more than 8 per-

1 Formed in August 1919 from the law enforcement militia groups established at the Budapest university, the Turul Alliance (Turul Szövetség) became one of the most influential of the student fraternities (*bajtársi szövetségek*). By the second half of the 1920s, it had grown into the largest national higher education student organization, and by the 1930s, into a broad national mass-movement through its member associations. In terms of ideology, the association endorsed the "racial defense" program of Gyula Gömbös and was thus characterized by a right-wing radical stance, revisionism, militarism, and anti-Semitism. The Turul Alliance fully endorsed the numerus clausus, and its members were involved in a number of attacks on Jewish students.

2 MNL OL, K636, item 257/10. Submission of the United Christian National League, the Turul Alliance, and the Association of Awakening Hungarians to parliament, September 1, 1920.

Figure 5. Prime Minister Gyula Gömbös (center) with the leaders of the Turul Alliance in 1933. Source: Wikimedia Commons.

cent of the raw materials and also limiting the proportion of Jews employed by the ministries that distributed raw materials to 8 percent.[3] Additionally, a proposal was made to introduce a quota in the press, with printing paper distributed according to the proportion of the various "nationalities," and Jewish-owned newspapers marked with some Hebrew letters.[4] Another proposal was to extend the Jewish quota to secondary schools,[5] while yet another to exclude Jews from state tenders. In addition to these economic sanctions, one proposal also sought the introduction of the so-called "racial defense" laws, which would exclude Jews from teaching subjects that were part of forming the "national and Christian spirit" and would ban Christians from domestic service in Jewish households. Jews would also be excluded from public service and have their political rights revoked.[6]

3 Motion by Károly Ereky, April 27, 1920, in *Az 1920. évi február hó 16-ára összehívott nemzetgyűlés irományai*, vol. 1 (Budapest, Pesti Könyvnyomda Részvénytársaság, 1920), 281; and address by László Budaváry on August 7, 1920, in *Az 1920. évi február hó 16-ára összehívott nemzetgyűlés naplója*, vol. 4: 287–89.

4 The proposals on the press came from István Friedrich. "Levelek," *Budapesti Hírlap*, April 22 and 23, 1920.

5 MNL OL, K636, item 257/10. Submission of the United Christian National League, the Turul Alliance, and the Association of Awakening Hungarians to parliament, September 1, 1920.

6 Motion by Gyula Zákány, April 28, 1920, in *Az 1920. évi február hó 16-ára összehívott nemzetgyűlés irományai*, vol. 1: 381.

Although the voices demanding these wide-ranging Jewish laws died down within a year or two, during the years of Bethlen's postwar recovery efforts, certain anti-Semitic politicians (Ottokár Prohászka and Gyula Gömbös, a defining figure of Hungarian interwar rightwing radicalism who would become prime minister between 1932 and 1936, for example) nonetheless continued to promote the idea. Gömbös was still demanding a numerus clausus for every sector of the economy in 1922: "I would ask that action be taken systematically in every aspect of government in order to build up the economic base of Christian Hungary. . . . I would ask that these limits be expanded (that is, the Jewish/non-Jewish limits) to at least parity with the relevant proportions. That is the very least that Christian Hungarians can ask."[7]

The numerus clausus as an education law

The push for a comprehensive Jewish quota was not related primarily to higher education. Yet, subsequent attention has nonetheless focused on the numerus clausus in the universities because, in the end, higher education was the only field into which an official Jewish quota, set in law, was introduced in 1920. There were no new quotas introduced for the next eighteen years, until 1938.

At the start of the 1919–20 academic year, the situation in higher education (albeit temporarily) was truly dire. The students who had interrupted their studies to fight, either in the war or in the revolutions that followed, all turned up at the same time. There were twice as many students registering at the Faculty of Medicine as there had been in 1914. The faculty was simply unable to undertake the teaching of that many students.[8]

In theory, it would have been possible to alleviate the situation in Hungary by instituting extra semesters during the summer and by relaxing some requirements. This is what many other European countries died. This solution was, in fact, tried in Hungary in 1918, but the experience of the extra semesters led to the heightening of anti-Jewish tensions, since the Christian students showed

7 Minutes of the parliamentary session of December 16, 1922, in *Az 1922. évi junius hó 16-ára hirdetett nemzetgyűlés naplója*, vol. 7: 48.

8 Katalin N. Szegvári, *Numerus clausus rendelkezések az ellenforradalmi Magyarországon* (Budapest: Akadémiai Kiadó, 1988), 97–98. There were 6,500 students enrolled to the Faculty of Medicine for the 1919–20 academic year, in contrast to 3,524 in 1914. See Kovács, *A zsidóság térfoglalása Magyarországon*, 31.

less enthusiasm for the extra semesters than their Jewish colleagues. By that time, the proportion of Jewish students—including those enrolled for the summer semesters—had risen to 34 percent.

The universities were also afraid that the flood of students immigrating from the territories lost by Hungary after the war would lead to permanent overcrowding. (This did not, in fact, come to pass, because the universities in the lost territories were soon moved into the territory of post-Trianon Hungary.[9]) Given that anyone with a secondary school diploma could apply to university freely and without any kind of limits, the universities themselves called for the system to be changed: the law should regulate the maximum number of students allowed to enroll in any one year; in other words, a "closed [fixed] number" system should be put in place—or, to give it its Latin name, a "numerus clausus."

The introduction of limits on the number of students in higher education would not necessarily—under different political circumstances—have gone together with the system of an anti-Jewish racial quota. In 1912, before the war, a debate was organized at Hungarian institutions of higher education on whether a numerus clausus should be introduced—following the German model—in some faculties but the debate did not include any sort of racial arguments, since the legal instrument of a "fixed number" is not, in itself, discriminatory.[10] Nonetheless, the numerus clausus in Hungary is still synonymous with the anti-Jewish system of quotas and this is justified in so far as the numerus clausus was linked to an anti-Jewish quota right from the moment of its introduction in the country. This was the case despite the fact that the number of students in higher education could have just as well have been regulated in Hungary—as in many other European countries—without the use of quotas, by selecting students on the basis of academic merit alone.

Numerus clausus without the Jewish quota?

It would have been possible for the law to introduce some sort of quota, without it being necessarily aimed at the Jews. Originally, on August 22, 1919, the Faculty of Medicine presented just such a proposal, and incidentally, this was

---

9 According to Ministry of Religion and Public Education data from 1921, 4,632 of the university students in Budapest (which was 37.5 percent of the total) had refugee status. Pálfy, "Nemzetállam és felsőoktatási piac," 153.

10 N. Szegvári, *Numerus clausus rendelkezések*, 42–44.

the first faculty to recommend a numerus clausus. The Faculty of Medicine's original recommendation, which was passed to the minister of education by professor of ophthalmology Károly Hoór, contained a proposal for a planned system of quotas, but it was aimed not at Jews but at women, and it also proposed excluding those who had taken part in the revolutions from higher education.[11] The preparation of the law took a full year and it was on July 22, 1920, that Minister of Education István Haller finally submitted the proposed bill. It still did not contain a Jewish quota.[12]

Discussion of a Jewish quota did not arise during the planning process regarding the proposal from the Faculty of Medicine. Rather, it first arose in the Faculty of Theology's response to the Faculty of Medicine's recommendation, which was approved by the dean of the faculty, Mihály Kmoskó. His reasoning was that the introduction of a fixed number system automatically dictated the next step, the introduction of a rule by which "the individual faculties should establish the proportions governing student enrollment on the basis of past behavior and race," because this was the only way of ensuring that "no domestic nationality, race, or religion should benefit from undue privileges . . . under the numerus clausus system of enrollment."[13] Since the Faculty of Theology had no Jewish students, Kmoskó was clearly not concerned with keeping Jewish students away from his own specialist field, but from the universities as a whole.

The various faculties responded differently to the proposal. Of the twenty-four professors at the Faculty of Humanities, fifteen (including the dean, Ernő Fináczy) expressed marked objection to the plan. The majority of professors at

11 Mária M. Kovács, *Liberalizmus, radikalizmus, antiszemitizmus: A magyar orvosi, ügyvédi és mérnöki kar politikája 1867 és 1945 között* (Budapest: Helikon, 2001), 76. The Faculty of Medicine's recommendation of August 22, 1919 states that "there is a need for a numerus clausus for students," but they do not suggest any racial or nationalities filter. Their recommendation would cap the number of students at 400 per year, and they envisaged their selection thus: 1) a restricted number of female students; 2) the students should be selected by a board of admission (in the higher years, year-end exams should be before a committee); and 3) those who played a role in the Commune [the Hungarian Soviet Republic] should be filtered out, or in other words, those who "were not restrained even by the idealism of youth from taking up roles in revolutionary mass-organizations in workers' or soldiers' councils or as agitators." Minister István Haller's draft law, as introduced at a cabinet meeting a year later on July 21, 1920, still made no reference to a system of quotas. N. Szegvári, *Numerus clausus rendelkezések*, 96, 114.

12 The parliament debated the draft of the law on seven occasions (September 2, 3, 16, 17, 18, 20, and 21, 1920). Nándor Bernolák's motion for an individual amendment, which was about the creation of the nationalities quota, was introduced on September 3, and the law was passed on September 21.

13 N. Szegvári, *Numerus clausus rendelkezések*, 97.

the Faculty of Law, on the other hand, agreed with Kmoskó's recommendation. It was also supported by the majority of the professors at the Faculty of Medicine, and later at the University of Technology.[14] Another full year passed before parliament made the recommendation into a law. Thanks to Kmoskó's contribution, however, it was not the educational impact of the numerus clausus that was at the center of the debates, but the anti-Jewish element.

The Jewish question would certainly have arisen in some form in connection with the numerus clausus even if the recommendation from the universities had not contained measures aimed at Jews. For in the case of a merit-based admissions system, the issue would have arisen that the proportion of Jewish students under a numerus clausus system would foreseeably have risen, since the average academic performance of Jewish students at secondary school level (excepting physical education) was higher in every subject than that of their non-Jewish counterparts.[15] Consequently, the proportion of Jews in the student population would have increased in proportion to the extent to which better academic results were reflected in the admissions process. Alajos Kovács also concluded that "without the establishment of proportionality in the numerus clausus (i.e., the limitation of the proportion of Jews), it would have resulted in an even higher proportion of the next generation of the intellectual elite being Jewish than before its introduction."[16]

The introduction of a numerus clausus in higher education, then, would in any event have drawn attention to the Jewish question, even under different circumstances. Supporters of the numerus clausus understood that if a fixed number system was introduced without a Jewish quota, then the proportion of Jewish students would actually increase. But in 1919–20, the Jewish ques-

---

14 With institutional roots going back as far as the early eighteenth century, the University of Technology was founded in Buda in 1872 under the name Royal Joseph Technical University. In 1934, the university was reorganized and officially renamed Palatine Joseph University of Technology and Economics.

15 Karády, *Iskolarendszer és felekezeti egyenlőtlenségek*, 118–19. Karády looked at the academic results of the students at twenty-four secondary schools between 1873 and 1930. The average difference in grades between Jewish and Catholic students was 0.32 in Hungarian Language and Literature in the Jewish students' favor, while the average difference in grades between Jews and other religions was 0.22. In Latin, the same study found (with the same categories in the same order as above) a difference of 0.27 and 0.26; in German 0.33 and 0.25; in mathematics 0.22 and 0.13, all in favor of the Jewish students. In physical education, however, the difference was against the Jewish students, at 0.22 and 0.19.

16 Alajos Kovács, "Értelmiségünk nemzeti jellegének biztosítása," *Társadalomtudomány* 6, no. 4 (1926): 267.

tion was in any event a tinderbox for social tensions. The loss of the war, the left-wing revolutions that had a high proportion of Jewish participants, and the general political and economic crisis resulting from the Trianon Peace Treaty meant that the Jews were cast in the role of scapegoats.

"An orgiastic cacophony of the basest human motives"

Anti-Semitic forces accused the whole of Hungarian Jewry of treachery and betrayal of the country. At the same time, they blamed them for the war-induced shortages, war profiteering, price increases, the apparently disproportionately low number of Jewish war dead, the harsh peace terms imposed by the Entente powers, the dissolution of historic Hungary, their prominent role in the leadership of the Hungarian Soviet Republic, and for the suffering caused by both capitalism and communism in general. After 1919, the traditional concept of Jewish capitalism was joined by the idea of Judeo-Bolshevism as an element of political anti-Semitism: the figure of the left-wing Jewish revolutionary was now conflated with the Jewish plutocrat as a target for the anti-Semitic movements.

Rational arguments did not carry much weight in the atmosphere of political hysteria. The country had been "overtaken by an orgiastic cacophony of the basest human motives," as Ödön Beniczky put it in parliament in the summer of 1920 (Beniczky had been minister of the interior in the Friedrich and Huszár governments).[17] It did not matter that it was merely a small fraction (two to three thousand people) of the several hundred thousand strong Jewish community in Hungary that had taken part in the communist movement, even if the leaders of the movement were in large part Jewish. It did not matter that the vast majority of Jews remained just as passive during the Hungarian Soviet Republic era as the population overall, that the victims of the Red Terror included Jews as well as non-Jews, and that Jews also supported the counter-revolutionary efforts and took an active part in diplomatic efforts surrounding the question of Hungary's borders.[18]

Anti-Semitic posters went up in the streets, Jewish shops were attacked, Jewish passengers were thrown off trams, the buildings of Jewish religious

17 Minutes of the parliamentary session of July 15, 1921, in *Az 1920. évi február hó 16-ára összehívott nemzetgyűlés naplója*, vol. 9: 575.

18 Gábor Kádár and Zoltán Vági, "Rendszerváltások és pogromok," *Népszabadság*, June 20, 2008.

communities were burgled, and Jewish students were prevented from entering university.[19] There were lynchings nationwide as hundreds of Jews, who had had nothing to do with and showed no sympathy for the revolution, and indeed some who had previously supported actions distinctly opposed to the Soviet Republic, fell victim to detachments of officers seeking retribution for the Hungarian Soviet Republic from the autumn of 1919 onwards.[20] The detachments often used the flag of political anti-Semitism as a cover for common criminality, as in the famous case of Izsák, where in the summer of 1920, an armed group of twenty men robbed and murdered three rich Jewish wine merchants in the name of the Association of Awakening Hungarians, even though the merchants had nothing to do with the 1919 Soviet Republic. The Jewish families fled, the detachment occupied their houses, and anyone who tried to return home later was beaten and driven away once again; meanwhile, their wine harvest was sold off in Switzerland.[21] On the day of the signing of the Trianon Peace Treaty, there was an anti-Semitic demonstration in Budapest, as a result of which 85 Jews were wounded.[22] It was in a similar atmosphere that the parliamentary election campaign, encouraged by the Entente, was conducted in the winter of 1919. Prior to the election, the government led by Károly Huszár confined the Social Democratic politicians in internment camps, and the party—which could have counted on a tenth of the votes cast—ended up boycotting

19 Szabolcsi, *Két emberöltő*, 292–95.

20 Of the 480 victims of the Soviet Republic who lost their lives, 31 were Jewish. See the report on the activities of the National Office of Hungarian Jews 1929, MNL OL, K28, item 53. There are differing estimates in the historical literature of the number of victims who lost their lives at the hands of the officers' detachments during the White Terror. In any case, even the lowest estimates of between 800 and 900 persons included many Jewish victims. Ignác Romsics mentions more than a thousand, "probably close to two thousand" victims. Ignác Romsics, *Magyarország története a XX. században* (Budapest: Osiris, 1999), 132. Nathaniel Katzburg gives a figure of around 700 dead, see Nathaniel Katzburg, *Zsidópolitika Magyarországon, 1919–1943* (Budapest: Bábel Kiadó, 2002), 38–39. See also János Gyurgyák, *A zsidókérdés Magyarországon* (Budapest: Osiris, 2001), 112; and Krisztián Ungváry, "'Sacco di Budapest,' 1919: Gheorghe Mardarescu tábornok válasza Harry Hill Bandholtz vezérőrnagy nem diplomatikus naplójára," *Budapesti Negyed*, nos. 29–30 (2000: 3–4): 173–202. According to research by Gábor Kádár and Zoltán Vági, "the murders, lynchings, and torture in more than fifty places can be attributed with certainty to detachments that can be linked to Horthy's national army. But it was not only the perpetrators of [Iván] Héjjas and [Pál] Prónay's white terror who murdered: in numerous cases, the local population organized pogroms." Kádár and Vági, "Rendszerváltások és pogromok."

21 Countess Gyula Andrássy noted in her diary that this "was not about the Hungarians rising, nor about the Christian National movement, nor even those worried for the Hungarian race, but a union of wine merchants." MNL OL, P4 330, diary of Countess Gyula Andrássy.

22 Szabolcsi, *Két emberöltő*, 306. The demonstration was on June 4, 1920.

the elections.[23] In the elections the anti-Semitic extreme right secured a serious showing in parliament.[24]

Numerus clausus as anti-Jewish law—Russian precedents

István Haller, the minister of education, considered the numerus clausus with its Jewish quota to be an epoch-making innovation. "There is certainly no one who has preceded us in what we are about to enshrine in law."[25] But on this point, he was mistaken: in 1887, three decades before the introduction of the Jewish quota in Hungary, Russia had introduced a state-sponsored Jewish quota. In the cities of the Pale of Settlement, the number of Jewish university students was capped at 10 percent, while in other Russian cities it was set at 5 percent, and in Moscow and St. Petersburg at 3 percent.[26] Russian Jews, excluded from higher education, flooded west; at the turn of the century there were almost four thousand young Russian Jews studying at universities in Germany, Austria, and Switzerland, mostly enrolled in medicine.[27] At the turn of the century, there were more than two thousand Russian students in Germany alone.[28] German universities reacted to the influx of Russian Jews with their own form of fixed number system. This, however, unlike the Russian numerus clausus, did not contain any openly anti-Jewish measures. It merely decreed that the number of "foreign" students at German universities could not exceed nine hundred from 1913 onwards. This had the effect of reducing by two thirds the number of places that were available to young Russian Jews.[29]

The Russian numerus clausus quickly came to the attention of the Hungarian devotees of political anti-Semitism. In 1891, Géza Petrassevich, editor of the

---

23 The Huszár government issued the decree for internment on December 5, 1919, on the basis of which Social Democrat workers and Jewish small traders were also interned in the Hajmáskér internment camp. Romsics, *Magyarország története*, 135.

24 László Hubai, "A szociáldemokrata párt részvétele a választásokon, 1922–1947," *Múltunk* 42, no. 2 (1997): 119–45.

25 Minutes of the parliamentary session of September 2, 1920, in *Az 1920. évi február hó 16-ára összehívott nemzetgyűlés naplója*, vol. 5: 150.

26 Israel Cohen, *Jewish Life in Modern Times* (London, Methuen, 1914), 152.

27 Cohen, *Jewish Life in Modern Times*, ch. 2.

28 Peter Drewek, "Limits of Educational Internationalism: Foreign Students at German Universities between 1890 and 1930," *Bulletin of the German Historical Institute*, no. 27 (Fall 2000): 39–64.

29 In 1911–12, there were around 2,000 Russians studying in Germany and almost half of them were medical students. Half of all foreign students at German universities were still Russian in 1914. Drewek, "Limits of Educational Internationalism," 44.

journal *Alkotmány* (Constitution) recommended that Hungary adopt the Russian system. In 1907, Károly Hencz recommended in the parliament that limits be established on the number of Jewish students at the universities, while Károly Kmety urged the same for secondary schools. At the time, these recommendations were not taken up, and reappeared only after 1918 among the demands of anti-Semitic politicians.

Nonetheless, Minister of Education István Haller was right about some things. The classification of Judaism as a "race" really was the beginning of a new chapter in Hungarian history. The novelty of the situation was summed up thus in 1921 by Vilmos Vázsonyi, Hungary's former minister of justice (who was Jewish and who fled the country at the time of the revolutions): "I fled from the Communists a denomination, and returned a race."[30] Vázsonyi's interpretation was shared by many leading politicians throughout the 1920s. Klebelsberg, as minister of education, agreed with Vázsonyi that the law of 1920 was really a "racial" law, precisely in the sense that belonging to a "race" was determined by ancestry. According to Klebelsberg, the universities which treated the Jews as a race and therefore "counted converted Jews among the Jewish racial contingent . . . basically acted logically," or in other words, they interpreted the law of 1920 correctly. If "the universities interpreted the law in such a way that the converted Jew was included in the contingent of the Jewish race, then they were acting logically in accordance with the spirit of that law. For once Jews have been classified as a race, one cannot escape from race as one does, say, from a religious denomination by converting, or from a nationality by declaring oneself to be of another nationality."[31] The concept of "race," then, is different in Klebelsberg's conception from the concept of "denomination" or "nationality" in that belonging to a "race" is determined at birth, and this characteristic cannot be changed by voluntary conversion or assimilation to a different language. And, as Klebelsberg said in parliament, "anyone who reads the debate preceding the adoption of Law No. XXV of 1920 attentively cannot help but gain the impression that the members who passed that law did, indeed, intend at the time to define Judaism as a race."[32]

30 Szabolcsi, *Két emberöltő*, 335.

31 Minutes of the parliamentary session of February 23, 1928, in *Az 1927. évi január hó 25-ére hirdetett országgyűlés képviselőházának naplója*, vol. 9: 198.

32 Minutes of the parliamentary session of February 10, 1928, in *Az 1927. évi január hó 25-ére hirdetett országgyűlés képviselőházának naplója*, vol. 9: 12.

Nationality, religion, race

Throughout the 1920s many people debated and interpreted the precise meaning of the term "racial group" (*népfaj*),[33] which was used in the numerus clausus law. The crude nature of the law, the anomalies and inconsistencies in its application, coupled with the fact that the classification of the Jews as a "nationality" was against the law then in force, made it possible throughout this entire period for the term "race" to be a point of constant contention, and allowed the term to serve as a political weapon as well. When, for example, in 1925 Vilmos Vázsonyi asked Prime Minister István Bethlen in parliament whether the government actually considers the Jews a race or a religion, Bethlen's equivocal answer showed that the government applied one or the other depending on the political character of the individual in question:

> As for the question my right honorable friend [i.e., Vilmos Vázsonyi] poses, as to whether the Jews are a race or not, my answer is that the law establishing the numerus clausus declared the Jews to be a racial group or a nationality, respectively. Of this there can be no doubt, since, my honorable friend, even if he happened not to be present at those debates, will be aware that when the law was made, this section referred specifically to the Jews. This, naturally, does not mean that this is the position of this government. If it pleases the house, I consider those Jews who identify with the Hungarians, who were partners to this nation for better or for worse, to be Hungarians of the Jewish religion and not a separate racial group. On the other hand, I must also say that in this country there were Jews who declared themselves to be a separate racial group by refusing to associate themselves either in the past or even to this day with the interests of the nation.

Patriotic Jews—he said—should be considered "Hungarians of the Jewish religion," while the rest had declared themselves to be a "racial group."[34]

---

33 The term *népfaj*, which literally translates as "folk race" (and as such is similar to the German *Volksrasse*), could, based on context, mean both ethnicity and race. The translation "racial group," used in this volume, intends to convey some of this ambiguity, while making it clear that the term was used to justify a discrimination based on a racial understanding of the Jews.

34 István Bethlen's speech on the parliamentary session of December 17, 1925, in *Az 1922. évi junius hó 16-ára hirdetett nemzetgyűlés naplója*, vol. 38: 223.

We cannot say that the proponents of the numerus clausus did not want to clear up this confusion in 1920. The men who made the law knew that there was no such concept in Hungarian law as "racial group," and it did not allow for the differential treatment of citizens based on their origin. This was precisely why the anti-Semitic student groups and the Christian Socialist trade union demanded that parliament make a law that declared the Jews to be a race. "Jews are a separate race," they wrote in their submission of March 15, 1920, "and therefore we demand that the Jew—no matter if they be of any Christian religion—be judged on the basis of his race." This submission explicitly states that by doing this, they wanted to withdraw the possibility of assimilation and equal rights from the Jews, because "any attempt at assimilation is a suicidal design for the Hungarian race." "There has never been," they wrote, "a more opportune historical moment . . . than now" for the introduction of a racial law, "this brave endeavor," as the submission says.[35]

The reasoning of the authors of this submission was logical. They were right that without the law for which they were calling, the Jews could only be treated as a "nationality" or "racial group" by finding ways around the law then in force. The drafter of the law could theoretically have chosen a different solution, for example a system of quotas based on religion, but this too—just like the nationality/race-based quota—would have run counter to the obligations Hungary had taken on in the peace treaty, which ruled out limiting the equality of citizens before the law on the basis of nationality, religion, or race. But a system of denominational quotas would not, in the case of the Jews, have had the desired effect anyway, because the system would have had to treat Jews who had converted as Christians, and thus the number of people subject to the system would have been smaller. The other argument against a religious quota was that if such a system were introduced, it would have been necessary to establish the proportion of places for one Christian denomination versus another, and this would have involved serious political battles.[36] One thing, therefore, stayed in place: the classification of Jews as a "racial group" based on ancestry, but without establishing criteria for belonging to that "racial group."

35 Ladányi, *Az egyetemi ifjúság*, 142.

36 Nonetheless, the introduction of proportions on a religious basis did feature in the early recommendations for the introduction of the numerus clausus, from 1919. Ladányi, *Az egyetemi ifjúság*, 142.

In the end, there was no separate law about the classification of the Jews as a "race." This was left, in effect, to the relevant implementation decree of the numerus clausus law. Nonetheless, with the introduction of the Jewish quota, the law came out in support of the position of the extreme right. This was summed up in the summer of 1919, a year before the law was passed, by Albin Lingauer, an anti-Semitic journalist (and a member of the parliament of 1920) as follows: "we have a reckoning with the Jewish race and not with the religion. And there's no converting out of the race!"[37] The Hungarian government was still committed to this viewpoint in 1925, years after István Bethlen took office, when it defended the racial clause in an official statement to the League of Nations, saying: "With the Jews, race, religion, and nationalities are merged and they appear in different aspects in the different countries. . . . In the Law under discussion, all mention of religious minorities was deliberately omitted, for religion is something over which the individual has control, since he has the power to change it. Religion is, therefore, not a characteristic sufficiently consistent to determine a minority without excluding the possibility of abuses."[38]

Camouflaged changes to the legal status of Jews

Without officially classifying Jews as a separate nationality or race, the Jewish quota could only be introduced by creating a legal contradiction. Under the law in force in 1920, the concept of "Israelite" had an exclusively religious meaning and therefore could not be used in the nationalities-based system of quotas. The law on nationalities (Law No. XLIV of 1868) regarded language as the sole test of belonging to a nationality, and the law governing freedom of religion (Law No. XLIII of 1895) specifically stated that a religious classification could not be "of a national or racial character."[39] The lawmakers in 1920, therefore, could only introduce a Jewish quota by classifying the Jews in the implementation decree as a nationality—in direct contravention of the prevailing laws.

---

37 Márton Békés, "Az ellenforradalom két arca Vas megyében," *Vasi Szemle* 62, no. 6 (2008): 698.

38 The Hungarian Government's Submission to the League of Nations, May 19, 1925. Quoted in Nathaniel Katzburg, *Hungary and the Jews: Policy and Legislation, 1920–1943* (Ramat-Gan: Bar-Ilan University Press, 1981), 68.

39 Gábor Gángó, "Az 1868. évi nemzetiségi törvény és következményei," *Korunk* 20, no. 5 (2009): 3; and Andor Ladányi, "A kisebbséggé nyilvánítás kérdéséhez: A történelmi előzmények," *Múlt és Jövő* 17, no. 1 (2006): 100.

Thus, the change in the legal status of the Jews ended up being implemented without due parliamentary process, debate, or new legislation. The whole thing consisted of three words added to a table in the implementation decree: "Israelites are [to be] treated as a separate nationality." The cynicism behind the framing and the implementation of the law foreshadowed the political atmosphere of the new era. True, only a few years later, the minister of education, Kunó Klebelsberg, called this process "desultory lawmaking," but he never rejected—neither at the time, nor later—the political goal behind the "desultory" law.[40]

The proportions for the nationalities quota created by the numerus clausus were based on the language data of the census. Each "minority" could enter higher education in the proportion in which the relevant language was used by people among the overall population of the country. But for the Jews—and only for the Jews—there was a separate rule. Right from the introduction of the numerus clausus law, a person belonged to the Jewish "nationality" if their religion was Judaism, even if their native language was Hungarian. In their case, therefore, language counted for nothing. By making religion and not language the test for belonging to a "nationality" in the case of the Jews, the law took a big step towards introducing origin as a determining factor.

"Jewish by birth, by origin, and by race"

In theory, Jews who had converted should not have been subject to the restrictions imposed by the quota, since the quota applied to people belonging to "the Jewish religion." The application of the quota was therefore characterized by much debate and many conflicting practices. The University of Pécs, for example, did not count Jews who had converted as Jews. In some cases, when it came to converted Jews, even different faculties of the same university sometimes had different practices.

The presidential council of the University of Budapest pointed out in 1922 that it would be problematic to include converted Jews within the 6 percent limit, since this limit was adopted by the makers of the numerus clausus law

---

40 Kunó Klebelsberg, "Explanatory memorandum to the bill amending Law No. XXV of 1920 on the regulation of enrollment at the universities of arts and sciences, the University of Technology, the Faculty of Economics of the University of Budapest, and law academies," November 18, 1927, in *Az 1927. évi január hó 25-ére összehívott országgyűlés felsőházának irományai*, vol. 4: 398–400.

on the basis of the number of people of the Jewish religion in the country, and therefore—if it was to apply to those who had converted as well—the limit should have been set by looking at a larger section of the populace in the first place. The council went on to say that the calculations on which the Jewish quota was based were questionable, since "there is no data on Hungarian Jewry as a racial group or nationality." Furthermore, "if persons of the Christian religion but Jewish race had been counted as Jews as well, the proportion of Jews nationwide would have been greater than 6 percent," and in that case, more "Jews" would have had to be admitted to the universities.[41] The presidential council, therefore, was inclined not to have the university apply the quota to Jews who had converted.

By contrast, the Faculty of Medicine decided firmly upon the test of origin since, as the dean of the faculty said: "changing religion changes neither your origins nor your race." Therefore, applicants whose parents were "of the Mosaic faith belong to the Jewish race, even if they later adopt the Christian faith . . . and we will consider them still to be Jewish by birth, by origin, and by race, though they have changed their religion."[42]

Minister of Education Kunó Klebelsberg considered the attitude of the Faculty of Medicine to be correct: "It is quite clear that the intention of the legislature at the time [in 1920] was to declare Jews a race . . . Here was an explicit intention, which was included in the Hungarian Corpus Juris."[43] Despite the frequent claim in Hungarian historiography, that differential treatment based on ethnic origin first began in Hungary with the so-called Second Jewish Law of 1939, we can see that it started with the explicitly anti-Jewish quota of the numerus clausus law in 1920.

The use of the concept of "race" ran counter to the law then in force. Klebelsberg himself spelled out how this tension should be dissolved. It is always the most recent "law" that is in force, he said. "Since Law No. XXV of 1920 was introduced later than Law No. XLII of 1895, the former could change the

---

41 ELTE Archives, Rector's Office, Minutes of the University Council, 1922/I., ordinary meeting.

42 ELTE Archives, Rector's Office, Minutes of the University Council, 1922/I., ordinary meeting.

43 Minutes of the parliamentary session of February 23, 1928, in *Az 1927. évi január hó 25-ére hirdetett országgyűlés képviselőházának naplója*, vol. 9: 198. Klebelsberg, during the amendment of the law in 1928, highlighted that with the repeal of the Jewish quota the "clear legal viewpoint" of Law No. XVII of 1867 and Law No. XLIV of 1895, that in Hungary "Judaism is a religion and nothing other," would be "reinstated." *Az 1927. évi január hó 25-ére hirdetett országgyűlés képviselőházának naplója*, vol. 9: 198.

way the law stood, and in fact, did precisely that."[44] This meant that the one-line instruction in the implementation decree—"Israelites are [to be] treated as a separate nationality"—was enough to change the legal status of the Jews. This was spelled out by none other than the country's minister of the interior, who later became minister of religion and education.[45]

Supporters of the Jewish quota were bothered by neither the invalid legislative procedure nor the contradictions within the law. Their point of view was expressed most clearly by Pál Teleki, prime minister at the time the law was passed, who argued against the repeal of the Jewish quota a few years later. Anyone, he argued, who considers the repeal of the racial clause a return to the rightful legal position of the autumn of 1920 is mistaken, because "the chief characteristic of the law is not that it represents reality, but that it expresses a will."[46] Such measures—he said later, in support of the Second Jewish Law—express a "will" that with time became "part of the popular opinion of the nation, part of its popular sentiment, and thereby part of the Constitution."[47] In contrast, then, with the commonly accepted judgement that Teleki's basic political orientation was generally conservative, we can see that his detailed moral rejection of constitutionality and the principle of equality before the law puts Teleki closer to the radical right of the time.

Proponents of the Jewish quota ended up bridging this constitutional gap by not providing any kind of detailed definition of "racial group" in the law. How Jews should be distinguished from non-Jews on the basis of their "racial group" was ultimately decided at the level of university committees only. Practice, however, varied between universities. The admissions panel at the Faculty of Medicine in Budapest, for example, considered as Jewish anyone born Jewish, whether they belonged to the Jewish religion or not.[48] The decisions of these

---

44 Minutes of the parliamentary session of February 10, 1928, in *Az 1927. évi január hó 25-ére hirdetett országgyűlés képviselőházának naplója*, vol. 9: 126.

45 Klebelsberg was minister of the interior between December 3, 1921, and June 6, 1922, and minister of education from June 16, 1922, to August 24, 1931.

46 Speech in the Upper House "On the amendment of the numerus clausus," March 13, 1928, in Pál Teleki, *Válogatott politikai írások és beszédek*, ed. Balázs Ablonczy (Budapest, Osiris, 2000), 197.

47 Speech in the Upper House "On the Second Jewish Law," April 15, 1939, in Teleki, *Válogatott politikai írások és beszédek*, 384.

48 The practice of the University of Szeged differed, as is evident from the characterization of applicants in one of the 1923 records: "Those who applied to the medical faculty included five Christians, one who is a Christian after his mother [but] a Jew after his father and who later converted to the Roman Catholic faith. The other nineteen are Jews." Records of the Fifth Extraordinary meeting of

committees were made after 1921 within a new conceptual framework; in their reports, they listed those students who were "born Jewish" separately. Thus, the Jewish quota was applied unequivocally on the basis of origin and not on the basis of an individual's current status (taking into account their possible conversion).[49]

This, however, meant that the racial clause restricted the civil rights of Jews in another way as well. For by treating Jews who had converted to the Christian faith not as Christians but as "born Jewish"—or in other words, as Jewish—they were denying the legal force of their conversion, which was contrary to Law No. XLIII of 1895 on the freedom of religion.

The racial clause, then, ran counter to both the principle of equality before the law and the law then in force. This was spelled out by the Royal Curia itself, four years after the law entered into force, when it declared the classification of the Jews a "nationality" illegal: "Jews have no separate native language, but have always spoken the dominant language of their environment, and their native language changes accordingly. From a legal standpoint, we cannot speak of a Jewish nationality in Hungary today."[50] The Curia's decision surprised no one, since it was not a question of its lawyers having come to some new conclusion on a difficult point of law in those four years, but of the Curia coming out and stating something that was common knowledge when the law was introduced. As one member of parliament, József Pakots, put it:

> even the people introducing this law felt that there was something to hide in this measure, and that it would be best therefore to couch it in generali-

---

the Medical Faculty of the Royal Hungarian Franz Joseph Scientific University, held on January 12, 1923, Szeged University Archives, Papers of the Faculty of Medicine.

49 N. Szegvári, *Numerus clausus rendelkezések*, 130. At the universities of Szeged and Pécs, students were classed as Jewish not on the basis of their origins but rather their religion.

50 In its judgement of September 23, 1924 in the specific case of the far-right journalist Lehel Kádár, accused of incitement, the court ruled against the second circuit court's judgement quashing his conviction and with the first circuit court's sentence of a year's incarceration. In its justification, the Royal Curia established that "according to our laws, Hungarian Jewry is neither a separate nationality nor a social class. Given that on the basis of Law No. XLIV of 1868, concerning the equality before the law of citizens from various nationalities, the criterion for differentiating between nationalities is the mother tongue, a 'separate nationality' is to be understood as a cohesive ethnic group unified around a common language, with a common history based on that language and a commitment to maintaining it . . . therefore, from a legal perspective, we cannot talk of a Jewish nationality in Hungary today. . . . For the word 'Jewish' in its generally accepted meaning is used to denote the Mosaic faith and those who belong to it and does not signify any other notions." Ladányi, "A kisebbséggé nyilvánítás kérdéséhez," 100.

> ties and try to elevate its dubious measures onto the moral high ground. The numerus clausus law is not honest. Even a child knows that the point of the law is to restrict, insofar as possible, the presence of the youth of the Jewish religion within higher education. . . . The law, however, makes no mention of the word religion or denomination, but hides its ulterior goal under the cloak of "racial group or nationality." If someone unfamiliar with the background were to read the law, it would appear that the measures by which "the proportion of young people belonging to a given racial group and nationality residing in the country shall preferably reach the national proportion of the racial group or nationality concerned, but shall at least be nine-tenths of the national proportion" had some sort of protective purpose. But the aim is quite the opposite, i.e., the restriction of the enrollment of Jewish youth in higher education. If the law had wanted to be honest, it would have said the proportion of young people in higher education whose number exceeds the proportion of their ethnic group—viz., religion—within the population of the country as a whole, should be brought into line with that proportion.[51]

Pakots effectively highlighted the reason why the anti-Jewish quota system was formulated in terms of a sort of principle of ethnic/demographic equality. The body of the text did not speak about restrictions on the Jews, rather it said that every nationality had a "right" to take part in higher education in the same proportion at which it was represented demographically within the population of the country as a whole. The main body of the text essentially disguised the anti-Jewish nature of the measure behind a facade of "positive discrimination" for Slovaks, Ruthenians, Germans, and other nationalities, while the actual Jewish quota was hidden in the ministerial decree implementing the law.

At first glance, it is impossible to understand why—when leading politicians, including those in government, stated quite openly in parliament and in the press that the goal of the law was to restrict the rights of the Jews—the law itself nonetheless tried to create the illusion of impartiality. Who was trying to fool whom, and why?

51 Minutes of the parliamentary session of November 26, 1925, in *Az 1922. évi junius hó 16-ára hirdetett nemzetgyűlés naplója*, vol. 37: 473.

"Positive discrimination" or a foreign policy maneuver?

The answer to this question is to be found in Hungary's situation on the international stage and its foreign policy goals. Although the far right persistently demanded the introduction of the numerus clausus from the autumn of 1919 on, it was unclear right up until the autumn of 1920 whether the law would contain openly anti-Jewish restrictions. This was a crucial year from the point of view of Hungarian foreign policy. Right up until the spring of 1920, the Hungarian leadership was hopeful of being able to convince the Great Powers to take a more lenient view on the question of the country's new borders. The government received the final text of the peace treaty on May 5, 1920, and signed it on June 4. But the country's international standing remained important for Hungarian foreign policy, since the peace treaty left several territorial questions open and the Hungarian government did not abandon its longer-term plans for having the border revised even after signing the treaty.[52]

In this context, the introduction of the racial quota was clearly risky from a foreign policy standpoint, since it ran counter to the fundamental principles that underpinned the peace treaties, and especially their provisions on the protection of minorities. Years later, Kunó Klebelsberg's recollection (in a private letter to István Bethlen) was that the minority protection clauses of the Trianon Peace Treaty were formulated specifically with the Hungarian numerus clausus law in mind. What is more, they were formulated so as to be incompatible with the racial clause of the Hungarian numerus clausus law—which had been passed by then—and thereby allow the League of Nations to act against the law: "Hungary created the numerus clausus law before the Trianon Peace Treaty was signed. Lucien Wolf himself says that he personally exercised his influence over the throwing together of the religious and racial clauses and thus it is natural that—being acquainted with our law, which had kicked up a lot of dust—he formulated the religious and racial clauses in such a way as to be opposed to the third clause of our own law."[53]

Article 58 of the minorities clause of the peace treaty did indeed explicitly prohibit the restriction of the rights of national, religious, or racial minor-

52 Ignác Romsics, *Bethlen István: Politikai életrajz* (Budapest: Magyarságkutató Intézet, 1991), 127–28.

53 Szinai and Szűcs, *Bethlen István titkos iratai*, 256–57. Lucien Wolf represented Anglo-Jewry through the Board of Deputies of British Jews in the British delegation at the Paris peace conference, and was later active in the minority rights cases concerning Jews.

ities, in that it stated that every Hungarian citizen, regardless of differences of race, language, or religion, was equal before the law and enjoyed equal civil and political rights.

But the chronology that Klebelsberg presents is not accurate. The peace treaty was signed by the Hungarian government on June 4, 1920, but the very first official draft of the numerus clausus law was sent out to the universities only on July 4, exactly a month after the signing of the treaty. The law was only passed in September 1920. Moreover, the July draft contained no mention of the racial clause or the nationalities quota, stating merely that the minister of religion and education was getting ready to introduce a fixed number system in university enrollment.[54] Klebelsberg, therefore, could presumably not have been thinking of the law as passed.

Lucien Wolf, referred to in Klebelsberg's letter above, could not have been familiar with the draft law when the minorities clauses of the peace treaty were being drawn up. At most, he would have known what was accessible in the press. From this source, he could have known about the recommendation made on December 4, 1919, by the University Council of the University of Budapest, which really did already contain the plan for the racial quota: "If we do move to a numerus clausus system, then the admission of students to the faculties of applied subjects from the various religions and . . . races should be limited to their proportion within the overall population of the country."[55] Wolf may also have known that when the recommendation was made within the university, it already had an anti-Jewish edge, because—as Professor of Law Alfréd Doleschall said when presenting the recommendation to the University Council—"the real thrust [of the draft] is directed against the plethora of Jews." The "basic inter-

54 The complete text of the recommendation reads:
"1. Only so many students may enroll in the secular faculties of the universities of science and arts from the start of the 1920–21 academic year that can be assured of receiving a thorough education.
2. The number of students to be taken for each faculty will be established by the Ministry of Public Education on the basis of the recommendation of the faculty in question.
3. This law does not affect the right to enroll for those who had been enrolled as full-time students in previous years or as special students for at least two semesters.
4. Enrollment must be sought by written submission to the relevant faculty, on which the full assembly of professors of the faculty will decide. Their decision shall be final.
5. This measure does not apply to those wishing to enroll for pharmaceutical sciences or the public finance course of the faculty of law and political science. Nonetheless, the minister, on the recommendation of the faculties in question, may limit the number of students here as well." Ladányi, *Az egyetemi ifjúság*, 146.

55 ELTE Archives, 500/1919–20, ET.

ests of self-defense" of Hungarian society, he continued, "justify, nay demand, that destructive elements, whether they are so by nature of their nationality or their race, . . . should be forced into the background."[56] We cannot therefore rule out that the "law" mentioned by Klebelsberg in his letter and which came to Lucien Wolf's attention in Paris was not, in fact, the law as passed, but rather the press reports of the University Council meeting in Budapest.

Nonetheless, it is a fact that between the autumn of 1919 and the autumn of 1920, the debates around the numerus clausus could not be settled, primarily because of foreign policy concerns. Successive Hungarian governments did not wish to face the international repercussions of passing an anti-Semitic law. Professor Doleschall himself expressed doubts whether a quota imposed on Jews "is something that would be admissible in our present and future international situation" and whether "it would not be preferable to leave the practical implementation to the admissions committees of the faculties, instead of openly propagating the principle?"[57]

The foreign policy concerns were exacerbated when, in March 1920, the head of the Hungarian peace delegation in Paris, Count Albert Apponyi, wrote to the government, warning them that the conditions in the country, the news of anarchy, anti-Semitic paramilitaries, and violence filtering out abroad were doing untold harm to the delegation's negotiating position. It was impossible to argue in the interests of retaining or regaining areas with mixed populations or more lenient borders that the Hungarian state was patient and tolerant of the ethnically non-Hungarian population when news of violence and the planned restriction of the rights of the Jewish minority followed each other thick and fast.[58] Referring to the referendums that were expected to take place, Apponyi warned that "the attraction of a state will naturally wane if it is incapable of defending the basic freedoms of its citizens and where the rule of law is placed in question by the violence of individuals."[59] He asked the government to restore the rule of law immediately and thereby allow the delegation's work to progress.[60] Prime Minister Sándor Simonyi-Semadam read the letter in parliament.

---

56 ELTE Archives, 500/1919–20, ET.

57 ELTE Archives, 500/1919–20, ET.

58 Minutes of the parliamentary session of March 17, 1920, in *Az 1920. évi február hó 16-ára összehívott nemzetgyűlés naplója*, vol. 2: 124.

59 *Az 1920. évi február hó 16-ára összehívott nemzetgyűlés naplója*, vol. 2: 124.

60 *Az 1920. évi február hó 16-ára összehívott nemzetgyűlés naplója*, vol. 2: 124.

Its reception was scandalous: shouting broke out from the extreme right. "Please accept," Simonyi-Semadam called through the tumult, "that Jew-hatred, antipathy towards the Jews, is not worth sacrificing Hungary's integrity. Please put aside this mood, put aside all antipathy at this crucial moment. . . . Please tell those young men that it is not some heroic deed to assault, beat up, or harass someone in the street, on the tram, or in a cafe, because they think he looks Jewish . . . because by doing so, they are putting at risk our most sacred efforts."[61] Simonyi-Semadam's muddled speech is a kind of testimony to how the country's leaders were aware of the strictures of the country's situation abroad. Following his argument, the reason why it is wrong to beat someone up on the tram who looks Jewish is not because that person has done nothing wrong, but because it puts Hungary's international standing in danger. The radicals have to accept that Hungary cannot afford to introduce anti-Semitic legislation, because this runs counter to the country's international interests.

It was the same logic—one appealing to the country's international interests—that defined the statements concerning the numerus clausus of Minister of Religion and Public Education István Haller, who was well known for his anti-Semitic views. In the spring of 1920, Haller hemmed and hawed for months before committing himself on the question of the Jewish quota. Haller's original reasoning was that the numerus clausus in itself—even without a Jewish quota—would be enough to prevent the enrollment of Jewish students, since the university admissions councils would of themselves—in their exercise of the right to make the admissions decisions the law arrogated them—enact the anti-Jewish conception behind it.[62]

The extreme right-wing forces outside government, however, were not troubled by international concerns. They saw these as an excuse that the government used against them to buy themselves time. The Association of Awakening Hungarians and other anti-Semitic organizations demanded that the politicians they had supported in the electoral campaign of the winter of 1919 (including Haller, the minister of religion and education) make good on the campaign promises they had made to the associations in exchange for their support. The radical right was not afraid of violence either. Groups from the Turul Alliance and the Awakening Hungarians occupied the entrances to the universities and

61 *Az 1920. évi február hó 16-ára összehívott nemzetgyűlés naplója*, vol. 2: 124.

62 Ladányi, "A numerus clausustól a numerus nullusig," 56.

Figure 6. Demonstration by the Association of Awakening Hungarians against the ratification of the Trianon Peace Treaty in front of the National Museum in Budapest the fall of 1920. Source: Fővárosi Szabó Ervin Könyvtár Budapest Gyűjtemény.

prevented the start of teaching. They inspected the papers of professors and students heading to university and prevented Jewish students from entering, even for exams. They announced that they would keep occupying the universities until the numerus clausus law was passed.[63] "Christianity's life and death struggle will be decided at the universities," Dezső Szabó declared in March 1920, hinting that the numerus clausus law was in fact to be the dress rehearsal for a series of anti-Jewish measures planned by the far right.[64]

The radical right made it clear that foreign policy considerations could not deflect them from pressing for anti-Semitic laws. In parliament, Béla Fangler replied on behalf of the Association of Awakening Hungarians to Apponyi's words calling for restraint, by saying:

---

63 "As long as we do not see," wrote the right-wing student paper, "the institutional defense of the nation being guaranteed at the colleges, we do not want the status quo. We renounce the blessings of functioning universities." *Ifjak Szava* [Voice of youth], November 30, 1919, 7. Quoted in Ladányi, *Az egyetemi ifjúság*, 125.

64 Ladányi, *Az egyetemi ifjúság*, 136.

> Threatening us with the Entente Powers to keep us from daring to speak out and daring to act against the Jews, saying that if we do, we'll get a damaging treaty from them, is nothing but hollow words. The Entente would give us a treaty just as damaging even if the cabinet here were made up entirely of Jews, it would give us the same treaty if the ministers who sat here had legs that were not quite the same length as each other, if they had crooked noses and beards and moustaches so vivid in hue that sparks could fly out of them. The Entente is guided not by sentiment, but by the desire to ruin us totally.[65]

The deputies representing the Association of Awakening Hungarians produced a whole string of submissions in April 1920 demanding that parliament introduce anti-Jewish measures without delay. "The main goal," they wrote, "is the nationwide defense of the breadwinning professions."[66] They demanded that the state introduce a numerus clausus for the market in raw materials and for the Jews working in the ministries that allocated them.[67] They also demanded the expropriation of Jewish shops, the introduction of the numerus clausus "in the commercial sphere as well," and "that there be only so many Jewish merchants as are entitled to shops according to their overall proportion in the population."[68] They further demanded the introduction of the numerus clausus in higher education, its extension to secondary schools, and that Jews should be banned from teaching "subjects that are especially useful in developing a sense of national and Christian spirit."[69]

István Haller rejected the introduction of a Jewish quota in higher education as late as the spring of 1920, citing foreign policy concerns. He made it understood that he agreed with "the main goal," but that the country's international situation did not allow for it.

---

65 Minutes of the parliamentary session of April 10, 1920, in *Az 1920. évi február hó 16-ára összehívott nemzetgyűlés naplója*, vol. 2: 55.

66 MNL OL, K636, item 257/10. Submission of the United Christian National League, the Turul Alliance, and the Association of Awakening Hungarians to parliament, September 1, 1920.

67 Motion by Károly Ereky on April 27, 1920, in *Az 1920. évi február hó 16-ára összehívott nemzetgyűlés irományai*, vol. 1: 281.

68 Béla Fangler's address on the parliamentary session of April 19, 16, 1920, in *Az 1920. évi február hó 16-ára összehívott nemzetgyűlés naplója*, vol. 2: 65.

69 Motion by Gyula Zákány, April 28, 1920, in *Az 1920. évi február hó 16-ára összehívott nemzetgyűlés irományai*, vol. 1: 381. A few weeks later, on June 2, deputy Balázs Szabó asked whether the government was willing to restrict the role of Jews in all economic, industrial, mercantile, and scientific fields "to a point equal to their proportion of the population." Minutes of the parliamentary session of June 2, 1920, in *Az 1920. évi február hó 16-ára összehívott nemzetgyűlés naplója*, vol. 3: 212.

Figure 7. Picture of the first Teleki government (July 1920–April 1921), with Prime Minister Pál Teleki (sitting in the middle, third from the right) and Minister of Religion and Public Education István Haller (sitting first from the left). Source: Wikimedia Commons.

> At the moment we must pay careful attention in all our actions to certain considerations that we may be able to ignore sometime in the future, but which at the moment . . . represent a danger for us. . . . It was for this very reason that I did not consider a hasty solution and final settlement of this question to be opportune, and tried to persuade those concerned to seek a solution which would achieve the end itself, but which would be unassailable and for which the country and the nation would not face any difficulties anywhere.[70]

The Ministry of Religion and Public Education wanted to calm the debate raging around the numerus clausus. This explains why it took nine months from the genesis of the universities' recommendation for a fixed number system for the ministry to finally send the universities the draft of the planned numerus clausus law at the beginning of July 1920. The ministry at this point also presented the draft law to the cabinet.[71]

70 Minutes of the parliamentary session of April 29, 1920, in *Az 1920. évi február hó 16-ára összehívott nemzetgyűlés naplója*, vol. 2: 395.

71 The cabinet debated the recommendation on July 21, 1920.

There was no reference to the Jewish quota in the text, which merely foresaw a fixed number system to be introduced in higher education admissions. Haller knew that this draft would be a disappointment for the extreme right, since—as he pointed out—the draft "contained no mention of a numerus clausus in the sense that a lay person might understand it."[72] And indeed, the draft was greeted with vociferous outrage from the anti-Semitic side. "They've robbed us of our numerus clausus," the journal *Virradat* (Dawn) wrote, because "the draft operates on the principle that in the context of the peace treaty there can be no restrictions on the advancement of any race or religion."[73]

A breakthrough: A decision from the government

Events only gathered pace after Pál Teleki's investiture as prime minister in July. In his speech outlining his political program, he promised that his government would take steps "institutionally to defend the interests of Christian society."[74] He made it clear that as prime minister he would support the state-sponsored restriction of opportunities for Jews. At the same time, Teleki expressed willingness to end street violence and bring the anti-Semitic paramilitary groups under control. At this point, he was still keen to dispel the impression that his government was going to take a tough stance with the extreme right in order to improve Hungary's international standing since (as he said in his speech) foreign observers "are once again completely mistaken in their perception of an alleged white terror."[75]

But it was not a position he could maintain for long. Five days after his speech, on July 27, a group of supporters of the Awakening Hungarians forced their way into a cafe on Budapest's main boulevard, beat the Jewish guests bloody, and killed a bank director and a Jewish lawyer.[76] Teleki reacted forcefully. He promised that the perpetrators would be caught and punished, since (as he said) the murders put the country in a bad light internationally; as if this were not precisely the connection he had been denying only a few days before. "The

72 Ladányi, *Az egyetemi ifjúság*, 146.
73 *Virradat*, July 13, 1920, quoted in Ladányi, *Az egyetemi ifjúság*, 146.
74 Balázs Ablonczy, *Teleki Pál* (Budapest: Osiris, 2005), 172. Teleki presented his program on July 22, 1920.
75 Ablonczy, *Teleki Pál*, 171.
76 Zinner, *Az ébredők fénykora*, 72.

Figure 8. The leadership of the Association of Awakening Hungarians in the 1920s, with László Budaváry (in the middle). Source: MNM Történeti Fényképtár.

country is presently engaged in a monumental struggle," he announced in parliament, "one fought both internally and externally. . . . I can say with conviction that these efforts to disturb the peace are nothing short of treason. This is how I see this question, and that is why I have ordered the most thorough investigation possible; this is also how I want all those who will be involved in this case to see it."[77]

The day after the murders in the cafe, on July 28, one of the leaders of the Awakening Hungarians, deputy László Budaváry, submitted a motion for a comprehensive Jewish law, more radical than ever before, which more or less presaged the main points of the Jewish laws brought twenty years later, in 1939 and 1941. Budaváry said that "after eleven agonizing months of waiting" since the fall of the Soviet Republic, the legislature must now bring anti-Jewish measures not only in higher education but in all fields of life. He called his motion a "racial defense" law, one not designed to conform to a concept of justice, but to pro-

77 Minutes of the parliamentary session of July 30, 1920, in *Az 1920. évi február hó 16-ára összehívott nemzetgyűlés naplója*, vol. 4: 122.

tect Hungary from the "gravest danger," namely Jewry.[78] The motion encompassed all aspects of economic and social life. It would have deprived the Jews of their political rights and their right to own or rent land, would have expropriated all property exceeding one house in Jewish hands, and would have banned Jewish immigration, deported all Jews settled in the country since 1914, and expropriated their assets without compensation. It would have introduced a Jewish quota in every school, public office, factory, workshop, and bank, would have nationalized one part of the country's theaters and forbidden Jews from heading any of the rest, would have banned Jewish schools, and would have barred Jews from the higher management of newspapers. Government tenders and trading licenses from the government would have been available only to "Christian" businessmen. Foreshadowing the Third Jewish Law of 1941, it would have banned "Jews [from employing] Christians for personal service (servant, cook, driver, butler, etc.)."[79] Budaváry's motion was considered fit for debate by a majority of the members of parliament present at the time. But Budaváry's motion was not the deciding factor in the racial quota of the numerus clausus law; it merely served to radicalize the atmosphere.

The solution: A hidden Jewish quota

The breakthrough came with the work of Ottokár Prohászka, president of the governing party, the Christian National Union Party (KNEP). It was Prohászka who, a few days after Teleki's appointment, found a framework for incorporating the anti-Jewish element into the numerus clausus law then being drafted in such a way as to minimize the level of international risk to which the Hungarian government would be exposed. As it turned out, Prohászka's calculations were not without basis: though the international reception of the numerus clausus law was very bad, the Hungarian government was able to successfully delay its being strictured for racial discrimination under the principles of international law for six or seven years.

The plan for the hidden Jewish quota was presented by Bishop Prohászka on August 5, 1920, at a meeting of the far-right university student organization,

78 László Budaváry's speech, see the minutes of the parliamentary session of August 7, 1920, in *Az 1920. évi február hó 16-ára összehívott nemzetgyűlés naplója*, vol. 4: 280–89.

79 For the full text of the motion, see the Appendix to this volume.

the National Union of Hungarian University and College Students (Magyar Egyetemisták és Főiskolai Hallgatók Országos Szövetsége, MEFHOSZ). The meeting was attended by a number of parliamentary deputies. Some argued that it would not be proper to include racial or religious elements in the law, given the terms of the peace treaty. The position that absolutely no reference should be made in the law to race, religion, or nationality was all but set to win at the meeting. At this point, however, Prohászka had an idea to "save the day." The law should specify that university admission limits should apply not only to Jews, but to all the "races" and "nationalities" in the country, according to their proportion within the overall population in the country. Prohászka wondered whether "we couldn't phrase it so that admissions would be based on the numbers of the 'races and nationalities'"?[80] In this way, the law would not explicitly deal with the restriction of admission rights for Jews, but the end result would be the same—university places for Jews would be limited to their 5 percent proportion within the population overall. The meeting adopted Prohászka's recommendation. They also determined that their student activists would approach deputies involved with the law individually and encourage them to support the "Prohászka formula."

The recommendation was discussed twice by the governing party in August, in both cases with Prohászka presiding. At the second discussion, on August 24, the assembly accepted the formula and decided that it should be introduced to parliament as an amendment by Nándor Bernolák (professor of law in Debrecen) on September 3. In the end, it was the Prohászka-Bernolák amendment that contained the racial paragraph, clause three of the law, which read:

> When granting admission, in addition to the requirements of loyalty to the nation and moral reliability, on the one hand, consideration shall also be given to the intellectual ability of the applicant, on the other, and to the requirement that the proportion of young people belonging to a given racial group and nationality residing in the country shall preferably reach the national proportion of the racial group or nationality concerned, but shall at least be nine-tenths of the national proportion.[81]

---

80 Ladányi, *Az egyetemi ifjúság*, 150–51.

81 Parliamentary session of September 3, 1920, in *Az 1920. évi február hó 16-ára összehívott nemzetgyűlés naplója*, vol. 5: 184.

When the law was passed, it was the implementation decree for this amendment that actually brought the Jewish quota into being. Nándor Bernolák left no room for doubt that his amendment was aimed at restricting the Jews:

> The current distribution of university places between the races is not equitable. . . . Under these circumstances, I cannot deny that in the motion I lay before you there is the intention that the Jews should not participate in the professional fields in such overwhelming numbers. Yes, that is what I want—and I will say it quite clearly—it is profoundly in the interests of the Hungarian nation, as it is in the interests of the Jews living in Hungary, that the proportion of Jews in higher education should come down.[82]

The parliamentary debate on the law was then mostly dominated by the restrictions on the Jews. The majority of deputies who spoke supported Bernolák's motion, while seven argued against it, pointing out that the amendment contravened the principle of the citizen's right to equality before the law. It is worth noting that the opponents of the racial clause made a number of predictions that in the coming years were to become a reality. They said that the racial clause would hurt Hungary's international standing, that it would create counter-selection and lead to a "brain drain," and yet would not improve the chances of higher education for the children of the poorer classes. Being able to foresee the consequences, however, was of little use; rational arguments were overruled by anti-Semitic feeling.

Passing the law

The law, which represented a historical watershed for Hungarian Jews, being the first step in the destruction of the equality before the law they had been granted by their emancipation, was passed by parliament in an unusual manner on September 21, 1920. Most of the government and 71 percent of the deputies, including István Bethlen, absented themselves from the vote. Klebelsberg left the chamber before the vote, something he explained years later, saying that

82 Parliamentary session of September 3, 1920, in *Az 1920. évi február hó 16-ára összehívott nemzetgyűlés naplója*, vol. 5: 185, 187.

he thought the wording of the law was unfortunate right from the start.[83] The prime minister, Pál Teleki, was also absent, being also foreign minister until the day after the vote. Of the 13 members of the government, a mere three were present, two of whom—István Haller (minister of religion) and Gyula Rubinek (minister of trade)—voted against the law. Only István Szabó de Sokorópátka, the Smallholder minister without portfolio, voted for it.[84]

Nonetheless, Minister of Religion and Public Education István Haller's contribution to the debate provides a good summary of the Teleki government's change of position in July and August. Haller, who as late as April had rejected the idea of an anti-Jewish quota for foreign policy reasons, was by September (in the debate before the passing of the law) saying that this question was "of no interest internationally" because "they're looking for a firm hand, and if our hand proves firm, they'll want it, without bothering about what else is going on here."[85] During the course of the debate, Haller became more and more open in his support of the Jewish quota, which he had earlier opposed out of foreign policy considerations. He then proceeded to vote "no" to the law which his own ministry had introduced. The motive behind his voting is presumably the same as that behind Prime Minister Teleki's absence from the vote (on a law he otherwise agreed with). Haller later (in 1926) published a monograph in defense

---

83 Ilona Újszászi, "Időutazás a Délmagyarral: Perpatvar és numerus clausus," *Délmagyar.hu*, October 17, 2008 (accessed December 1, 2009).

84 Voting "yes" were: János Nagy, Dániel Oláh, Imre Örffy, Géza Paczek, Dénes Patacsi, György Perlaki, Ottokár Prohászka, Vilmos Prőhle, Móric Putnoky, Richárd Reischl, János Sabel, János Sallay, Károly Schandl, Henrik Schiessl, István Somogyi, Balázs Szabó, János Gy. Szabó, István Szabó (de Sokorópátka), József Szabó (Budapest), Jenő Szabóky, Ferenc Talányi, Béla Taszler, Ferenc Thomas, Béla Túri, Ferenc Usetty, Elek Avarffy, János Bartos, Imre Bárány, Béla Bernáth, Nándor Bernolák, László Budaváry, Imre Csontos, János Czakó, Béla Dánér, Antal Eberhardt, Károly Ereky, Gyula Fáy, István Gerencsér, Miklós Griger, Jenő Gunda, József Haller, Miksa Herrmann, Imre Héjj, Tivadar Homonnay, Zoltán Hornyanszky, János Huber, Károly Huszár, János Iklódy-Szabó, Antal Javos, Jenő Karafiáth, Emil Kovács, József Kovács, András P. Kuna, Pál Legeza, Albin Lingauer, Pál Lipták, and Viktor Mátéffy. Voting "no" were: Attila Orbók, Sándor Pető, Gyula Rubinek, Ernő Bródy, István Haller, István J. Kovács, and Zoltán Meskó. Minutes of the parliamentary session of September 21, 1920, in *Az 1920. évi február hó 16-ára összehívott nemzetgyűlés naplója*, vol. 5: 482. Absent from the vote from the government were: István Sréter (Minister of Defense), Ágost Benárd (Minister of Health and Employment), Jakab Bleyer (Minister without Portfolio for National Minorities), Gyula Ferdinandy (Minister of the Interior), Frigyes Korányi (Minister of Finance), József Vass (Minister of Food), Vilmos Tomcsányi (Minister of Justice), and István Szabó de Nagyatád (Minister of Agriculture). Pál Teleki was also Foreign Minister on a temporary basis until the day of the vote, the office being handed over to Imre Csáky only on the following day, September 22, 1920.

85 Minutes of the parliamentary session of September 21, 1920, in *Az 1920. évi február hó 16-ára összehívott nemzetgyűlés naplója*, vol. 5: 464.

of the Jewish quota, called *The Fight over the Numerus Clausus.*[86] Haller's "no" vote was nothing more than a tactical stroke, just like Teleki's absence, since they were both vociferous supporters of the Jewish quota.

For some deputies who were not present at the debate, the law clearly was not an important issue. Of 219 members of parliament, only 64 were present.[87] Others, however, like many Smallholder deputies, walked out before the vote because although they did not wish to support the law, they also could not vote against it, for the sake of their cooperation with the Unity Party.[88]

The number of "yes" votes was 57 overall. The law was therefore passed by barely more than a quarter (26 percent) of the members of parliament. Those who had voted for the law were in fact 18 fewer than had signed the (Prohászka-Bernolák) amendment to introduce the racial quota only a few weeks before.[89] There were those who had signed the Prohászka-Bernolák amendment but had changed their minds a few days later, such as Károly Rassay. Rassay had signed the amendment in the belief that it was intended to correct the practices of the previous academic year, when no Jewish students at all had been admitted to the universities, and that the 5 percent quota it wanted to introduce was aimed at guaranteeing that at least some Jewish students would be admitted. Rassay realized that this was not the case before the vote and did not attend.[90] It is conceivable that there were some who did not attend because they took it for granted that the law would be passed without them. Yet, others did not consider the law stringent enough, and therefore refused to vote for it. Finally, there were those

86 Haller, *Harc a numerus clausus körül.*

87 The precise number of deputies was not stated on September 21, 1920. The number of deputies in parliament changed frequently during the course of 1920 because the distribution of mandates was continuous due to the disorganization in electoral districts. In April 1920, the house consisted of 168 deputies. The number of deputies given in the parliamentary diary closest in date to the vote in September 1920 was 208 in February 1921. Klebelsberg said in 1927 that the parliament had 219 members in September 1920. Ladányi, "A numerus clausus-törvény 1928. évi módosításáról," 1128.

88 Bethlen, *A magyar zsidóság almanachja*, 60. Address by Miklós Forgács. The Unity Party (*Egységes Párt*), officially known as the Christian Peasant, Smallholder, and Civic Party (*Keresztény-Keresztyén Földmíves-, Kisgazda- és Polgári Párt*), was—under various names and following several transformations—the ruling government party in Hungary from 1922 to 1944.

89 The law introducing corporal punishment, which also carried some political risk, was approved by more than a hundred deputies. There were 167 deputies on June 17, 1920, and 208 in February 1921. Minutes of the parliamentary session of September 16, 1920, in *Az 1920. évi február hó 16-ára összehívott nemzetgyűlés naplója*, vol. 3: 446.

90 Minutes of the parliamentary session of May 13, 1927, in *Az 1927. évi január hó 25-ére hirdetett országgyűlés képviselőházának naplója*, vol. 4: 94. At this point, Rassay was still a member of the KNEP, but went on to found the Independent Smallholders' Party.

who presumably made their decisions contingent on what the leading politicians would do—and they absented themselves from the vote to a man. During his political career, Teleki absented himself from unpleasant or risky events more than once, for example when—as foreign minister—he decided not to go to Paris to receive the terms of the peace treaty. On the day of the final vote on the numerus clausus law, he was apparently recuperating in a sanatorium.[91] Nonetheless, we have no reason to suppose that Teleki (who two months before the vote had promised the institutional "defense" of "Christian society," and who later—in the 1920s—as an ardent supporter of the racial clause, fought for the maintenance of the anti-Semitic law) had any objection to the racial clause. As prime minister, ultimate responsibility for the passing of the law still lies with him, even if he spent the day itself resting in a sanatorium in Buda.

The fact that Teleki, Bethlen, and Klebelsberg all stayed away suggests that they were all aware of the risks associated with the law. They knew that the law represented a break with the traditions of the constitutional state, and that politicians who voted for the law might easily lose their standing on the international scene. At the same time, neither Bethlen nor Klebelsberg were willing to vote against the law and thereby come into conflict with the political forces pushing for the Jewish quota and their supporters. Teleki himself agreed on principle that the Hungarian parliament should legislate to "restrict" the Jews.[92]

As a result of the Bernolák–Prohászka amendment and the implementation decree issued by István Haller, the numerus clausus became an anti-Jewish law inscribed on paper. With that, the government took unnecessary international risks even from the standpoint of its anti-Semitic supporters, since it would have been enough to create boards of admission in order to restrict Jews from higher education. It is worth noting that both Ministers of Religion and Public Education Haller and Kunó Klebelsberg were of the opinion that the boards of admission, whose creation was mandated along with the fixed number system, would have been sufficient for the restriction of Jews without any further racial paragraph or quota system.

Many people at the universities were of the same opinion. Among them was Károly Hoór, professor of ophthalmology, who tried to dissuade the government from introducing the racial clause on behalf of the Faculty of Medicine,

---

91 Ablonczy, *Teleki Pál*, 180.

92 Péter Tibor Nagy, "A numerus clausus—hetvenöt év után," *Világosság* 36, no. 2 (1995): 72–80.

precisely with the restriction of Jews in mind. Since, as Hoór wrote to the minister of religion, the faculty was "mostly composed of members who are fully aware that the reduction of the Jewish element in the faculty and in the medical profession is an immediate necessity." It was, therefore, unhelpful to "bind the hands" of the university boards of admission by any sort of quota under the law, because the boards needed the flexibility to be able to deviate from the proposed 5 percent "either upwards or downwards."[93]

Hoór was most probably right. Constituted with the appropriate political bias (as they could well have been), the university boards of admission would have been able to work to prevent the admission of Jewish students without the need of any kind of legislation. This assumption is supported by the fact that at the polytechnics which were not subject to the numerus clausus law, the proportion of Jews was reduced just as much as at the other universities and polytechnics. At the College of Veterinary Medicine, the proportion of Jews decreased from 24 percent in 1914 to 4 percent in 1925, while at the College for Economics, it went from 8 percent in 1918 to 1.8 percent in 1925.[94] In other countries, such as the United States, where certain elite universities and medical schools were just deciding to restrict the number of Jews they would admit, it was precisely the system described by Hoór that was employed without reference to any state initiative or legislation.

Barely eight years later, when István Bethlen amended the racial clause, it was this same technique that was brought into being in Hungary. The universities did not admit a significantly larger number of Jewish students than when the racial clause had been in force. It is, therefore, no exaggeration to suppose that had the numerus clausus law been limited to mandating that all applications to universities be decided on by university admissions boards (without a racial quota), the exclusion of Jewish students from the universities would have begun just the same.

The ideology behind the Jewish quota: Prohászka

Prohászka proposed the idea of an anti-Jewish numerus clausus in May 1918, even before the left-wing revolutions. In a high-profile article, he counter-

93 Haller, *Harc a numerus clausus körül*, 73.
94 Haller, *Harc a numerus clausus körül*, 146.

posed Christian youth doing its duty at the front with Jews sitting at their university desks.

> Let us go through the winding fronts and we will see that the closer one gets to danger, the more Christians there are, and the farther one gets from the front, the more Jews. The one keeps dying while the other saves his skin—much to the benefit of our future Hungarian culture, of course! . . . Let us help our youth in their studies, let us help them succeed, or else we will have lost the battle after their victory! These insights illuminate the statistical data like watch-fires, and at the same time come to us like tongues of flame from the fires of Pentecost, to ensure that we don't exchange this world war for the extinction of our nation, heroism for slavery. . . . Our university-age youth are out shouldering the great and heavy burden of defending the homeland and have no time to study, while their space at the universities and polytechnics is taken up by others who are all too plentiful at home—who could stay home because (there is no other conclusion I can reach, so I will say it) they are degenerates.[95]

The bishop explained several times during the course of 1918 that the new political movement, christened by him "Hungarizmus," aimed for the comprehensive restriction of the economic rights of the Jews.[96]

"What exactly is my so-called anti-Semitism?" he asked in his article "Have We Had Enough?" His reply was that "it is not about going out and committing violence against Jews, no—it is about waking up the Hungarian people, with the whip of statistical data if need be, from their torpor and make them take back and hold on to what they have—all that to which their being, their faith, and their traditions tie them, and which they are in danger of losing."[97]

But what purpose was Prohászka's "whip of statistical data" really meant to serve? We are presented with numbers concerning the proportion of Jews in various branches of the economy, and how they relate to the proportion of

---

95 Ottokár Prohászka, "Pro Juventute catholica," in *Iránytű*, ed. Antal Schütz (Budapest: Szent István Társulat, 1929), 184–86. First published in *Alkotmány*, May 26, 1918; and Máté Gárdonyi, "Az antiszemitizmus funkciója Prohászka Ottokár és Bangha Béla társadalom- és egyházképében," in *A Holokauszt Magyarországon európai perspektívában* (Budapest: Balassi Kiadó, 2005), 195.

96 For example, *Népújság* [People's Paper], September 15, 1918.

97 Ottokár Prohászka, "Elég volt-e?," in *Iránytű*, 190. The article appeared on September 11, 1918, in the journal *Alkotmány*.

Figure 9. Bishop Ottokár Prohászka.
Source: Wikimedia commons.

Jews in the country overall. This includes data on bankers, landowners, businessmen, engineers, doctors, lawyers, and students at universities and polytechnics. These, then, are the fields in which the proportion of Jews will have to be measured using statistical data. And from this data will have to be made that "whip" which will help to change the inner balance of economic life.

The idea of a Jewish quota was complete in Prohászka's writings before the left-wing revolutions. He had introduced the theme of the proportional overrepresentation of Jews, or, in other words, that although Jews made up only 5 percent of the country's population, their proportion in certain economic fields was much higher. He had also outlined a program that would "cure" this overrepresentation of Jews. He said that "Christian Hungarians" must be "roused" to "take their rightful place," to stop and reverse the growth of the proportion of Jews.[98]

Following the revolutions, Prohászka merely adapted the thoughts he had previously laid out. It was not, therefore, a case of his radical anti-Semitism being a product of the left-wing revolutions. The bishop now incorporated the program for the Jewish quota into the ideological framework of the struggle between the races. It was in this same ideological framework that he found explanations for the revolutions. According to this ideology, the "Jews" "tricked" the "Hungarians" and dragged them into revolution. The victims of this "trickery," the "Hungarians," were therefore absolved of blame. All responsibility lay with the "Jews":

> I ask you, what is revolution? This revolution is totally alien to Hungarian thinking, alien to all Hungarian feeling. This revolution has cursed us with some sort of moral blood poisoning. It has plunged us into a world of alien

98 Prohászka, "Elég volt-e?"

> ideas, or if you'll allow me to say so within quotation marks, an odd sense of morality. It has given us new insights, but I would say that if a Zionist caravan from Tarnopol were to tramp its way across Hungary on its way to the Holy Land, and were to stop at the edge of some village to cook and wash there, its culture and morality would be just as far from the thought and feeling of the people of the village as this revolution was from the spirit of the Hungarian people. . . . All sorts of ideas formed in curly or un-curly heads have confused the public feeling. But if there was a Hungarian revolution and I ask, where was there anything Hungarian that revolted, it was most certainly not in the Károlyi or so-called Red revolutions, but in the crucible of reactionary Christian nationalism. . . . This is the reaction, the revolution that I can boldly and openly call, in the name of morality, a national Christian revolution.[99]

Prohászka kept the program of institutional anti-Semitism alive throughout the twenties. In his 1922 article, "The Christian Hungarian Way in Business," he wrote that Hungary needed a comprehensive change, which "by making every part of social activity part of the nation concentrates the society of the nation itself."[100] The article does not say what makes a "concentrated" society, but this much is clear: the anti-Jewish state intervention that Prohászka thought necessary goes far beyond the walls of the universities and affects every branch of the economy. Prohászka outlined a similar program in his article entitled "Awakening Hungary." There, he wrote: "It's not about beating the Jews to death—this is a purely defensive war. What we want is to stay here, to be the lords of our own manor. . . . That is not the case today. Whoever does well in trade is the real lord of the manor. Money talks, dogs bark. . . . The foundations have to be laid in the economy, otherwise the work we do will be like building a house from the first floor down."[101] Once more we are told that the purpose of the anti-Jewish measures is nothing other than to rearrange the conditions prevailing in the economy at the time.

---

99 Minutes of the parliamentary session of February 26, 1920, in *Az 1920. évi február hó 16-ára összehívott nemzetgyűlés naplója*, vol. 1: 63.

100 Ottokár Prohászka, "A magyar keresztény irányzat a kereskedelemben," in *Iránytű*, 297. First published in *Fejérmegyei Napló*, February 21, 1922.

101 Ottokár Prohászka, "Ébredő magyarok" [Awakening Hungarians]. In *Iránytű*, 288.

This is the broader connection that Prohászka brought to the attention of his audience during the parliamentary debate on the numerus clausus law as well. "It is very important," he said, "that we ourselves should be clear about what it is precisely that we want."[102] It would not be right to see the numerus clausus as merely a little "tweaking" of the higher education issue. The numerus clausus was a much more significant issue. It was just the "beginning" of a wide-ranging program that would transform all of Hungarian economic life. "It is clear that we have to begin the reorganization of Hungarian national upbringing right across the board. We are not quite ready for that yet, but are starting with the universities."[103] Prohászka thus considered the numerus clausus part of a longer process whose significance went far beyond the world of the universities.

Prohászka was brutally frank about the possibility of the introduction of the numerus clausus leading to violence. The processes that the numerus clausus had set in train, he said in parliament, contained the hidden risk that they could spill over into racial persecution. But, he continued, the Jewish quota had to be introduced nonetheless, even if the risk of it giving rise to "racial persecution" existed, although that was something that he, personally, would not support. "To my Jewish fellow-citizens, I say that you should not take this [the numerus clausus] as a sign of hatred, nor as racial persecution. It might spiral into that, but I would neither encourage nor praise its doing so."[104] Prohászka, then, saw the political risk associated with the numerus clausus as the process it had initiated could "spiral out of control" and lead to outright "racial persecution." He nonetheless recommended that the law be passed even after taking this danger into account, because he considered the great "national interest," which spoke for the law, to outweigh the risk.

Prohászka—in contrast to what he said in parliament—did not, in reality, condemn the persecution of Jews. A host of his personal comments serve as excellent examples of how support for the numerus clausus law and support for anti-Jewish street violence were not mutually exclusive. In fact, they were more interrelated in nature. Prohászka himself was a leading member of the Association of Awakening Hungarians (ÉME), which organized the anti-Semitic violence. As a bishop, he gave the Catholic Church's blessing to the

102 Minutes of the parliamentary session of September 16, 1920, in *Az 1920. évi február hó 16-ára összehívott nemzetgyűlés naplója*, vol. 5: 344.

103 *Az 1920. évi február hó 16-ára összehívott nemzetgyűlés naplója*, vol. 5: 344.

104 *Az 1920. évi február hó 16-ára összehívott nemzetgyűlés naplója*, vol. 5: 347.

organization's existence. It was in Prohászka's presence that the ÉME members of parliament made their "Christian-National" oath. Prohászka defended and encouraged the organization against the government's efforts at postwar stabilization even in 1921:

> They accuse the Association of Awakening Hungarians of being an organization bent on the destruction of Jewry. This is not the case—the Awakening Hungarians do nothing more than defend the Hungarian race. It does not matter, then, that this or that great person may say that the rule of law and equality wants everyone to be equal before the law. Is that even possible? Let me give just one example. The skunk is an animal, just like any other. As such, skunks could well demand a place in the henhouse. Whoever has that image in their mind's eye is ready to respond to the philosophers' piffle. . . . My dear awakening brothers! I want the rising Hungarian people to organize, to march together side by side, and organize consciously, in every street, like a [National] guard.[105]

In light of the above, any interpretation which would have Prohászka seeing the numerus clausus as a temporary crisis measure limited to higher education in order to take the wind out of the sails of street violence against the Jews becomes untenable. He saw it precisely for what it was: a watershed, the start of a new era in which—just like in the period before their emancipation—the restriction of Jewish rights would be possible once again. As he put it in his English language pamphlet *The Jewish Question in Hungary*, Hungarian society had in the past the means of defense and security against the Jews, but only as long as the legal rights of the Jews were circumscribed.[106] This security could only be reinstated if Jewish rights were restricted once again. In Prohászka's thinking, then, the interests and true security of Hungarian society could only be secured by a vast process of redistribution in every sector of the economy and society; something which it was imperative to undertake, even if that pro-

---

105 "Ébredő magyarok: Beszéd az ÉME nagygyűlésén, 1921. október 22," *Fejérmegyei Napló*, October 30, 1921. Quoted in András Nyerges, "Kis Prohászka-breviárium—Szemelvények a püspök megnyilatkozásaiból," *Mozgó Világ* 35, no. 2 (2009): 49–54.

106 "The legal restrictions placed on the Jews up until then—which protected and reassured Hungarian society—ceased, and with the extension of their rights, the country was suddenly exposed to the unrestricted advance of an intelligent and cunning race." Ottokár Prohászka, *The Jewish Question in Hungary* (The Hague: 1920), 3.

Figure 10. The Jesuit theologian and journalist Béla Bangha.
Source: Fortepan, 100296, Jezsuita Levéltár.

cess involved the restriction of the rights of the Jews and indeed could lead to their persecution.

The leading figure in the voluble Catholic press campaign for the introduction of the numerus clausus, the Jesuit Béla Bangha, shared Prohászka's views. The origin of Bangha's anti-Semitism, like Prohászka's, considerably predated the left-wing revolutions.[107] Bangha's tours of Kecskemét in May 1917 and Kiskunfélegyháza in May 1918, during which he spoke about the need to restrict the Jewish press, were followed by anti-Semitic disturbances.

Bangha considered a comprehensive anti-Jewish program (or "clean-up") necessary and supported the numerus clausus law in the hope of realizing this wider agenda. He wanted to restrict the participation of Jews in the banking sector, trade, the press, and cultural life, while he also planned to completely exile the Jews from the villages: "Above all, we must clean the villages of their Jewish liquor merchants and general traders, taking away their shopkeepers' and

107 Péter Bihari, "Antiszemitizmus az első világháború Magyarországán," *Beszélő* 13, no. 2 (February 2008), http://beszelo.c3.hu/cikkek/antiszemitizmus-az-elso-vilaghaboru-magyarorszagan (acessed September 24, 2009).

liquor licenses, putting cooperatives (consumer, credit, agricultural, and produce cooperatives) in their place all the way down the line. In fact, it would be best if the villages never even so much as set eyes on a Jew."[108]

In order to "solve the Jewish question," Bangha (in his own words) advocated the use of "radical" institutional means, which would break with the "naive," "short-sighted," and "soft" philosophy of liberalism and the principle of Jewish equality. Although Bangha would not, in principle, have opposed the "complete sidelining" of the Jews, he did not think it possible for two reasons. Firstly, because it would lead to economic disaster, and secondly, because the Jews also had to support themselves somehow since, as he wrote (though his words now sound naive to us), "it is nonetheless physically impossible to deport more than a million Jews from the country."[109] As it turned out two and a half decades later, Bangha's judgement of what was and was not possible had been mistaken...

The "proportionality" program: Alajos Kovács

The more prosaic version of the program so vehemently propounded by Prohászka and Bangha was worked out by Alajos Kovács. Kovács was a well-respected statistician of the day, department head, and later director (from 1925) of the Central Statistical Office, and a close colleague of Pál Teleki.[110] Kovács not only took part in the preparatory work for the numerus clausus, but was also one of the drafters of the 1938 Jewish law. It was his work that created the "whip" envisioned by Prohászka from the "statistical data" that was to be used to "whip up" public opinion to support action against the Jews.

Alajos Kovács—like Prohászka—thought that statistics had to be made into a tool of political mobilization. "In the struggle of self-defense," he wrote in his 1922 work *The Jewish Takeover of Hungary*,

> which has now begun against the expansion of the Jewry, we have to have a good knowledge of the battle stations of the Jews if we want to succeed. Let us take in turn, therefore, the positions that Jewry occupies, so that we

108 Béla Bangha, *Magyarország újjáépítése és a kereszténység* (Budapest: Szent István Társulat, 1920), 161–62.
109 Bangha, *Magyarország újjáépítése és a kereszténység*, 161–62.
110 Alajos Kovács and István Bethlen both took part in the work of the office created in August 1919 by Pál Teleki tasked with preparing for the peace talks.

> can see where and with what force we have to take up the struggle, which must put the Christian Hungarian people into a position concomitant with its proportion and importance against Jewry, which is even now endangering the existence of the Hungarian nation.[111]

For this great undertaking, considered Kovács in 1922,

> we either need an operation that goes right to the root of the problem, or long but regular treatment. The choice of treatment is a matter for the politicians. It is a matter for the politicians in whose hands the fate of the country is today placed in trust. Their task, that of solving the Jewish question in such a way as not to bring down upon our heads philosemitic international opinion while nonetheless allowing the Hungarian people—now suffering repression and exclusion in its own homeland—to succeed in accordance with its proportion, will not be easy.[112]

The "solution to the Jewish question," then (just like in Prohászka's thinking), was to restrict their position in society and the economy by means of the state and to take over some portion of the material goods in Jewish hands. In Kovács's mind, the "Jewish question" would have been "solved" if the Hungarian state had—using official means—been able to ensure that the Jews did not take a greater part of the benefits of, or positions in, the economy than their proportion within the overall population of the country. Since, according to Kovács's calculations, the part of national wealth and income in Jewish hands was approximately 20–25 percent, whereas the proportion of Jews within the overall population was a mere 5 percent, the proportionality program effectively meant that about three quar-

Figure 11. Alajos Kovács. Source: MNM Történeti Fényképtár.

111 Kovács, *A zsidóság térfoglalása Magyarországon*, 7.
112 Kovács, *A zsidóság térfoglalása Magyarországon*, 53.

ters of the goods in Jewish hands had to be transferred somehow into non-Jewish ownership. In other words, this would entail a large-scale program of expropriation for which, logically, there would need to be a string of newer and newer Jewish laws modeled on the university numerus clausus.

This ideology was not born during the crisis years of the 1914–18 war nor was Hungary the first place where it appeared. It first appeared in Germany, decades before World War I, as a reaction to the emancipation of the Jews. The starting point for the German "process of normalization" program was that the Jews derived disproportionately large benefits from the privileged positions created by capitalist economics and urbanization and that this disproportionality was constantly creating further disproportionality in the opportunities for the Jews to improve their social position. It was this situation that the policy of "normalization" wished to put an end to (without much success). As part of this policy, the government urged Jews to change professions and the circumstances of their employment, with the intention of directing them towards the handicrafts sector and agriculture especially. It was from this intellectual background of the 1870s that the ideology of modern political anti-Semitism developed by the turn of the century, which suggested that "by solving the Jewish question, all current [economic and social] problems would be resolved as well."[113]

It was this German anti-Semitic tradition that Alajos Kovács applied to Hungary when he outlined the longer-term considerations behind the numerus clausus. Kovács's views were echoed by that influential supporter of the numerus clausus law, Bishop Ottokár Prohászka, who—during the debate on the draft of the law—came out and said: "Hungary only needs a certain percentage of Jews."[114] According to Kovács, the Jews' share of the national wealth and the national income was disproportionately high, at 20–25 percent. This percentage needed reducing by means of state intervention to that 5.9 percent of the overall population of Hungary that the Jews made up. In order to achieve this goal, there would have to be "measures" brought in against the Jews in all those fields of the economy where their share was disproportionately high. This was the view that prevailed in the Jewish Laws introduced after 1938, in

113 Reinhard Rürup, "Die 'Judenfrage' der bürgerlichen Gesellschaft und die Entstehung des modernen Antisemitismus," in *Emanzipation und Antisemitismus: Studien zur "Judenfrage" der bürgerlichen Gesellschaft* (Göttingen: Vandenhoeck und Ruprecht, 1975), 82–83, 91.

114 Minutes of the parliamentary session of September 16, 1920, in *Az 1920. évi február hó 16-ára összehívott nemzetgyűlés naplója*, vol. 5: 350.

whose elaboration Alajos Kovács took part, just as he had in the creation of the numerus clausus law.[115]

The key concept in Kovács's thinking was the principle of "proportionality." This was based on the idea that the relations in a given society are "proportional" when the proportions of the positions filled in various professions and the distribution of goods and capital in general were equal to the proportions that people of the various races and religions made up within the population overall.[116] In his own words:

> The crux of the Jewish question lies not in the large number of Jews, but in that thanks to their superior intelligence and commercial sense, they flood into those fields and professions that guarantee them intellectual or economic leadership, or at least a predominance well in excess of their proportion within the population as a whole. . . . While the Christian religions are proportionally represented in all the professions and the deviations from the national average in individual professions are insignificant, the Jews, with their 5 percent proportion of the population of the country, make up 11.7 percent of the *de facto* professional class and 15.2 percent of the jobs in industry and trade. Among the latter, the proportion of Jews in industry is 10 percent and 51.8 percent in trade.[117]

---

115 The writer Dezső Szabó, whom the members of the anti-Semitic student societies considered their spiritual leader, expressed the same sentiment: "The rule of law can only be guaranteed by a whole and complete system of laws and institutions, where every clause serves to support every other clause; and the resources of each and every institution serve to support all the others. Thus, for example, the principle of the numerus clausus in the polytechnics, on its own as it is, though it may look good, could even be dangerous. For one thing, the well-financed Jewish youth may easily go abroad and get a high-level education, then coming home, settle in thanks to the incredible cohesion of the Jews. Secondly, the Jews could establish a polytechnic here at home. Therefore, we have to extend the numerus clausus to all breadwinning professions, be they public or private. We have to create a system of laws which ensures equal chances for success for each race in the competition. And we must certainly turn the idea of a numerus clausus into law with respect to secondary schools as well." See article in *A Nép* [The People], May 26, 1921. Szabó, like so many of his contemporaries, considered the numerus clausus in higher education merely the first step in a broader "economic war" against the Jews, since—as he said—the Jews must be fought in the field where "the Jewish front is weaker and especially with those tools that are the natural tools of our race. The immediate tool of the Jews is their cunning, while ours is the open force of our protective legal system. Where, then, our cunning falls short, we must make up for it by this open force." See *A Nép*, May 26, 1921. Dezső Szabó clearly and logically expressed at the start of the 1920s how the introduction of the university numerus clausus would eventually lead to the philosophy behind the Jewish Laws introduced after 1938.

116 For the place Jews occupied in the occupational spectrum of the Hungarian population, see Viktor Karády, "Zsidóság és modernizáció a történelmi Magyarországon," in *Zsidóság és társadalmi egyenlőtlenségek (1867–1945): Történeti-szociológiai tanulmányok* (Budapest: Replika Kör, 2000), 7–40.

117 Kovács, *A zsidóság térfoglalása Magyarországon*, 40.

It is not difficult to discover in Alajos Kovács's calculations the signs of demagoguery pursued by statistical means. The strategic choice of his point of departure in large measure forecasts the end results and his conclusions. As the Christian Socialist Sándor Giesswein put it in parliament, this kind of statistical research did not help people see clearly, but rather it obscured their vision: "There are three kinds of lies," he said. "Lies you're forced to tell, lies you tell for comic effect, and statistics. I do not say this because the numbers themselves are deceptive, but because people have produced the greatest tricks and lies by the way they've used them."[118]

The employment statistics Kovács used served very well in highlighting the role of Jews in the creation of modern Hungarian capitalism and in showing that in several fields, especially connected to banking and modern trade, there really was a remarkably high proportion of Jews.[119] But even Kovács himself was aware that underlying this phenomenon were not racial, but primarily historical causes. The ban on Jewish ownership of land, which lasted almost right up to their emancipation, had the effect of steering Jewish businessmen towards retail, modern industry, and the banking sector in the first place. Moreover, the fact that civil service jobs were largely inaccessible to Jews led post-emancipation Jewish youth to seek their fortunes in modern graduate professions.[120]

The relatively low representation of the Jewish professional class in the civil service can be attributed to the fact that as Jews they had very little access to these offices, and as a consequence, Jews who undertook higher education focused on liberal professions. This meant that the proportion of Jews among lawyers was 51 percent in 1920, while among doctors it was 46 percent.

But Kovács interpreted and inflated the process and extent of Jewish "takeover" of the graduate intelligentsia with a political agenda—which is to say, in a way unbefitting a professional statistician. First of all, the concept of the Jewish "takeover" of positions in society and the economy made it seem as if Jewish students and graduates "took away" spaces from their non-Jewish colleagues, whereas until the introduction of the numerus clausus in 1920, there

118 Minutes of the parliamentary session of December 22, 1922, in *Az 1922. évi junius hó 16-ára hirdetett nemzetgyűlés naplója*, vol. 7: 204.

119 Karády highlights that among independent professionals in the financial lending sector, the proportion of Jews was 85 percent, of those in business 54 percent, and among the owners and directors of industrial concerns, it was 44 percent. Karády, "Zsidóság és modernizáció," 24.

120 Karády, "Zsidóság és modernizáció," 23–25.

were no numerical restrictions on university admissions. Anyone with a valid secondary school diploma could enroll. Therefore, insofar as there was anything "disproportionate" in the denominational makeup of the student body at the universities, the question to be asked should not have been why a larger proportion of Jews were trying to get graduate qualifications, but why the youth of the other religions were not doing the same. In any case, in light of the fact that the proportion of Jews with secondary school diplomas was five times as high as that among non-Jews, there is nothing surprising in the fact that a larger proportion of Jews applied to the universities than non-Jews. Later, a few years after the introduction of the numerus clausus, it turned out that the spaces that had become vacant thanks to the exclusion of Jewish students were not easily filled with non-Jewish applicants, since the exclusion of the Jews did not in itself alter the attitudes towards higher education of non-Jewish families nor did it change their material circumstances.[121]

Second, when making use of the national population figures, Kovács consistently ignored the fact that the "disproportionate" numbers between the religions among graduate professionals was primarily an urban phenomenon. The majority of the Jewish population was urban, while the majority of the non-Jewish population lived in the countryside. It is therefore natural that a comparison of the educational and professional data of the urban population with that of the population in the countryside would show that the proportion of university graduates and those working in the professions is higher in the city than it is in the countryside. In Hungary in 1920, almost two thirds of the Jewish population lived in towns, while almost two thirds of the non-Jewish population lived in the villages. As a demographer, Kovács would have known that this high degree of urbanization among Jews would in itself have meant that there would be a higher proportion of Jews (as city-dwellers) in higher education and, therefore, in the professions and the middle and lower-middle class occupations than the country's other, less urbanized, denominational groups.

But Kovács chose to explain the Jewish "takeover" of the professions not as a result of these specific historical and demographic circumstances, but as

121 Haller, *Harc a numerus clausus körül*, 144. István Haller complained in 1926 that Catholics and Protestants could not fill up "their" quota of places between 1921 and 1926. The reason for this was that there were not enough applicants for the places left free by the exclusion of the Jews because—as Haller pointed out—those social groups "even today are not in the right financial circumstances to be able to fill the quota allotted to them."

a result of the "racial" characteristics of the Jews. The "core of the Jewish question," as far as he was concerned, was that the Jews, because of their inherited racial characteristics, could not, or only in a small minority, be assimilated into Hungarian society.[122] Kovács thus saw the Jews—in contrast to Nazi racial theory—not as an inferior race, but quite the opposite. The Jews owed their successes, or as he would have it, their "triumphant surge forward," to "their racial characteristics" and "bodily and psychological makeup." He considered them to be a race with such advantageous characteristics that the supporters of a Christian "changing of the guard" could only take up the struggle by the use of political force. Kovács tried to make the aggressiveness of the program for "racial defense" acceptable with the use of the word "defense."

Just as conscious was the use of the term "Christian" society, which had the effect of lumping together the various religions of the non-Jewish population into one category. Kovács was well aware that, in terms of its cultural and material capital, "Christian" society was deeply divided and that there were significant differences between Catholics and Protestants as well. Kovács skated over this problem with unusual ideological tools: "The power relations of the various Christian religions balance each other out and complete each other harmoniously. Their development serves one unitary goal: the numerical, cultural, and financial strengthening of the Hungarian nation."[123]

In his study, branded "statistical pulp literature" (*statisztikai ponyva*) by liberal politicians, Kovács simply ignored the demographic and economic factors that did not serve to support his political goals.[124] This is particularly obvious in his analysis of graduate professionals which was undertaken for the purpose of supporting the racial clause of the numerus clausus. Noting that "nowhere else is the Jewish takeover as rapid as in the professional sphere,"[125] Kovács argued that the data he presented, "which show the terrific flood of Jews in higher education, should easily justify the Christian Hungarian people's right-

122 "Due primarily to their religious difference, their status as a unitary race, historical traditions, and generally their whole physical and psychological structure, the Jews are an indigestible, unassimilable race, which cannot be measured by the same standards as the other strata making up the nation, especially the Christian ones." Kovács, *A zsidóság térfoglalása Magyarországon*, 2.

123 Kovács, *A zsidóság térfoglalása Magyarországon*, 2.

124 Dániel Várnai's comment at the parliamentary session of December 26, 1922, in *Az 1922. évi junius hó 16-ára hirdetett nemzetgyűlés naplója*, vol. 7: 36.

125 Kovács, *A zsidóság térfoglalása Magyarországon*, 42.

ful efforts to be represented in higher education and in the professions according to its own proportion."[126]

Kovács was correct in saying that Jews were present in higher education in a proportion exceeding their proportion of the overall population. The average proportion of Jewish students in higher education oscillated around 24–26 percent between 1900 and 1918. During the war years, it sometimes reached 30 percent.[127] One contributing factor to the rising proportion of Jews is that Jewish families were more willing than non-Jewish families to send their daughters to university as well, and the growth in female university students itself boosted the number of Jews in higher education.[128]

However, given that half of Hungarian Jewry (52 percent) lived in or around Budapest, it was—from the point of view of statistical analysis—a misleading move to use as a point of comparison for the "proportionality" plan nationwide data from a primarily agrarian population. In the case of Budapest, the disproportionality claimed by Kovács, though considerable in some faculties, such as medicine, was not so great when taken overall. Although Jews did indeed account for 25–28 percent of the university students in Budapest, this, as mentioned earlier, happened against the backdrop of Jews making up around 20 percent of the city's population.[129] It is true, however, that seen in this light, the figures would have lost a good deal of their power to motivate politically. At the beginning of the 1920s, 86 percent of all students in higher education in the country studied in Budapest, and the selection of students was strongly influ-

126 Kovács, *A zsidóság térfoglalása Magyarországon*, 34. In his 1938 work on the Jewish population of post-Trianon Hungary, Kovács described the goal of the numerus clausus thus: "The original goal of the numerus clausus was to partially exclude the Jews from what are practically the professional fields and to bring down their proportions to the level to which they are represented in the population overall. We did not want the Jewry to take a disproportionately large role in the intellectual elite of the country, as it had done before. For it is shameful for the nation that its leading intellectual elite should be drawn in good part from an only superficially assimilated alien element which has forced its own worldview, morality, and business-oriented spirit onto the spiritual life of the nation. Besides, experience has shown that the Jews use this situation to gain power and in possession of that power will lead the nation on an erroneous path, and ultimately to ruin." Kovács, *A csonkamagyarországi zsidóság*, 20.

127 István Haller supported the necessity of the racial clause with the following data: In the 1917–18 academic year, at the University of Budapest, the proportions of Jewish students were 21.6 percent in the Faculty of Law, 51.6 percent in the Faculty of Medicine, 20–25 percent in the humanities, 34 percent in pharmacology, and 37.1 percent at the Technical University. Haller, *Harc a numerus clausus körül*, 13.

128 Karády, *Iskolarendszer és felekezeti egyenlőtlenségek*, 63.

129 The proportion of Jews in the overall population of Budapest in 1910 was 23.1 percent.

enced by their ability to live at home. The proportion of Jews among students in higher education should therefore have been compared to the religious breakdown of the population of Budapest as well. But such an analysis would have been less helpful in trying to support the racial clause of the numerus clausus.

This biased use of data from the capital and from the country as a whole was immediately apparent to some public opinion makers. Vilmos Vázsonyi, in parliament, pointed to the "fallacy" of the "proportionality" principle when based on national figures:

> The Honorable Minister consistently fails to remember when establishing the proportions for the numerus clausus—and herein lies the fallacy—that the majority of Hungarians of the Jewish religion live in the cities. Nearly half of Rump Hungary's[130] entire Jewish population lives in Budapest. Only a negligible fraction of Jews live in the villages. So, if I were to be looking to establish the proportion fairly, I should not be looking at the proportions in which the country overall sends its children to university, but the proportions in which the urban population does. This principle, I submit, cannot be put into operation, and the falseness of the numbers [used for] the numerus clausus—not the idea behind it—becomes clear when you consider that a large percentage of the urban population is Jewish. . . . I ask you to take into account location when looking at the proportions of university students in the population.[131]

Vázsonyi's reasons were especially valid because cultural policy in the early 1920s encouraged the universities in Budapest to take students from the capital first and foremost, while the rest of the universities—Pécs, Szeged, and Debrecen—were to fill their rosters from their local catchment areas.[132]

Vázsonyi pointed to another "fallacy" in Kovács's thinking, namely, that the "takeover" of spaces in higher education by Jews and their "overrepresentation" until 1920 came about in historical circumstances where, as mentioned earlier, admission to the universities and polytechnics was unrestricted (as long as one had a valid secondary school diploma). Given that every candidate with a valid

---

130 Meaning post-Trianon Hungary.

131 Minutes of the parliamentary session of December 12, 1925, in *Az 1922. évi junius hó 16-ára hirdetett nemzetgyűlés naplója*, vol. 38: 220.

132 Klebelsberg quoted in Ladányi, "A numerus clausus-törvény 1928. évi módosításáról," 1137.

secondary school diploma was admitted to university, the Jewish candidates were not, therefore, accepted at anyone else's expense and did not "take away" places from Christian applicants. Even István Haller, the minister of religion, admitted this in his justification of the numerus clausus.[133]

The number of Jewish students increased as a result of legislation following the 1867 Austro-Hungarian Compromise, which made it possible for Jews to enter professional occupations from which they were previously barred or could enter only by extraordinary permission of the crown (jurisprudence, for example). Responding to these new opportunities, Jewish students enrolled at university, while the career choices for the children of non-Jewish families remained the same as they had been before the Compromise.[134] If the Jewish students did, nonetheless, appear as competitors to their non-Jewish colleagues, this was not because Jews displaced other people in higher education, but because after starting their professional life, the career paths of the two groups developed differently.

Lastly, when formulating the "proportionality" principle, Alajos Kovács was biased in omitting the fact that Jews were taxpaying citizens in Hungary, just like non-Jews. According to Kovács's calculations, Jews provided 20–25 percent of the country's national income, and their contribution to the national budget was at least as large.[135] In light of this, the idea that Jews drew "disproportionate" benefits from the opportunities presented in the country's higher education system does not stand up. For if we divide the statistics for the population of the country along ethnic-religious lines, as Alajos Kovács does, then it turns out that Jews took part in higher education in more or less the same proportion in which they contributed to the country's economy.

---

133 According to Haller's calculations, the number of students at all the universities in 1867, including the law schools, was 3,352, of whom 396 or 11.8 percent were Jewish. In the 1913–14 academic year, the total number of students was 16,700, of whom 3,879 or 23.2 percent were Jewish. Thus, according to Haller's calculations, the number of Jewish students grew tenfold in the fifty years between 1867 and 1917, from 396 to 3879. If the number of non-Jewish students had grown in the same proportion as the Jews, then there should have been 33,700 students at the universities and law schools by 1917. However, only roughly half this number, some 16,700 students, were at university because the number of non-Jewish students had grown more slowly than those of Jewish students. Haller, *Harc a numerus clausus körül*, 92.

134 M. Kovács, *Liberalizmus, radikalizmus, antiszemitizmus*, 50.

135 The cost of each degree issued was about 15–20,000 crowns. Bethlen, *A magyar zsidóság almanachja*, 97.

The "proportionality" program and the extreme Right

The extreme right anti-Semitic associations, or in Prime Minister Huszár's words, "provocation parties" (*hecc-pártok*), played a key role in creating the political atmosphere necessary for the racial clause of the numerus clausus.[136] These associations were very powerful during the disintegration of the traditional political system, the military collapse, and the Romanian occupation and subsequent withdrawal.[137] Their organized actions—imbued with a military spirit and often in military uniform, with a clear chain of command and making use of the railways—served to significantly boost the strength of these associations and the impression these interventions made during the power vacuum at the end of 1919 and during the weak, short-lived governments that followed.

The Association of Awakening Hungarians, which drew tens of thousands of people, put up anti-Semitic posters in the countryside, and organized terror attacks and pogroms. The Awakening Hungarian leaders and activists were a mix of people from the most varied social backgrounds. They included leading politicians, priests, teachers, instructors, judges, demobilized army officers, refugees, postmen, railwaymen, students, and the unemployed. There were some who had genuinely suffered under the 1919 Soviet Republic, while others had joined the ranks of the "Whites" precisely to wipe away the memory of their role during the short-lived republic, and finally, there were the common criminals, who hid their acquisitive greed behind a convenient political screen. Between 1919 and 1921, the Association of Awakening Hungarians was found to have been responsible for 73 murders. The goods of the mostly Jewish victims were distributed by the association among the local members.[138] The military leaders of the association, authorized by various types of documents, could stop anyone and inspect their papers, as well as place them under arrest and confiscate their belongings. As Ödön Beniczky, the minister of the interior under the Friedrich government, said in parliament in 1921, a good deal of these actions came about "not from patriotic zeal, but from the simple desire to rob on the part of a band of organized criminals, hidden behind a grandiose

136 Gratz, *A forradalmak kora*, 269; and Zinner, *Az ébredők fénykora*, 47.

137 Following the collapse of the Hungarian Soviet Republic, which was at war with Romania since April 1919, large parts of the country came under the control of the Romanian army. The Romanians withdrew from Budapest only in November 1919, and from the rest of the country in April 1920.

138 Zinner, *Az ébredők fénykora*, 41.

facade of suppressing Communism."[139] The Awakening Hungarians used university and school buildings for their meetings and in 1920 were tasked with keeping order around the universities, thus exacerbating the anti-Semitic mood already prevalent in the universities.[140] In Budapest, the Awakening Hungarians organized anti-Semitic terror attacks. They checked the papers of passersby on the street, while at night they beat up Jews.[141] In the spring of 1920, these nighttime attacks became daytime attacks, and a string of "cafe-attacks" began in the Lipótváros district of the city, culminating in the deadly July 27, 1920 attack mentioned earlier.

By the autumn of 1920, the Awakening Hungarians were operating with more than a hundred local chapters nationwide. They established their own investigation unit, organized their own strikes, established a food distribution network, and received allocated housing. As well as beating up Jews, then, the Association of Awakening Hungarians undertook more and more activities that made it appear to be some sort of shadow government. Taking their cue from the civil service, the association created "departments," among them an "investigative department," a "department of food," a "department of housing," and so on. Following a decree by the "department of housing" in November, the Awakening Hungarians occupied the Lipótváros Casino and moved people displaced from territories lost after the war who had been living in railway cars into its rooms.

While the government opposed the actions of the Awakening Hungarians, the police response was for some time uncertain and ambiguous. Investigations dragged on and perpetrators were often not found. The Awakening Hungarians also found sympathizers within the police who helped get rid of evidence.[142] The government's response was weakened by the fact that, with regard to the Awakening Hungarians, there was no agreement between the cabinet and Horthy. In January 1920, Horthy received a delegation from the Awakening Hungarians, and asked them to help maintain people's "proper behavior" once the peace terms were made public.[143] By doing so, Horthy himself contrib-

---

139 Minutes of the parliamentary session of July 15, 1921, in *Az 1920. évi február hó 16-ára összehívott nemzetgyűlés naplója*, vol. 9: 575.

140 Zinner, *Az ébredők fénykora*, 59.

141 Gratz, *A forradalmak kora*, 317.

142 The membership figures of the Association of Awakening Hungarians varied through the years, but Tibor Zinner mentions a membership of several tens of thousands around 1920. Zinner, *Az ébredők fénykora*, 69.

143 Zinner, *Az ébredők fénykora*, 55.

Figure 12. Members of the Turul Alliance, 1922. Source: Fortepan, 31756, István Fodor.

uted to the appearance of the Awakening Hungarians as some sort of law-enforcement body.

The government only cracked down on the Awakening Hungarians and other paramilitary organizations from the autumn of 1920. On November 11, in the presence of Pál Teleki, the police and army surrounded and then arrested the members of the terrorist detachments encamped at the Casino. The government suspended the Awakening Hungarians, and was prepared to respond with martial law in case of future attacks. Following the crackdown, membership began to drop and their illegal attacks became more infrequent—though they did not stop entirely. As late as 1922, they staged a terror attack on the Erzsébetváros Democratic Circle on Dohány Street, which claimed eight lives. In 1923, in protest against the Bethlen government's taking up foreign loans, they organized a bomb attack on the French embassy.[144]

The Awakening Hungarians had no political vision, plans for reform, or political program. Their vision of the future was based on raw anti-Semitism with popular appeal. Dezső Szabó summed this up by saying: "We have only one goal—and that is to break the Jewish race down completely."[145] At the

144 Zinner, *Az ébredők fénykora*, 159 and 165.

145 Zinner, *Az ébredők fénykora*, 60. Dezső Szabó's speech was made on March 28, 1920, in Debrecen, at the statutory meeting of the Association of Awakening Hungarians.

mass meetings of the Awakening Hungarians, the talk was of the expropriation and redistribution of Jewish property, and demands for the introduction of a "social, economic, and cultural ghetto system" for the Jews. They also decided on the restriction of Jewish participation in trade and industry.[146] In order to gain access to Jewish property, deputy László Budaváry recommended in the autumn of 1920 that "every Jew ought to leave the country within 24 hours."[147]

The Awakening Hungarians drew large crowds with their raw anti-Semitism focused on the expropriation of the Jews. But the mood of the crowd was translated into the language of everyday politics by the leading politicians who were members of the Awakening Hungarians. More than a tenth of the parliament of 1920, which is to say 26 deputies, were members of the leadership of the Awakening Hungarians, among them Bishop Ottokár Prohászka, the ideological mainstay of the numerus clausus law and its most influential propagandist.

Compared to the diffuse but effective anti-Semitism of the Awakening Hungarians, the extreme right-wing student organizations at the universities operated in a more targeted manner. True, the radical student organizations—such as the Turul Alliance for students of law and medicine; the Christian Socialist Centrum; the National Union of Hungarian University and College Students (MEFHOSZ), the umbrella group bringing together older student organizations; and Hungária at the University of Technology—could only mobilize a minority of students, with the exception of the Faculty of Medicine.[148] Thanks to their level of organization, however, they nonetheless had a good deal of influence, since most members of these organizations also belonged to the university public security battalions. The members of these battalions received regular remuneration from the state. Organizationally, they were placed under the leadership of the Budapest Public Security Headquarters and were used, among other things, to break strikes. Their membership stood at 2,400 in December of 1919, while the police force of Budapest had a strength of 3,200.

During the course of the year following the fall of the Soviet Republic, the student organizations kept the issue of the Jewish quota on the agenda with

146 Zinner, *Az ébredők fénykora*, 44.
147 Zinner, *Az ébredők fénykora*, 86.
148 For a time, MEFHOSZ served as the umbrella group for the other associations, with the exception of Hungária, but this unity ceased in the spring of 1920 when the Turul Alliance left. See Ladányi, *Az egyetemi ifjúság*, 74–78, 96.

Figure 13. Ball of the Foederatio Emericana (association of Catholic Hungarian university and college students), 1935. Source: Fortepan, 101583, Miklós Pápay.

street protests right up to the moment parliament passed the anti-Jewish law.[149] They prevented Jewish students from entering the universities and checked the papers of students in the corridors, ejecting those who were Jewish. They did not allow Jewish students to sit for their exams. It was enough for someone to merely look Jewish to fall under suspicion. In October 1919, the government closed the universities because of the anti-Semitic incidents and teaching only resumed the following spring.

Teaching resumed in the spring of 1920, but campaigning by the radical organizations enabled them to appoint two members to each of the five-member committees that vetted applicants and had oversight of admissions.[150] The anti-Semitic student organizations did not give up their anti-Jewish activities even after the racial clause was introduced. They organized a "guard" to ensure that the proportions stipulated by the law were respected and campaigned for the further strengthening of anti-Jewish measures.

---

149 Gábor Ujváry, "Egyetemi ifjúság a 'neobarokk társadalomban': A bajtársi szövetségekről," *Valóság* 34, no. 5 (1991): 64–65.

150 In the spring of 1920, a total of 12 Jewish students were allowed to enroll at the Budapest university. Ladányi, *Az egyetemi ifjúság*, 139.

Pál Teleki's role

A significant part of the political elite in power after 1919 agreed with the fundamental idea behind Kovács's "proportionality" program. At most, they disagreed on the educational and economic sectors in which they should introduce the proportionality principle, and the means by which the program should be pursued.

It is a generally accepted idea in Hungarian historiography that Pál Teleki supported the law as prime minister in order to put the brakes on the wave of anti-Semitic violence that followed the fall of the Hungarian Soviet Republic and to restrict it "within the framework of the law." This, however, is but one side of the coin. For, in Teleki's thinking, the numerus clausus was not merely some forced concession to the far right, but a tool—in itself justified—of a broader-conceived social policy.

Teleki, like Prohászka, considered the emancipation of the Jews a historical error, the careless product of a period awash with prosperity. It was a mistake that now could only be corrected at the price of taking away legal rights. He thought that the Hungarian people had been "corrupted" by the Jews, that it was their fault that the Hungarian middle class had imploded during the post-war revolutions, and that this middle class had to be saved by means of anti-Jewish measures, above all the numerus clausus.[151] Accordingly, he frequently expounded the program of "scientific anti-Semitism" from the summer of 1919 onwards, according to which the state had to restrict the rights of the Jews, and "if possible the advancement of the Jews in the professional sphere must be reduced proportionately."[152] In his introductory speech as prime minister in the summer of 1920, he alluded to the "institutional defense of the interests of Christian society," or in other words, he made it clear that as the head of the Hungarian government, he would support the restriction of the Jews by legal means. It was actually as part of this rationale that he supported the introduction of the numerus clausus in higher education.[153]

151 Cf. the speech by deputy János Esztergályos at the parliamentary session of February 21, 1928, in *Az 1927. évi január hó 25-ére hirdetett országgyűlés képviselőházának naplója*, vol. 9: 123; Ablonczy, *Teleki Pál*, 146–47; and Krisztián Ungváry, "Szobrot Teleki Pálnak?" *Népszabadság*, February 17, 2004.

152 *Pesti Élet*, September 15, 1919, 3; and Géza Malasits's recollections at the parliamentary session of February 16, 1928, in *Az 1927. évi január hó 25-ére hirdetett országgyűlés képviselőházának naplója*, 9: 91.

153 Minutes of the parliamentary session of July 22, 1920, in *Az 1920. évi február hó 16-ára összehívott nemzetgyűlés naplója*, vol. 4: 15.

Teleki made it clear that he thought the racial quota to be appropriate and necessary later on as well. When Prime Minister István Bethlen proposed the amendment of the racial quota in 1927, Teleki defended the racial clause even against him. There was only one aspect of the numerus clausus that he was willing to criticize and that was that it defined the area within which the Jews could be restricted too narrowly.[154] It applied only to higher education and did not take in other areas of life. But, he maintained, the higher education law in itself did not accomplish much, since it would not "solve the fundamental problems Christian youth are facing in terms of employment prospects."[155] He added further, "We cannot think that by merely enacting a law, that law will afterwards act for us, and we can sit back because we've passed this law."[156] Christian youth graduating from university should be able to expect the state to continue to care for them "in life," and in order for that to happen, the distribution of power then existing in the economic field would have to be changed. "We ask nothing more for Christian society," he said, "than space for ourselves according to our proportion and importance."[157]

In Teleki's thinking, then, the numerus clausus was just one of the anti-Jewish measures—which were to be welcomed—that he expected with time to reorganize the ethnic balance of the division of property, to the detriment of the Jews. He also expected them to put an end to the preponderance of Jews in certain sectors of the economy, at the price of discriminating against them, if need be.[158] Another eleven years had to pass after the events of 1928 before Teleki, now prime minister for a second time, was able to help bring about an anti-Jewish measure that was more strict and comprehensive than ever before, the so-called Second Jewish Law. In connection with this law, he himself directed attention to the close links between the 1920 numerus clausus and the Jewish laws introduced from 1938 onwards, pointing out that the new laws had their roots in the tra-

---

154 Speech in the Upper House "On the amendment to the numerus clausus," March 13, 1928. In Teleki, *Válogatott politikai írások és beszédek*, 188–205.

155 Teleki, *Válogatott politikai írások és beszédek*, 202.

156 Teleki, *Válogatott politikai írások és beszédek*, 190.

157 Teleki, *Válogatott politikai írások és beszédek*, 204.

158 Balázs Ablonczy, in his survey of Teleki's political legacy, reached a similar conclusion. He attributed Teleki's conviction in this regard to the events of 1918–19: "1918–19 matured in him the thought that there was—in his eyes—a middle class with alien origins, which was blocking the development of the Hungarian Christian middle class, or national elite. Therefore a competitive advantage had to be ensured over them, even at the price of discrimination." Balázs Ablonczy, "Vázlat a magyar konzervativizmusról," *Confessio: A Magyarországi Református Egyház figyelője* 29, no. 4 (2005): 16.

dition created by the 1920 law. As he said, the numerus clausus created the conditions, "an intellectual and emotional mood" in Hungarian politics of which the new Jewish law was an almost "necessary" and "natural consequence."[159] His biographer, Balázs Ablonczy, was right to conclude that though Teleki did not live to see the time of the deportations, he played an active role in starting that process in which "first the status, then the property, later the capacity to work, and finally the very existence of the Jews, became prized targets."[160]

It is therefore erroneous to claim that Teleki supported the numerus clausus law merely out of necessity.[161] It is true that Teleki did not contribute to the debate preceding the law, nor did he take part in the final vote. But the reason for his absence was not that he objected to the law, but that he did not wish to compromise his international standing.

What is certain is that Teleki did not oppose the numerus clausus law. We can also exclude the possibility that Ottokár Prohászka, the leader of the governing party, faced opposition from Teleki when he decided to introduce his amendment on the racial clause. We must also note that Teleki would have had the opportunity to voice his disapproval, had he in fact disapproved of the racial clause. Further, Teleki strenuously defended the Jewish quota during the course of his later career. It is also true that there were several other anti-Semitic measures during Teleki's premiership, even if they were not enshrined in law. Teleki approved that Jews who had immigrated to Hungary from 1914 onwards should be interned prior to their expulsion from the country, the withdrawal of licenses for Jewish-owned cinemas, and the ban on letters written in Hebrew being carried in the post. Finally, he also took part in the February 1921 decision of the Hungarian cabinet which stipulated that Jews—as unreliable elements—should be placed into separate army units.[162]

---

159 Teleki, *Válogatott politikai írások és beszédek*, 378–79.

160 Ablonczy, *Teleki Pál*, 411.

161 Konrád Salamon's textbook for fourth-year secondary school students, which is widely used, claims that the numerus clausus was only supported by a far right "minority." Teleki's name does not even come up in this regard. "In September, the right-wing and far right minority in parliament pushed for a nationalities quota to be included in the numerus clausus then being prepared to reduce the overproduction of intellectuals.... The measure affected primarily Hungarians of Jewish origin negatively." Konrád Salamon, *Történelem IV: A középiskolák IV. osztálya számára* (Budapest: Nemzeti Tankönyvkiadó, 1993), 56.

162 Ablonczy, *Teleki Pál*, 181. The Jewish units ultimately failed to materialize as the peace treaty forbade conscription.

In light of all this, we have to question the idea, so widespread in Hungarian historiography, that Teleki only introduced the government's numerus clausus law as a concession to the mood of the streets. It is true that the law was introduced at roughly the same time as the crackdown on extreme right paramilitaries, but this does not necessarily mean that there was a causal link between the two—in other words, that the paramilitaries were able to be brought under control because Teleki had introduced the numerus clausus. Teleki did not suppress the paramilitaries with the numerus clausus law, but with determined action from law enforcement agencies.

The coincidence of timing does not mean that Teleki's sole aim was to use the law to "disarm" the anti-Semitic mood of the masses after the revolutions and to "take the wind out of the sails" of the radical right.[163] It is true that the government committed itself to resolute steps to put an end to the attacks in the streets at the time when the law was introduced. This proved that the government could create order in the streets and do away with the anti-Semitic terror groups. But the same government certainly did not do everything in its power to rein in the anti-Semitic students running riot in front of the gates of the universities.[164] Quite the opposite: it made use of the radical student associations as allies. In November 1920, when parliament had to ratify the Trianon Peace Treaty, the government used the university police detachments as garrisons and entrusted them with the guarding of key locations, such as telephone exchanges and the post office.[165]

The government did not get in the way of the attacks perpetrated by the anti-Semitic student groups. Twenty days after the numerus clausus law was passed, the minister of education had these words of encouragement to say to the anti-Semitic students: "Let the people with the crooked ears take note—only that which is Hungarian can exist in this country and the Jews should be prepared for when the trumpet of the awakening Hungarian people reduces their castles to dust."[166]

163 In the words of Ignác Romsics: "Teleki tried to defuse and to some degree satisfy the anti-Semitic mood with the so-called numerus clausus." Romsics, *Bethlen István*, 124.

164 Zinner, *Az ébredők fénykora*, 79. The Association of Awakening Hungarians was at the forefront of the campaigns taking place at the universities.

165 Ladányi, *Az egyetemi ifjúság*, 182.

166 Report from the Győr meeting of the Christian Socialist Party, MTI News Release, October 11, 1920.

The Teleki government gave the rector of Budapest University no assistance in stopping the beatings of Jewish students. In October 1920, the rector tried to contact the minister of education on five separate occasions, but the government preferred to talk with the student organizations instead.[167] Nor did the police respond to a call from the prorector of the evacuated universities of Kolozsvár and Pozsony asking for assistance concerning the beatings of Jewish students.[168]

Hungarian historians usually explain Teleki's behavior by saying that he needed to introduce the racial quota in order to strengthen his position at a moment when his government was preparing to crack down on the paramilitary groups. This explanation does not take into account the possibility that Teleki of his own free will—and without any special strategic purpose—supported the introduction of the racial quota because he fundamentally agreed with it. It does not take into account that Teleki, as premier, made use of the chaotic period leading up to the restoration of the rule of law in order to preside over the establishment of the institutional framework of political anti-Semitism. This would have been more difficult to do later, since the removal of the paramilitaries from the streets would have meant the disappearance of the sort of violent anti-Semitism that otherwise could have been used to justify the introduction of an anti-Jewish law as part of the postwar stabilization process. By putting an end to the attacks of the extreme right, then, Teleki also put an end to that obvious source of danger which would have served as justification for the introduction of the numerus clausus.

The interpretation which suggests that Teleki introduced the racial clause for the purpose of quieting the far right is further weakened by the fact that the passing of the law did nothing at all to restrict the far right. In fact, quite the opposite is true—the day after the law was passed, Károly Ereky launched a parliamentary attack on the government, saying that "nothing is being done to bring down the Jews."[169] A few days later, the Association of Awakening Hungarians began

---

167 Ladányi, *Az egyetemi ifjúság*, 171.

168 Zinner, *Az ébredők fénykora*, 173. Prorector Schneller's account of the joint council meeting of the universities of Kolozsvár and Pozsony, October 26, 1920; and minutes of the parliamentary session of October 26, 1920, in *Az 1920. évi február hó 16-ára összehívott nemzetgyűlés naplója*, vol. 6: 143.

169 "While the Association of Awakening Hungarians restrains the awakened crowds who even now wait with clenched fists and see that nothing is being done to bring down the Jews, it is making a huge effort on behalf of the country." Minutes of the parliamentary session of September 22, 1920, in *Az 1920. évi február hó 16-ára összehívott nemzetgyűlés naplója*, vol. 5: 504.

making preparations for an anti-government coup.[170] "It has been confirmed," Minister of the Interior Gyula Ferdinandy told the cabinet, "that in October, the organization in question [the Association of Awakening Hungarians] was actively considering the takeover of power by coup-like means."[171]

The anti-Semitic student groups resumed their attacks from where they had left off before the law was passed. In October, they cordoned off the entrances to the Faculty of Humanities and the Faculty of Medicine in Budapest several times, and checked the papers of anyone entering. They took away documents from Jewish students, tore them up, and beat and ejected many of the students from the university.[172] Enrollment had to be suspended on October 14, as it had been the year before. The Árpád and Turul associations demanded that the government make a new law that would take away the "acquired rights" of the Jewish students to continue their education. They also demanded that the admissions boards contain delegates chosen by the right-wing student groups, and that the numerus clausus be extended to all higher education institutions.

The numerus clausus did not "take the wind out" of the sails of the far right, but rather swelled that wind, just like the Jewish laws of the 1930s. It served to strengthen with legal norms the political ideas behind the anti-Semitic street violence. It contributed to an explicit ideology and policy of racial defense at the universities directed against the Jews which was coming into force throughout this entire period.

István Bethlen and the numerus clausus

The dividing line between the conservative and radical right on the issue of the numerus clausus was far from as sharp as it could have been. Although it is true

170 Ferdinandy, the minister of the interior, reported on the planned putsch at a cabinet meeting on November 19. The minister for trade recommended that the organization be disbanded, while the minister of education recommended only new leaders and a change of the basic principles. The foreign minister thought that "insofar as the government is not willing to stand up firmly against the organization, this will be interpreted as a retreat on the government's part. Even if the organization restrains itself, we'll be in exactly the same position again within a month as we are today." In the end, the cabinet decided to suspend the Association's Aszód branch. MNL OL, K27, Minutes of the Council of Ministers, November 19, 1920, 19–22. On November 5, the "foreign policy section" of the Association attacked the government saying it was preparing to ratify Trianon. Two days later, following a resolution from the Association's "housing department," its members occupied the Lipótváros Casino and moved displaced persons into its halls.

171 MNL OL, K27, Minutes of the Council of Ministers, November 19, 1920, 19.

172 Ladányi, *Az egyetemi ifjúság*, 169.

that the conservatives differed from the radicals on the question of the numerus clausus, the concerns of the former had less to do with the discriminatory, anti-Jewish content of the racial clause and more to do with the negative impact of the racial clause on Hungary's international standing. They believed that it was important to prevent Hungary from sacrificing other important goals on the "altar" of anti-Jewish legislation. These goals included obtaining foreign loans in order to finance economic stabilization and the ability to use foreign policy positions to try and mitigate the repercussions of the Trianon Peace Treaty. As Bethlen put it in 1923, the problem in Hungary was not that some political circles were voicing anti-Semitic demands, since the "Jewish question exists" in Hungary and "has to be dealt with."[173] However, in Bethlen's reasoning, it would be distinctly improper to allow the domestic political struggles over the Jewish question to cut across the country's foreign policy goals, for (in his words) "the nation has much greater problems than . . . the Jewish question," and the resolution of these greater problems cannot be made subordinate to any "second-tier" problems.[174]

Bethlen's objection to the radical right was not, therefore, that they had fought for and labored to maintain the numerus clausus, but that they wanted to place their anti-Semitism at the center of Hungarian political life. They wanted to make it "the lone star dominating the firmament of Hungarian political life," and forgot about "the much greater, much more urgent, more grave problems which threaten the very existence of our nation, as if these latter were not the ones that should be the primary guides for the compass of Hungarian political life."[175] Bethlen thought that in dealing with these problems—which he considered more urgent than the Jewish question—it was better not to antagonize the Jews but to win them over as allies.

Bethlen's reasons for not supporting the numerus clausus were entirely pragmatic. He believed that obsessive anti-Semitism would paralyze Hungarian

173 Minutes of the parliamentary session of July 27, 1923, in *Az 1922. évi junius hó 16-ára hirdetett nemzetgyűlés naplója*, vol. 15: 176.

174 Speech by István Bethlen on the parliamentary session of July 23, 1923, in *Az 1922. évi junius hó 16-ára hirdetett nemzetgyűlés naplója*, vol. 15: 176. Bethlen summarized the foreign policy priorities as follows: to restore "balance" in the economy, establish economic ties with neighboring countries, "postpone" the question of reparations—or in other words, delay Hungary's pecuniary obligations, protect Hungarian minorities in the lost territories, and, finally, join the European international framework. See István Bethlen's speech on May 8, 1922, in Debrecen, in *Bethlen István gróf beszédei és írásai*, vol. 1 (Budapest: Genius, 1933), 236.

175 *Bethlen István emlékirata, 1944* (Budapest: Zrínyi Kiadó, 1988), 128.

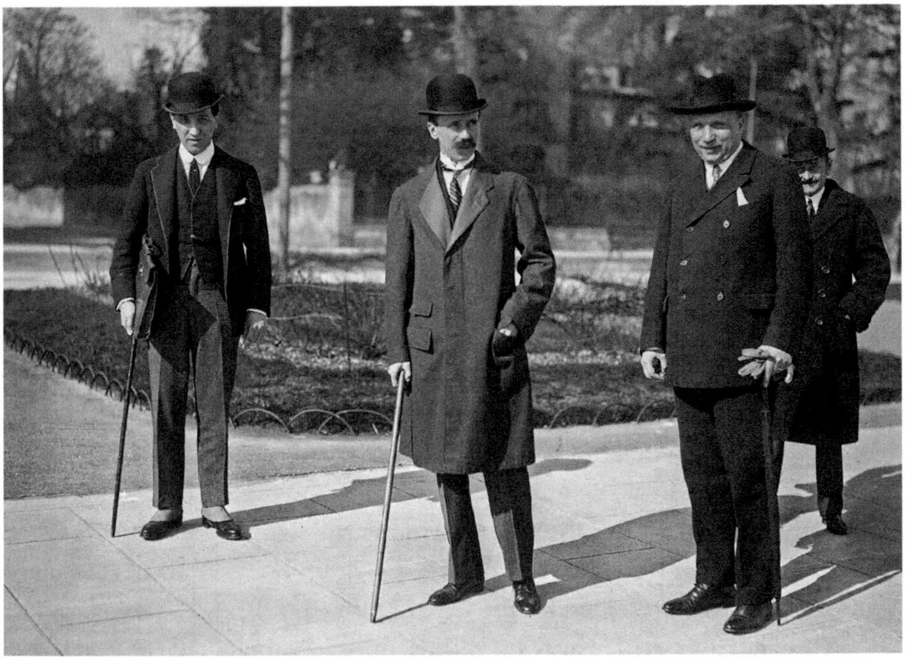

Figure 14. Prime Minister István Bethlen (center) with Minister of Foreign Affairs Lajos Walkó (second from right) in Geneva, 1926. Source: Fortepan, 217617, Bibliothèque nationale de France.

political life in its ability to solve problems. We have no record, however, of any moral objections to the Jewish quota on his part. What is known is his opinion that the numerus clausus was a tool that could help weaken the position of the Jews in Hungary until the members of the non-Jewish middle class, who "represent the appropriate race in historical tradition . . . will lead the nation once again."[176] At any rate, it is a fact that Bethlen—while he increasingly distanced his government from political anti-Semitism throughout the 1920s—waited until after the League of Nations started proceedings against Hungary before repealing the racial clause. When he did amend the law in 1928, he approved his minister of education's recommendations which served to perpetuate the exclusion of the Jews, albeit no longer on a racial basis but through express quotas on certain professions.

176 Romsics, *Bethlen István*, 201. According to Romsics, Bethlen—though he never spoke publicly on the issue—"probably" agreed with the anti-Semitic measures in the numerus clausus. Romsics, *Bethlen István*, 113.

Bethlen was unequivocally opposed to any escalation of anti-Semitic measures beyond the numerus clausus, and in fact there were none during his decade-long premiership. After his appointment as prime minister, he stated on several occasions that Hungary's foreign policy and economic interests both dictated that anti-Semitism quiet down on the domestic political scene. As he said in parliament in 1921 when discussing the need of the rule of law for the economy to function: "equality before the law is a basis and guarantee of the life of the nation that must not be touched or interfered with."[177]

Lajos Szabolcsi, the editor in chief of the Jewish weekly *Egyenlőség* (Equality), considered István Bethlen's policy of political and economic stabilization in the 1920s to be, from the point of view of the Jews, "distasteful" but successfully managed. In his 1942 memoirs, he dedicates space to explaining Bethlen's position regarding the racial clause. According to Szabolcsi, Bethlen simply "did not comprehend" the importance of the numerus clausus because "his vision, attuned to broader horizons, did not even pick up on the darkness that the numerus clausus represented for life here in Hungary."[178]

"Count István Bethlen was no philosemite," Szabolcsi wrote.[179] Indeed, despite his political clear-sightedness, Bethlen's thinking about the Jewish question was surprisingly unsophisticated. Referring obliquely to the Jews in 1911, he spoke of a "poison" that under the name of "internationalism" or at other times under the name of "radicalism" was engaged in a "power struggle" with the Hungarian nation.[180] After the 1919 Soviet Republic, he believed, as mentioned earlier, that "a large part" of the Jews had taken part in the revolutions, disregarding the fact that the overwhelming majority of the Jews played no part in the events whatsoever.[181] Bethlen ascribed the outbreak of the revolutions to the behavior of the Jews as well, without—as his biographer Ignác Romsics points out—taking into account how much the country's defeat had fanned

177 April 19, 1921, in *Az 1920. évi február hó 16-ára összehívott nemzetgyűlés naplója*, vol. 9: 188.

178 Later historians have a somewhat different view. Ignác Romsics, for example, believes that Bethlen did not repeal the racial clause for years because he generally agreed with it remaining in force. János Gyurgyák has a slightly different take on this, maintaining that Bethlen had committed himself to repealing the racial clause since the early 1920s, but he believed its repeal could not be carried through politically until 1927. However, Szabolcsi, Romsics, and Gyurgyák all agree in detecting ambivalence in Bethlen's words and deeds in connection with the racial clause, and they believe this ambivalence requires an explanation.

179 Szabolcsi, *Két emberöltő*, 333.

180 Quoted in Gyurgyák, *A zsidókérdés Magyarországon*, 123.

181 Gyurgyák, *A zsidókérdés Magyarországon*, 123.

the tensions arising from social inequality and the dissatisfaction of national minorities, completely independently of the Jews.

When talking about Jews, Bethlen—like so many of his contemporaries—meant financially successful Jews, ignoring the poorer Jews who made up the majority of Jewish society: the stonemasons, tailors, skinners, shoemakers, bakers, waiters, junkmen, peddlers, haulers, and workers. Unlike Alajos Kovács, however, he attributed the financial success of the Jews not to racial characteristics but to historical processes, that is, that the Jews were forced into mercantile occupations because the other middle-class professions were closed to them.[182]

Bethlen nonetheless thought that a certain amount of anti-Semitism had to be considered the norm in Hungarian society, so much so that "every good Hungarian" should be anti-Semitic to some degree.[183] The emphasis, however, was on the degree. "I am opposed to any kind of brash anti-Semitism," he said in 1921. In this short statement, we find the full extent of Bethlen's ambivalent rhetoric. His condemnation of "brash" anti-Semitism at the same time implies that one can live with the quieter kind.

Bethlen's uniquely ambivalent way of speaking came through once more in his 1921 speech to parliament in which he indicated that he considered the Jews to be alien to Hungarian society, while at the same time saying that he condemned anti-Semitic politics. "I accept," he said, "that a Jewish question currently exists in this country. But the solution to this question is for us to become economically the same without them as we are with them. This is in their interest as well, because at the very moment they are no longer indispensable, harmony will be restored."[184]

Despite his distant and indeed often negative attitude towards the Jews, Bethlen opposed all anti-Semitism that tried to place the Jewish question at the center of political life for pragmatic, or as he put it "sober" reasons. He believed that Hungary had far greater problems to solve than the Jewish ques-

182 See "Bethlen a zsidókérdésről" [Bethlen on the Jewish question], in Katzburg, *Zsidópolitika Magyarországon*, 234.

183 In his memoirs, he wrote when describing Gyula Gömbös: "Gömbös was an anti-Semite at heart, but no more anti-Semitic than any other good Hungarian in response to the times of Mihály Károlyi and Béla Kun, when everyone was disgusted by the behavior of a large part of the Jews." In *Bethlen István emlékirata*, 128.

184 Minutes of the parliamentary session of April 19, 1921, in *Az 1920. évi február hó 16-ára összehívott nemzetgyűlés naplója*, vol. 9: 189.

tion, and that putting it center stage weakened the country's ability to solve its major issues. As he said in parliament in 1923:

> I do not deny that this question bears some topical importance. For I am of the opinion that a Jewish question exists in Hungary.... But I would most strenuously condemn our making this the touchstone of our political debate. This question should not be the one around which the different political camps form. For, if it's bad enough that this question has such topical importance then we should not make things worse by trying to split the political parties because of it. If that were to happen, parliament and the entire public life of the country would become a battleground between the anti-Semites on the one hand and those who want to oppose them by bringing Jewish interests into the foreground. This would be a great danger and a great pity from the point of view of the country's broader interests.... The fact that we don't want to make the Jewish question the central one, that we do not consider it to be the most important issue facing us does not mean that this party is divided in principle. For the nation has much graver problems than the Jewish question. The chopping up of its territory is a much graver problem, the defenseless position in which we find ourselves is a much graver problem, the pressure with which our neighbors are squeezing us is a much graver problem, as are the eradication of our Hungarian blood in the territory taken away from us and our worsening financial and economic position. These are the questions we must strive together to find solutions for, and we can agree to disagree on issues of secondary importance.... Because what we want is a national democracy and we want to protect the country from any form of extremes. We want to protect the country from the kind of shocks which the passions of something like anti-Semitism, on the one hand, and the unreflective revolutionary ideals of radicalism, on the other hand, carry with them.[185]

Bethlen condemned Gyula Gömbös and the radical right in general for blowing the Jewish question out of proportion throughout this entire period. He held them heavily responsible for the preponderance of "damaging, hollow slogans and the kind of goals that, pushing aside day by day all other serious

185 Minutes of the parliamentary session of July 23, 1923, in *Az 1922. évi junius hó 16-ára hirdetett nemzetgyűlés naplója*, vol. 15: 176.

problems, have obscured our perception of the true state of the country."[186] He thought the radical right's efforts to start a campaign of serious expropriation of Jewish property distinctly dangerous, because he believed that the Hungarian economy could not continue to function without the Jews.[187] Bethlen did not support the Jewish Laws of the 1930s, resigning from parliament the day after the Second Jewish Law was passed. In his farewell letter to his supporters, he wrote: "The prophets of our nation today are those who—in the holy name of the nation—eat Jews for breakfast, counts for lunch, and before retiring redistribute all the land and property that doesn't belong to them. . . . The artificially created waves of radicalism must pass before common sense can have its say. Let us pray that it will not be too late, that when sobriety returns, the wounds and the damage done will not be irreparable."[188]

During the months of the German occupation, Bethlen considered the persecution of the Jews not only to be barbarian, but also a source of irremediable danger to "Christian Hungarian" society. In June 1944, distraught, he asked Horthy to make the government put an end to the raging anti-Semitism,

> to that inhuman, idiotic, and brutal persecution of the Jews—unworthy of the Hungarian spirit—with which the current government has besmirched the name of Hungary in the eyes of the world; which has become the source of the most unbridled corruption, robbery, and theft, and into which a significant portion of the country's intelligentsia have also sadly drifted. Though it will hardly be possible to remove this stain from our good name, we must nonetheless put an end to this barbarity. Otherwise, Christian Hungarian society itself will be incurably infected.[189]

186 *Bethlen István emlékirata*, 123.
187 Katzburg, *Zsidópolitika Magyarországon*, 235.
188 Romsics, *Bethlen István*, 277.
189 Miklós Szinai and László Szűcs, eds., *Horthy Miklós titkos iratai* (Budapest: Kossuth, 1972), 460.

Chapter Two

The First Decade of the Numerus Clausus and the Racial Clause

The quantitative impact of the Jewish quota on Jewish graduate professionals

The Jewish quota was a delicate subject in the statistical literature of the time, since Hungary was under pressure from the League of Nations, which accused it of racial discrimination for almost a decade. For this reason, the government's figures left a lot of data obscure, and information was published more than once which was manipulated in such a way as to help the country's defense against the League of Nations' accusations. Government statisticians, however, did not use the numbers in a biased manner merely for foreign policy goals, but also because in the inner circles of higher education—at the universities and the ministry of education—people could see that the basic concept behind the law was discredited very quickly, within two or three years of its introduction. The law was meant to "make space" for Christian youth by excluding the Jews. But by the mid-1920s, it had become apparent that the gap that had developed due to the exclusion of Jewish students could not be filled with Christian secondary school graduates and that there were not enough Christian applicants to the universities to maintain the prewar student numbers.

About statistics at the time

We cannot, therefore, merely accept the contemporary student data when making our judgement. What is more, the Jewish quota was enforced at the time of admission to university, but the contemporary official student figures regularly reflected the second semester of the academic years. The published statistics also did not reflect how many of the Christian and Jewish students who were offered places actually matriculated, and how many transferred to other universities during the academic year, or in other words, how the composition of the academic intake changed from the moment of admission until the end of the academic year.

In order to be able to judge, we must also carefully separate the data regarding those first-year university students who were accepted from those students in higher academic years, for the Jewish quota of the numerus clausus applied only to first-year admissions and not to students in higher years. The Jewish quota did not apply retrospectively to students admitted before 1920. In order to answer the question, then, to what degree the quota was enforced at the various universities, we have to look at the data for first-year students exclusively.

The proportion of Jews at university overall—including the higher years—exceeded 6 percent every year from 1920 to 1928. It was these figures that the Bethlen government pointed to in its own defense against the League of Nations. But the higher years included Jewish students who had begun their studies before 1920 and—according to the law—had "acquired rights" to continue their studies. As we shall see, there were indeed universities that in fact did "not respect" the law—not in the sense that their use of the quota was more relaxed, but quite the opposite; they excluded even those Jewish students in their higher years to whom the Jewish quota did not apply.

The birth of whitewashing myths about the implementation of the law was helped by the fact that the student statistics giving the proportion of Jewish students compiled at the end of the year, did not provide data on the underlying admissions process or dropout rate. In other words, they did not include data on the true scale of anti-Jewish restrictions, because the comparative proportions of the two variants—the "Jewish" and "Christian" groups of students—changed significantly throughout the academic year itself. Some of the Christian students who had been admitted did not, in fact, matriculate at the beginning of the academic year, thereby increasing the proportion of Jewish students. But from the perspective of the Jewish students who had not been admitted, it did not matter that the proportion of Jewish students had increased in the class to which they were not admitted. All that mattered was how many people were actually given places at the university at the end of the admissions process.

Let us illustrate with the admissions data for the University of Technology in 1926. These demonstrate nicely why the percentages for the proportion of Jewish to non-Jewish students presented at the end of the year cannot give us a clear picture of the implementation of the Jewish quota. In 1926, the minister of education authorized the admission of 670 students to the university.[1] The admissions board thereupon accepted 39 of the Jewish applicants, making up 5.8 percent of the authorized admissions. The University of Technology therefore adhered strictly to the Jewish quota. At the same time, however, fewer Christian students applied for the 670 places than were expected. The total number of applicants in the end, both Jewish and non-Jewish, was 558. Of these, only 472 had sufficiently strong academic results to meet the admissions criteria. In the end, the class consisted of 472 students. Thus, the proportion of Jews—because of a shortage of Christian applicants—rose to 8.26 percent. This increase did not take place because the university admitted more Jews than the Jewish quota allowed, but because it turned out during the admissions process that there were fewer Christian applicants than places authorized by the ministry. In the following year (1927–28), the minister authorized the admission of 643 students. Of these, the university allowed 6.22 percent to be Jewish students (a total of 40 persons). However, instead of the 603 Christian students expected to enroll in the class, only 430 did in fact enroll, of whom 20 failed to turn up at the beginning of the year. The total number of students admitted to the class of 1927–28 was therefore only 450. As a result, the proportion of Jewish students rose to 8.88 percent, while at the same time not one more Jewish student was admitted than the Jewish quota legislated for.

The statistical "trajectory" of the seven Jewish students admitted to the Department of Architecture is enlightening. They made up 7 percent of the government allocation of places (for 100 students). However, so few Christian students applied that the university could fill only 59 places with them. Including the seven Jewish students, the number admitted was 66. But of that number, the Jewish students now made up 10.6 percent. In the end, nine of the Christian students did not enroll, and therefore the proportion of Jews grew to 12.3 percent during the course of September–October. Thus, the proportion of Jews increased between the spring and autumn of 1927 from 6.22 percent to 12.3 percent without the university admitting a single extra Jewish student in the meanwhile.[2] According to the official published statistics, the proportion of Jewish students admitted to the Department of Architecture was 12.3 percent in the

1 BME Archives, Minutes of the University Council, 3/a, 5, 1926, November 11, 1926.

2 BME Archives, Minutes of the University Council, 3/a, 5, 1926, November 11, 1926.

second half of the academic year. But this proportion was achieved not because the department was not enforcing the Jewish quota. Rather, it was because the planned proportion of 93.78 percent Christian students decreased to 87.7 percent during the course of the admissions process and enrollment in the autumn.

In order to judge properly, we also have to treat the universities in the capital and in the provinces separately. For instance, at the small universities in Pécs and Szeged, a high proportion of Jewish students were admitted in the higher years for a long time, since these universities had hardly any Christian applicants. The numerus clausus did not forbid this, since the Jewish quota did not apply to the higher years. As for the first-year students, these universities, too, adhered to the quota more or less, even if they did occasionally exceed 6 percent by one or two percent. Nonetheless, the Bethlen government consistently presented the statistics for all the year groups of the universities of Szeged and Pécs alongside the national statistics; these were not merely the figures for first year admissions, but the data for the universities as a whole, counting the higher years as well. But if we separate out the first and higher years, we will see that these two universities also applied the Jewish quota for first-year admissions, just like the universities of Budapest and Debrecen.[3]

Data

The number of non-Jewish university graduates in Hungary increased by 12,879 between 1920 and 1930 (from 57,966 to 70,845). During the same period, the number of Jewish university graduates decreased by 1,558 (from 15,509 to 13,945).[4] The only extant figures for the number of Jewish students rejected by the universities are from the Ministry of Religion and Public Education and run only up to 1925–26. Up to this date, 4,644 Jewish students were rejected from the first year of university and we can assume that this number would have risen above 5,000 by 1928.[5] We have no data as to the number of people who did not even bother applying to university because of the numerus clau-

3 With its institutional roots going back to the Calvinist College of Debrecen founded in 1538, the Royal Hungarian University of Debrecen was established in 1912. In 1921, it was renamed the Royal Hungarian Tisza István University.

4 Data from the censuses of 1920 and 1930.

5 This was the number of students rejected, not the number of rejections, since there were students who applied more than once. The numbers above show how many people were rejected. Haller, *Harc a numerus clausus körül*, 133.

Table 3. Number and proportion of Jewish students among higher education students in the second semester of each academic year, according to the Central Statistical Office, 1910–1943

Academic year	Total number of students in the 2nd semester	Jewish students	
		by number	by percentage
1910/1911	14,021	3,490	24.9
1911/1912	14,233	3,387	23.8
1912/1913	14,575	3,553	24.4
1913/1914	15,414	3,879	25.2
1914/1915	n.d.	n.d.	n.d.
1915/1916	n.d.	n.d.	n.d.
1916/1917	n.d.	n.d.	n.d.
1917/1918	n.d.	n.d.	n.d.
1918/1919	18,449	6,719	36,4*
1919/1920	10,005	558	5.6
1920/1921	14,258	1,721	12.1
1921/1922	17,306	2,318	13.4
1922/1923	20,815	2,388	11.5
1923/1924	17,329	1,861	10.7
1924/1925	15,582	1,533	9.8
1925/1926	15,200	1,372	9.0
1926/1927	15,020	1,284	8.5
1927/1928	15,459	1,290	8.3
1928/1929	15,675	1,378	8.8
1929/1930	15,497	1,473	9.5
1930/1931	16,053	1,689	10.5
1931/1932	16,002	1,967	12.3
1932/1933	15,766	1,965	12.5
1933/1934	15,694	1,816	11.6
1934/1935	15,088	1,465	9.7
1935/1936	14,216	1,175	8.3
1936/1937	13,821	1,017	7.4
1937/1938	13,228	820	6.2
1938/1939	13,219	510**	3.9
1939/1940	13,815	437**	3.2
1940/1941	17,161	532**	3.1
1941/1942	19,900	584**	2.9
1942/1943	21,732	580**	2.7

* The exceptionally high proportion of Jewish students this year is explained by the fact that Jewish students applied for the supplementary semesters announced at the end of the war in a higher proportion than their Christian counterparts.

Source: Hungarian Statistical Yearbooks, 1910–1943; and Kovács, *A csonkamagyarországi zsidóság*, 73. For the data marked with **, see Ladányi, "A numerus clausustól a numerus nullusig," 68.

Table 4. Number and proportion of Jewish students among first-year university, technical university, and law school students subject to the numerus clausus according to the database of the Ministry of Religion and Public Education, 1910–1925

Academic year	Total number of students	Number of Jewish students	Percentage of Jewish students
1910/1911	11,926	3,470	29.1
1911/1912	12,274	3,368	37.4
1912/1913	13,608	3,534	26.0
1913/1914	13,487	3,858	28.6
1914/1915	8,556	2,646	30.9
1915/1916	5,076	1,540	30.3
1916/1917	5,597	1,812	32.4
1917/1918	17,748	6,027	34.0
1920/1921	13,696	1,712	12.5
1921/1922	16,849	2,307	13.7
1922/1923	17,764	2,323	13.1
1923/1924	14,331	1,798	12.5
1924/1925	12,972	1,450	11.2
1925/1926	12,326	1,283	10.4

Source: Haller, *Harc a numerus clausus körül*, 130.

sus, but we can estimate their number to be a few thousand. Because of all this, the proportion of Jews among university students decreased from the 25–28 percent of the prewar years to around 10 percent in the 1920s.

The tables below convey two sets of data about the numbers of university students; those of the Central Statistical Office and those of the Ministry of Religion and Public Education (see tables 3 and 4). The figures obtained from the Central Statistical Office on the number of students in higher education are higher than those of the ministry. The reason for this is that the data from the Central Statistical Office includes all university and polytechnic students, regardless of whether they attended an institution covered by the numerus clausus or not.[6] The Ministry of Religion and Public Education, however, kept

6 Haller, *Harc a numerus clausus körül*, 144–46. In 1926–27, there were a total of 39 higher education institutions in the country. These included four universities of arts and sciences, one faculty of economics, one technical university, 17 colleges of theology, three law schools, five trade polytechnics, and eight other schools (veterinarian, forestry and mining, physical education polytechnics, and the academy of dramatic arts). Of these, 12 were in Budapest. Minutes of the parliamentary session of February 10, 1928, in *Az 1927. évi január hó 25-ére hirdetett országgyűlés képviselőházának naplója*, vol. 9: 3.

a separate database of those universities (the universities of arts and sciences, the University of Technology, and the law schools) which were covered by the numerus clausus and those polytechnics where the law did not apply. This difference, however, hardly affects the percentage of Jewish students presented by the Central Statistical Office, because the polytechnics mostly applied the Jewish quota despite the fact that the law did not apply to them.

The reduction in the number of Jewish students in the first year of the Jewish quota

In the 1917–18 academic year, there were 6,027 Jewish students in the universities and law schools which would fall under the purview of the numerus clausus after 1920.[7] By 1920–21, this number had shrunk to 1,712. There were thus 4,315 fewer Jewish students in the first year of the implementation of the law. The greatest reduction was at the University of Budapest, where the number of Jewish students decreased by 3,880.[8]

This huge reduction was possible because several thousand Jewish students in the higher years with "acquired rights" were not allowed to register, even though the Jewish quota was theoretically only meant to apply to first-year admissions. The law did not extend the quota to the higher academic years: "The provisions of § 1 shall not affect the right of further enrollment of regular students who have already been enrolled in previous academic years, nor of non-ordinary students who have been enrolled with a secondary school graduation certificate in the faculties of humanities (humanities, languages, history and quantitative sciences) and medicine, provided that they are absolutely reliable in terms of their loyalty to the nation and moral standing."[9] This was reinforced by the decree implementing the numerus clausus law, which repeated the text of the law almost verbatim.[10]

The acquired rights of the Jewish students in the higher academic years were not, however, taken into account at all at the University of Budapest,

7 Haller, *Harc a numerus clausus körül*, 130. The data does not include the polytechnics. There were 237 Jewish students at the law schools that year. Only data from the 1921–22 academic year is extant for the polytechnics (with the exception of the academy of dramatic arts). In that year, there were a total of 24 Jewish students at these institutions.

8 Haller, *Harc a numerus clausus körül*, 135.

9 For the full text of Law No. XXV of 1920, see the Appendix to this volume

10 Decree No. 123.033 of 1920 of the Royal Hungarian Minister of Religion and Public Education, in *Magyarországi rendeletek tára, 1920* (Budapest: Pesti Könyvnyomda Részvénytársaság, 1920), 1455.

and they, too, were prevented from enrolling. Their exclusion became possible after István Haller, the minister of religion and education, decreed in 1920 that race defender students could also be part of the university admissions boards. The racial clause was not altered, however, so on paper this continued to apply only to first-year students. But with the cooperation of the professors on the admissions boards, the race defender students did not issue the certificates of national loyalty for the Jewish students, thus preventing the majority of Jewish students in the higher years from enrolling too. As a result of the cooperation between Haller and the racialist students—according to the summary of admissions figures in the university archives—the proportion of Jewish students in the second year of the faculties of humanities was 5.4 percent, in the third 7.5 percent, and 6.6 percent in the fourth, despite the fact that the proportion of Jewish students in the higher years between 1913–14 and 1917–18 was somewhere between 35–40 percent and those students had not all finished university by 1920.[11] The number of Jewish students at the University of Budapest had decreased by 3,880.

Some of the around 3,000 Jewish students forced out of the University of Budapest—about 500 individuals—were taken in by the universities of Pozsony and Kolozsvár which had been evacuated into the body of post-Trianon Hungary.[12] The leadership of the Faculty of Medicine in Budapest, however, were infuriated: "We can see that . . . our two sister universities have admitted all those . . . we did not consider reliable, primarily in terms of their loyalty to the nation, since that is the only way that the number of students belonging to the Jewish race among the student body of the two sister universities is 70–80 percent in certain age groups."[13] The majority of Jewish students in higher years (second to fourth) forced out of the University of Budapest, namely, 1,599 persons, were medical students.[14] Since these rejections were against the

11 Haller, *Harc a numerus clausus körül*, 124 and 134.

12 There were a total of 777 Jewish students at the universities of Pécs (Pozsony) and Szeged (Kolozsvár) in 1920–21. Haller, *Harc a numerus clausus körül*, 134. Given that in 1917–18, the two universities had 311 Jewish students and that of these, excepting those who had graduated in 1918–19, the Jewish students with "acquired rights" remained students of the universities, the two universities' "own" Jewish students numbered between 250 and 300.

13 Quoted in N. Szegvári, *Numerus clausus rendelkezések*, 132.

14 Pécsi Tudományegyetem, Egyetemi Levéltár (University of Pécs, University Archives, hereafter PTE Archives), Elnöki iratok, 89/1920–21 P.R.sz. Minutes of the first joint meeting during the 1920–21 academic year of the combined council of the Royal Hungarian Universities of Kolozsvár and Pozsony temporarily functioning in Budapest, held in Budapest on October 19, 1920.

law, Minister of Religion and Public Education István Haller mooted quashing these rejections, but he never in fact did so.[15]

Nonetheless, the statement made so often—even in the historiography—that the evacuated universities would not have respected the Jewish quota even for first-year admissions (or they would have taken significantly more than their 6 percent of Jewish students) turns out to be nothing more than a myth. This myth came about because the proportion of Jewish students at the provincial universities across all the years really was higher than in the capital. These proportions, however, were bolstered by the number of Jewish students attending the higher years. The question, then, of whether the 6 percent quota was respected in the first year (to which the law applied) or not—both in Budapest and in the provinces—cannot be answered on the basis of the overall proportion of Jews in all the academic years.

The fate of the Jewish students with "acquired rights" in the higher academic years

In 1920, around 4,800 Jewish students wanted to enroll in the higher academic years at the four universities of arts and sciences, the University of Technology, and the law schools on the basis of their "acquired rights." If not a single Jewish student had been admitted to the first year, but all the students with "acquired rights" had been allowed to enroll in the higher years, as the terms of the numerus clausus law set out, then the proportion of Jews at the universities affected by the law at the start of the 1920s would have had to have been at least 20–25 percent.

This, however, was not how it turned out. The proportion of Jews in all academic years nationwide shrank to 12.5 percent. This decrease was brought about by three factors. First, the universities in the capital extended the Jewish quota to students in the higher years who had so-called "acquired rights," although the law in theory did not allow for this.

Second, the majority of Jewish students with "acquired rights" from the higher years who were excluded from the universities of the capital were not given places at provincial universities either. This was that group of around 3,000

15 PTE Archives, Elnöki iratok, Minutes of the first joint meeting during the 1920–21 academic year of the combined council of the Royal Hungarian Universities of Kolozsvár and Pozsony temporarily functioning in Budapest, held in Budapest on October 26, 1920.

Jewish students that the Hungarian higher education system carried with itself for years after the introduction of the numerus clausus law like an "albatross." This same group raised the proportion of Jewish students at the provincial universities, while at the level of first-year admissions the prescribed Jewish quota was more or less achieved. This was the only way possible for the proportion of Jews in the Hungarian higher education system overall to be reduced to 8.5 percent by 1926. There would not, in any case, have been room at the provincial universities for the roughly 3,000 students excluded from the capital. Most of them were medical students—almost all the students with "acquired rights" in the higher years were excluded from the Faculty of Medicine in Budapest. While there were 2,947 Jewish students at the Faculty of Medicine in Budapest in 1917–18, there were only 245 in 1920 (see table 5).[16]

Table 5. Number of Jewish students admitted to the Faculty of Medicine in Budapest in 1920

Year of studies	Number of Jewish students	Percentage of Jewish students
1st	30	4.6
2nd–5th	215	7.9
1st–5th	245	7.0

Source: N. Szegvári, *Numerus clausus rendelkezések*, 129.

Third, for first-year admissions, the provincial universities also adhered to the Jewish quota (within a margin of 1–3 percent). As we shall see below, this is what both the fragmentary surviving data and archival sources suggest. In other words, the claim that the Jewish quota was not enforced on a nationwide scale for first-year admissions is nothing more than an imagined apologia unsupported by the actual statistical data.

The statistical data deployed in an effort to support this apologia, which give the proportion of Jewish students for all academic year groups and not separately for each, do not, in fact, prove this. This data, which the Bethlen government first put together at the time of the League of Nations inquiries, have been consciously manipulated. The Bethlen government took these manipulated numbers to Geneva, where it presented the numbers for the provinces and not Budapest, and for higher education overall incorporating the higher-year groups as well, instead of just the first year.

16 N. Szegvári, *Numerus clausus rendelkezések*, 129.

The Jewish quota for first-year admissions

But the apologia devised by the Bethlen government for the League of Nations proved long-lived. In reality, the medical faculties in Budapest and the evacuated universities had agreed among themselves by 1920 that none would take more Jewish students than the quota allowed, and this was an arrangement more or less respected in the following years (see tables 6 and 7).[17] The first-year intake of the Faculty of Medicine in Szeged in 1921, for example, included only 7 percent Jews, which is to say 11 persons, despite the fact that in the third, fourth, and fifth years, the intake was made up of more than 70 percent Jewish students with "acquired rights."[18] Mihály Pekár, the dean of the medical faculty of the University of Pécs (Pozsony) stated that the proportion of Jews among first-year students admitted to the Faculty of Medicine in Pécs was 6 percent in 1920, while in the higher years it was 30 percent.[19]

Klebelsberg, the minister of education, confirmed in parliament in 1924 that the University of Pécs had also enforced the Jewish quota among first-year students. It was a different matter, he said, that this was not necessarily reflected in the end of year statistics because some Christian students who had been admitted did not turn up at the start of the academic year, or transferred away during it, causing the proportion of Jews to rise even among the first-years.[20] The nume-

17 SOTE Archives, Minutes of the combined meeting of the medical faculties of the Budapest university and the evacuated universities, November 22, 1920.

18 N. Szegvári, *Numerus clausus rendelkezések*, 132; and Károly Hoór's contribution, SOTE Archives, Minutes of the meetings of the Faculty of Medicine of the Royal Hungarian Pázmány Péter University of Budapest, 1/a vol. 48, 320 (ordinary meeting of the faculty on January 17, 1922). Hoór complained at the meeting that the University of Szeged was admitting Jews excluded from the capital.

19 SOTE Archives, Minutes of the meetings of the Faculty of Medicine of the Royal Hungarian Pázmány Péter University of Budapest, December 23, 1920.

20 Klebelsberg said the following about the high number of Jewish students at the University of Pécs: "In this regard, I sought clarification from the University of Pécs, and they have given me the following information on why the number of Jewish students is higher at the university than the national average allowed by law. There are three reasons for this. First, they require permission to enroll. Permission is granted to Jewish youths in proportion to the number granted to Christian youths. It often happens, however, that the Christian youths do not make use of these permissions, withdraw, and attend a different university. The Jewish youths who get permission to enroll at the University of Pécs enroll without exception. As a result, their numbers are greater even at enrollment than the percentage permitted. This, however, can hardly be said to be the university's fault. Second, it frequently happened at the University of Pécs that Christian students—second, third, and fourth years—transferred to other universities, which we can hardly prevent since to some extent this wandering between universities is to be desired (having such a beneficial effect in Germany, as we know). The proportion thus changed again with the migration of the Christians. The third factor they alluded to was that anyone who was previously enrolled for two semesters at a Hungarian university

rus clausus did not apply to the higher years, and the University of Pécs was acting lawfully in admitting Jewish students with "acquired rights" to the higher years, or in other words, was not infringing the tenets of the Jewish quota.[21]

Table 6. Number and proportion of Jewish students at the universities (second half of the academic year), 1910–1926, according to the figures of the Ministry of Religion and Public Education

6.a. University of Budapest (Royal Hungarian Pázmány Péter University*)			
Academic year	Total number of students	Number of Jewish students	Percentage of Jewish students
1910/1911	6,763	2,361	34.9
1911/1912	6,863	2,244	32.7
1912/1913	7,019	2,392	34.1
1913/1914	7,407	2,598	35.1
1914/1915	4,808	1,220	25.4
1915/1916	3,030	1,095	36.1
1916/1917	3,452	1,301	37.7
1917/1918	10,634	4,288	40.3
1918/1919	n.d.	n.d.	n.d.
1919/1920	n.d.	n.d.	n.d.
1920/1921	5,800	459	7.9
1921/1922	6,594	525	8.0
1922/1923	6,896	5,258	7.6
1923/1924	5,816	456	7.8
1924/1925	5,569	428	7.7
1925/1926	5,232	403	7.7

6.b. University of Kolozsvár/Szeged** (Royal Hungarian Franz Joseph University)			
Academic year	Total number of students	Number of Jewish students	Percentage of Jewish students
1910/1911	2,107	296	14.0
1911/1912	2,157	311	14.4
1912/1913	2,124	280	13.2
1913/1914	2,119	266	12.6
1914/1915	1,077	138	12.8
1915/1916	583	80	13.7

has the right, under the previous law, to be enrolled regardless of the numerus clausus since, as you know, the numerus clausus only came into effect four years ago. There were numerous students who went abroad after their first two semesters and came home. Now, since these semesters only count partially, they have received permission to enroll as second, third, or fourth years to the University of Pécs." Minutes of the parliamentary session of June 4, 1924, in *Az 1922. évi junius hó 16-ára hirdetett nemzetgyűlés naplója*, vol. 24: 473.

21 Haller, *Harc a numerus clausus körül*, 136.

1916/1917	420	70	16.7
1917/1918	1,730	254	14.7
1918/1919	n.d.	n.d.	n.d.
1919/1920	n.d.	n.d.	n.d.
1920/1921	1,291	407	31.5
1921/1922	971	240	24.7
1922/1923	1,103	211	19.1
1923/1924	1,032	152	14.7
1924/1925	1,033	133	12.9
1925/1926	1,043	127	12.2

6.c. University of Debrecen (Royal Hungarian István Tisza University*)			
Academic year	**Total number of students**	**Number of Jewish students**	**Percentage of Jewish students**
1914/1915	227	19	8.4
1915/1916	163	13	8.0
1916/1917	197	25	12.7
1917/1918	567	68	12.0
1918/1919	n.d.	n.d.	n.d.
1919/1920	n.d.	n.d.	n.d.
1920/1921	441	31	7.0
1921/1922	665	88	13.2
1922/1923	806	110	13.6
1923/1924	723	108	14.9
1924/1925	839	104	12.4
1925/1926	783	95	12.1

6.d. University of Pozsony/Pécs (Royal Hungarian Elizabeth University)**			
Academic year	**Total number of students**	**Number of Jewish students**	**Percentage of Jewish students**
1914/1915	184	18	9.8
1915/1916	127	15	11.8
1916/1917	152	13	8.6
1917/1918	413	57	13.8
1918/1919	n.d.	n.d.	n.d.
1919/1920	n.d.	n.d.	n.d.
1920/1921	646	370	57.3
1921/1922	1,489	835	56.1
1922/1923	1,530	805	52.6
1923/1924	1,217	593	48.7
1924/1925	1,106	362	32.7
1925/1926	959	243	25.3

6.e. University of Technology			
Academic year	Total number of students	Number of Jewish students	Percentage of Jewish students
1910/1911	1,676	577	34.4
1911/1912	1,868	586	31.4
1912/1913	2,115	675	31.9
1913/1914	2,450	815	33.3
1914/1915	1,485	540	36.4
1915/1916	619	259	41.8
1916/1917	661	295	44.6
1917/1918	3,115	1,175	37.7
1918/1919	n.d.	n.d.	n.d.
1919/1920	n.d.	n.d.	n.d.
1920/1921	3,851	296	7.4
1921/1922	4,203	366	8.7
1922/1923	4,048	348	8.6
1923/1924	3,033	271	8.9
1924/1925	2,213	194	8.8
1925/1926	2,124	176	8.3

* Named as such in 1921
** Moved from former city to latter in 1919–1921
Source: Haller, *Harc a numerus clausus körül*, 183–84.

The Jewish quota at the universities of Pécs and Szeged

Christian students initially only applied in small numbers to the universities of Pozsony (evacuated to Pécs) and Kolozsvár (evacuated to Szeged). If these universities had not taken in some of the Jewish students forced out of the capital, Pál Bethlen wrote in 1925, then "both universities would have had to be closed due to a shortage of students."[22]

The low number of Christian students is primarily attributable to the fact that the Christian students who had been studying at these universities before the war did not continue their studies at the two evacuated universities, but enrolled at the university in the capital. The rector of the University of Pécs "placed the blame squarely on the Christian youth and wondered why they had abandoned their universities and flooded to the University of Budapest."[23]

22 Bethlen, *A magyar zsidóság almanachja*, 152.
23 PTE Archives, Papers of the Rector's Office, 317/1921–22.

Table 7. Proportion of Jewish students at the various Hungarian universities according to the figures of the Central Statistical Office

Academic year	University of Budapest	University of Debrecen	University of Kolozsvár/ Szeged	University of Pozsony/Pécs	University of Technology
1910/1911	34.9	n.d.	14.0	n.d.	34.4
1911/1912	32.7	n.d.	14.4	n.d.	31.3
1912/1913	34.1	n.d.	n.d.	n.d.	31.9
1914/1915	37.9	8.4	12.6	9.8	36.4
1915/1916	36.2	8.0	12.8	11.8	41.8
1916/1917	37.7	12.7	13.7	8.6	39.2
1917/1918	40.3	12.0	16.7	13.1	37.2
1918/1919	40.2	12.3	n.d.	n.d.	35.3
1919/1920	0.25	7.2	9.8	0.0	12.3
1920/1921	7.9	7.0	31.5	57.3	7.4
1921/1922	8.0	13.2	24.7	56.1	8.7
1922/1923	7.4	13.6	19.1	52.6	8.6
1923/1924	7.8	13.5	14.7	41.3	8.9
1924/1925	8.3	12.4	12.9	32.7	8.8
1925/1926	8.2	10.8	12.3	24.0	8.3
1926/1927	8.2	10.1	11.9	17.5	8.3
1927/1928	8.4	8.9	11.6	12.4	9.1
1928/1929	8.4	14.1	12.1	11.0	9.0
1929/1930	9.2	16.1	12.3	10.6	9.7
1930/1931	10.5	17.3	13.7	11.2	10.7
1931/1932	12.4	21.4	15.8	14.2	11.8
1932/1933	12.6	18.2	16.7	14.7	14.8
1933/1934	11.8	14.7	14.5	14.9	14.9
1934/1935	8.9	12.3	11.8	11.1	13.2
1935/1936	7.5	8.3	11.5	9.8	11.9
1936/1937	6.9	6.8	9.3	8.2	11.3
1937/1938	5.6	5.6	8.5	6.3	9.3

Source: Hungarian Statistical Yearbooks, 1911–1939

It was critically important for the universities of Pécs and Szeged, fighting for survival, to be able to start teaching in their various academic year groups. Although they had fewer Christian applicants than they needed, they had a crowd of Jewish students excluded from Budapest at their very doors. The numerus clausus law placed no obstacles in the way of the provincial universities accepting Jewish students with "acquired rights" for the higher years. The universities of Pécs and Szeged did just that, in fact (see table 8). This was how the two universities managed to get all their year groups running. In addition to the 777 students deemed to be Jewish in the 1920 academic year, they also managed to obtain 1119 students deemed Christian, even if there were a few converted Jews among the "Christians."[24] The minister of education presented detailed data on the Jewish students accepted to the universities of Pécs and Szeged. He did so only for the higher years because, as he explained, for the first year, all universities "had established the maximum amount of Jewish students admissible at 6 percent."[25]

Table 8. Proportion of Jews among higher-year university students at the universities of Budapest, Pécs, and Szeged during the 1920–21 academic year, according to the data of the Ministry of Religion and Public Education

Academic year	Departments	Budapest	Pécs	Szeged
2nd	Law	8.0	n.d.	8.1
	Medicine	6.2	77.0	51.5
	Humanities	5.4	n.d.	25.0
3rd	Law	9.5	n.d.	9.8
	Medicine	6.2	89.0	49.0
	Humanities	7.5	n.d.	33.3
4th	Law	15.6	n.d.	5.5
	Medicine	15.4	84.0	47.5
	Humanities	6.6	n.d.	22.2
5th	Medicine	15.0	46.6	75.0

Source: Haller, *Harc a numerus clausus körül*, 124.

The universities of Pécs and Szeged, ignoring the practice adopted at the University of Budapest, considered Jews who had converted to Christianity. There was no legal barrier to this either, since the implementation decree did not specify who should be considered a Jew and on what basis. But the race defender professors at the University of Budapest, under the leadership of Károly Hoór, the dean of the Faculty of Medicine, protested against this practice at the universities of Pécs and Szeged, saying that Jews who had converted were still Jews. Otherwise, as Hoór said, following this logic, "a Chinaman born of Chinese parents who converted to Christianity" would also cease to be "Mongol."[26]

24 Haller, *Harc a numerus clausus körül*, 134–35.

25 Haller, *Harc a numerus clausus körül*, 123.

26 Hoór, *A numerus clausus a szegedi és a pécsi egyetemen*, 8.

Because of these attacks from the race defenders, the University of Szeged in 1922 sent a letter to the minister of education asking "on the basis of what documents relating to religion or origin should membership of a particular race or minority be judged?"[27] The request was forwarded by Minister of Education Klebelsberg to the University of Budapest for their opinion. The various faculties gave their opinions separately. According to the Faculty of Law, the only guideline as to who was to be considered Jewish was religion, since the 6 percent quota itself had been established on the basis of the number of Jews in the country, and if Jews who had converted were to be included, a higher quota should have been established. According to the Faculty of Medicine, however, being Jewish was "to be established purely on the basis of origin and never on the basis of religion, since changing religion changes neither a person's origin nor their race" and "the law of 1920 does not distinguish between religions, but explicitly says nationalities and races."[28]

Although the debate ultimately remained unsettled, it is nonetheless a fact that Jews who had converted began to feature less and less often among the Christians in the admissions practices of the universities in the capital as well as the universities of Pécs and Szeged. Four years later, in 1926, however, during the Bethlen government's efforts to mollify the situation with the Jews, Klebelsberg returned to the issue with a decree. The new decree ran counter to the interpretation of the race defenders and ordered that Jews who had converted be considered for the purposes of admissions as Christians and not Jews.[29] At the same time, the minister stated in the press that Judaism was not a race but a "religion."[30]

But Klebelsberg considered this a political concession and not the rectification of a legal iniquity, since—as he said two years later (in 1928) in parliament—after 1920 it was really those universities and faculties who acted "logically" and interpreted the law correctly who "counted converted Jews as part of the Jewish racial contingent." As he said, if one was to look at the intention of the people who passed the 1920 law, there is no doubt that they were on the side of a racial and not a religious definition.[31]

27 ELTE Archives, Rector's Office, Minutes of the University Council, 1922/I., ordinary meeting.
28 ELTE Archives, Rector's Office, Minutes of the University Council, 1922/I., ordinary meeting.
29 MTI Weekly Release, no. 38, September 21, 1926, 2.
30 Ladányi, "A numerus clausus-törvény 1928. évi módosításáról," 1124.
31 Minutes of the parliamentary session of February 23, 1928, in *Az 1927. évi január hó 25-ére hirdetett országgyűlés képviselőházának naplója*, vol. 9: 198.

Thus, contrary to another popular view which occasionally appears in the academic literature, the universities of Pécs and Szeged did not "ease" the enforcement of the Jewish quota by taking in Jewish students with "acquired rights" for their higher academic years, for the law did not apply to the higher years right from the start, even if the University of Budapest illegally extended it to do so. There was also nothing in the law that said that universities could not accept students in the higher years from other universities. It is another question that the universities in Budapest—in contravention of the law—did not allow higher-year Jewish students with "acquired rights" to enroll either.

Not enough Christian applicants in Pécs and Szeged

Significantly fewer Christian youth applied to the universities of Szeged and Pécs than expected. Many of the Christians admitted simply did not turn up at the beginning of the year, or as the admissions board of the University of Szeged put it, "the Hungarians went missing" by the beginning of the academic year.[32] But these universities could not even be sure of the Christian students who had actually enrolled. In the autumn of 1920, for example, 52 of the 146 students admitted to the Faculty of Medicine in Szeged left in the space of two days to transfer to the University of Budapest.[33] Clearly, this increased the proportion of Jewish students at Szeged without of course a single extra Jewish student having been admitted over and above the original intake.

The University of Szeged experienced a chronic lack of Christian applicants for years. The official state allocation of places at the Faculty of Medicine was 750, but there was not a single year between 1921 and 1926 that the university managed to fill all these places.[34] (In 1921–22, there were only 484 students; in 1922–23 only 488; in 1923–24 there were 400; in 1924–25, there were 353; and in 1926–27, there were 361 students at the faculty).

Though they did manage, in the first year of the numerus clausus (1920–21) to take in 150 students, only 108 turned up for the start of teaching.[35] The sit-

32 Archives of the University of Szeged, meeting of the Faculty of Medicine, January 12, 1923.

33 Archives of the University of Szeged, 4th extraordinary meeting of the Faculty of Medicine, October 21, 1921.

34 Hoór, *A numerus clausus a szegedi és a pécsi egyetemen*, 7.

35 Hoór, *A numerus clausus a szegedi és a pécsi egyetemen*, 4. Hoór also says that the number of Jewish students was 17, but does not go on to say how many of them had converted. In any case, 17 students correspond to 16 percent of the 108 students, but only 11 percent of the approved number of places,

uation turned out "even worse" the next year, when out of the combined 150 places allocated for the mathematics and natural sciences faculties, only 57 were filled.[36] Out of them, 10 went to Jewish students. They were admitted within the framework of the original quota, so that Jews would make up 6.6 percent of the planned year group. Since, however, more than half (66 percent) of the planned Christian students did not enroll, the proportion of Jews grew to 18 percent without the university taking a single Jewish student over and above what the Jewish quota dictated for admissions in September.

By 1922, the Faculty of Medicine in Szeged was more cautious and took care that the number of Jews should not exceed the proscriptions of the quota because of the low number of Christian students. For the first year, the official allocation of places made it possible for them to take in 150 students, of whom 9 could have been Jewish on the basis of the Jewish quota. But instead of the 141 Christian applicants foreseen, only 85 applied, all of whom were offered places. But they no longer adjusted the proportion of Jewish students to the official number of places (150) as they had done the year before, but rather to the number of actual Christian applicants. As a result, of the 170 Jewish applicants, only five were admitted.[37] They determined that if there were any further Christian applicants, then they would also recalculate the number of Jews they would admit in accordance with the proportion prescribed in the Jewish quota.[38] The following year, in 1923–24, the Faculty of Medicine again could not fill the official allocation of 150 places because of the low number of Christian

and we can assume that among them the proportion of students who were Jewish by religion was according to the quota.

36 Hoór, *A numerus clausus a szegedi és a pécsi egyetemen*, 4–5.

37 Archives of the University of Szeged, Minutes of the first extraordinary meeting of the Faculty of Medicine of the Royal Hungarian Franz Joseph Scientific University on September 7, 1922. Characteristic of the meticulous implementation of the numerus clausus in the first-year admissions process, the minutes listed the Jewish applicants by name: "The committee recommends for admission to the first semester 5 applicants, calculated for the 85 Christian students, namely: Irén Singer, Imre Kemény, Tibor Frankl, Miklós Fischer, and Ernő Bach. In the eventuality that there should be subsequent Christian applicants to fill the allocation of 150 or 170 places, respectively, the committee recommends other applicants for a waiting list. They are: Eleonora Stern, Gyula Máté, Erzsébet Winkler, Sándor Wilheim, and Aranka Weisz, whom the Dean would take as regular students in proportion to the number of Christian applicants."

38 Archives of the University of Szeged, Ordinary meeting of the Faculty of Medicine of the Royal Hungarian Franz Joseph University on September 4, 1922. However, due to the insufficient number of non-Jewish applicants, and the dropout rate among those accepted, the Faculty of Medicine recommended "rejecting the applications of all Jewish applicants, as the number of Jews enrolled in the first semester already exceeds the legal percentage due to the absence of Hungarians." See the report of the Faculty of Medicine at Szeged in January 1923 on the application of the Jewish quota for first-

applicants and could only take 68 Christian students for the first year. Of the Jewish applicants, the university took only four, or in other words they adjusted the number of Jews to be admitted not to the official allocation of places but to the number of actual Christian applicants.[39] The situation at the Faculty of Natural Sciences at Szeged can also be attributed to the low number of Christian applicants. In 1922–23, only 91 of the 400 places authorized by the ministry were filled by students.[40]

The situation was similar at the University of Pécs in the early 1920s. The university had very few Christian applicants and thus filled the higher years with Jewish students excluded from the University of Budapest. In the first half of the 1920–21 academic year, the proportion of Jewish students was 77 percent (45 people) in the second year, 89 percent (57 people) in the third, 84 percent (42 people) in the fourth, and 75 percent (37 people) in the fifth. The numerus clausus law contained no guidelines for the higher years, and the University of Pécs therefore was not breaking any rules. But in the first year, the university also stuck to the Jewish quota, so the 12 Jewish students accepted for the first year made up only 6 percent of the overall year group.[41] The Faculty of Law took a higher proportion of Jewish students for the 1921–22 academic year, when they accepted 98 Christian and 14 Jewish students, although four of the Jewish students had been evacuated from the territories lost at Trianon and therefore did not count for the purposes of the Jewish quota.[42] If the university had been able to fill the official allocation of places for Christian students,

---

year admissions, University of Szeged Archives, Faculty of Medicine, Dean's office, Meeting of the Faculty of Medicine, January 12, 1923.

39 Archives of the University of Szeged, Extraordinary meeting of the Faculty of Medicine of the Royal Hungarian Franz Joseph University on September 7, 1923. The number of Christian applicants remained permanently low. The faculty still had only 73 Christian first-year applicants in 1927, as compared to 61 Jewish applicants. The allocated number of places was not filled. Instead, having admitted the 68 Christians who had the necessary academic results, they then admitted only five Jews. See MNL OL, K 36, 1928-23-69628. Dean's Office of the Faculty of Medicine of the Royal Hungarian Pázmány Péter University in Budapest, compilation from the provincial universities.

40 Hoór, *A numerus clausus a szegedi és a pécsi egyetemen*, 6.

41 Because of this fluctuation, the data changed for the second semester. I have given the figures for the first semester throughout the text (the official allocation of places also changed for the second semester). During this year, only the Faculty of Medicine and the Faculty of Humanities of the University of Pécs were operational within Hungary itself, and of the five humanities students, one was Jewish. PTE Archives, VIII. 1a, 1921–22. (1396/1921–22. R.) When, therefore, the race defenders said that the proportion of Jewish students at the University of Pécs was 20 percent, they were referring to this single Jewish student.

42 PTE Archives, Elnöki iratok, VIII. 104a, 1921–1922.

the proportion of Jews would have worked out precisely in keeping with the terms of the Jewish quota.

The University of Budapest, however, continued to attack the universities of Pécs and Szeged because of their high proportion of Jewish students. It was a particular source of outrage that the University of Szeged accepted Jewish students from among the students who had fled the lost territories. At the University of Szeged, for instance, of the 57 students accepted into the pharmaceutical and mathematics courses in 1921–22, four were Jews who had fled the lost territories. In the same academic year, twenty-one of the 111 first-year students accepted into the Faculty of Medicine were Jews who had fled. The latter were accepted not within the framework of the 6 percent Jewish quota, but based on the provision that students who had fled the lost territories were to be given priority.[43]

Unlike the University of Budapest, neither István Haller nor his successor as minister of education, Kunó Klebelsberg, objected to this practice at the universities of Pécs and Szeged. They considered the survival of the evacuated universities to be symbolically important. Hungary, by keeping these universities alive, was signaling that it maintained its claim to the lost territories of Slovakia and Transylvania. Their maintenance, however, bordered on the absurd from the point of view of the numerus clausus. While the law was meant in theory to reduce the number of students, and specifically Jewish students, in higher education, the capacity of the higher education system, with the addition of these two universities, grew by approximately 2,000 places a year, for which there were not enough Christian applicants.[44] The paradoxical situation of the provincial universities was brought up in parliament by Rezső Rupert in 1922.

> It was a waste to locate the universities in Szeged and Pécs. Our great hope that they would flourish there and would even attract the youth of the neighboring occupied territories did not come to pass. The universities are completely depopulated, there are hardly one or two students hanging around them. . . . But at the time, we were guided by the belief that we were working towards the integrity of the country . . . that sooner or later there would come a moment when the country's borders would expand and then the territories,

43 Hoór, "A numerus clausus," 5–6.

44 Haller, *Harc a numerus clausus körül*, 134–35.

> which we could then reoccupy, we would have to let go as we would not be able to sufficiently fill them, unless we had prepared for this great moment.[45]

But none of this interested the race defenders, who called the University of Pécs the "shame of the numerus clausus."

Lack of students in the years of the numerus clausus

Throughout this conflict, Haller identified a problem for which the numerus clausus law could not and did not provide any solution, namely, that a sufficient number of Christian students would be required in order to implement the Jewish quota. The law was silent on how to enforce the Jewish quota in the absence of Christian applicants. This was natural, since the entire law was built on the premise that more people wanted to go to university than there were places. As soon as this assumption proved false, the whole law became untenable. "If 300 places were allocated [by the ministry] to one of the faculties," wrote Haller, "then the number of Jews within that group could have been 18 on the basis of the 6 percent quota. But in reality, 300 people did not apply to the faculty—only a hundred did. If they then admitted 18 Jewish students, the real proportion would be 18 percent rather than 6 percent."[46]

In contrast with the official ideology of the numerus clausus law, a number of universities from the second half of the twenties onwards were struggling not with a surplus of applicants, but with the very opposite in fact. They could not fill the apportioned number of places for Christian students for lack of Christian applicants. True, some faculties and classes—especially in the capital—sometimes had to reject even Christian applicants, but these were mostly women and their rejection can be attributed not to an excess of applicants, but to a general rejection of female university students. From the point of view of male Christian applicants, the problem was not that the state allocated too few places and therefore some students did not get into higher education. Rather, the problem was that there were often not enough Christian applicants to fill the state allocation of places, which was consistently reduced

45 Minutes of the parliamentary session of February 7, 1922, in *Az 1920. évi február hó 16-ára összehívott nemzetgyűlés naplója*, vol. 16: 353.

46 Haller, *Harc a numerus clausus körül*, 125.

from 1923 onwards.[47] The problem now was not that there were too many applicants for the universities but that the number of non-Jewish applicants had waned significantly. From the higher number of students typical of the early twenties, the number of students in higher education in 1924 dipped to roughly 15,000 per annum, or to the level of the last year before World War I, and more or less stayed constant until 1940. Most universities still struggled to fill their classes with Christian students even with the restrictions of the Jewish quota. Thinking it through, there is nothing surprising about this, since in order to reach the prewar number of students, the universities had to take in 20–25 percent more Christian students than before the war, thanks to the strictures of the Jewish quota.

But, as table 9 below shows, the number of Christians graduating from secondary school did not grow at this pace, so the resupply of the entire system began to break down.[48] The necessary students could initially be supplied on an ad hoc basis from the backlog of cancelled wartime school years, but this was difficult to sustain in the long term. This is clearly illustrated by comparing the 1911–12 and 1925–26 academic years. In the 1911–12 academic year, when there was no Jewish quota, the total of 12,274 students enrolled at the universities and the law schools required only 8,906 Christian students, since the other 3,368 places were filled by Jews.[49] But in 1925–26, when the total number of students reached the level of 1911–12 once again, that is, a total of 12,326 students, 11,043 of them were Christian.[50] This meant that more than 2000 extra Christian students were required to meet the total number of students in 1925–26 than was necessary fourteen years previous.

From the mid-1920s onwards, the number of Christian applicants could not even fill the reduced official allocations of places.[51] A few years after the intro-

47 There were 13,696 applicants for the 13,767 places officially allocated for the 1920–21 academic year, but by 1921–22 there were only 16,829 applicants for the 17,928 places allocated. And in 1922–23, there were only 16,829 applicants for the 19,905 places allocated. The allocations of places at educational institutions subject to the numerus clausus are to be found in Ladányi, *Az egyetemi ifjúság*, 167–68. For the number of students enrolled at the universities and the law schools, see Haller, *Harc a numerus clausus körül*, 130.

48 Of those accepted to the Technical University and the Faculty of Economics in the 1920s, 9–10 percent had their secondary school diplomas from the Trade High School (Felsőkereskedelmi iskola). József Asztalos, *A magyar főiskolai hallgatók statisztikája az 1930/31 tanévben,* (Budapest: Magyar Királyi Központi Statisztikai Hivatal, 1932), 31.

49 Haller, *Harc a numerus clausus körül*, 130.

50 Haller, *Harc a numerus clausus körül*, 130.

51 For example, there were only 558 applicants for the 670 places allocated at the Technical University for 1926. Of these, only 472 were qualified for admission. Budapesti Műszaki és Gazdaságtudományi

Table 9. Number of Christian and Jewish secondary school graduates between 1911 and 1924

Academic year	Number of students successfully graduating from secondary schools (*gymnasium, reáliskola*)	Christian	Jewish	Accepted to higher education institution affected by numerus clausus	Accepted students (in institutions affected by numerus clausus) as a percentage of all secondary school graduates
1910/1911	5,015	3,900	1,115	2,805	55.9
1911/1912	5,348	4,128	1,220	3,187	63.5
1912/1913	5,690	4,452	1,238	3,153	55.4
1914/1915	6,081	4,682	1,399	2,240	36.8
1915/1916	7,295	5,682	1,613	1,387	19.0
1916/1917	6,009	4,461	1,548	1,695	28.2
1917/1918	6,426	4,828	1,598	1,927	30.0
1918/1919	3,824	2,656	1,168	1,707	44.6
1919/1920	4,079	3,017	1,062	1,938	42.6
1920/1921	4,697	3,533	1,164	2,234	47.6
1921/1922	4,579	3,420	1,159	2,399	52,4
1922/1923	4,426	3,242	1,184	2,010	45,5
1923/1924	4,729	3,558	1,171	2,246	47.5
1924/1925	4,547	3,512	1,035	2,343	51.5
1925/1926	4,871	3,819	1,052	2,638	54.25

Source: Hungarian Statistical Yearbooks, 1910–1926

duction of the numerus clausus law, even the anti-Semitic statistician Alajos Kovács—who had fought so hard for its introduction—noted that "life ... itself is taking care of the question" since "the number of students" at university "is progressively decreasing."[52] Kunó Klebelsberg was already saying in 1925 that despite the exclusion of Jews from higher education, "the children of

Egyetem Levéltára (Archives of the Budapest University of Technology and Economics, hereafter BME Archives), Minutes of the University Council, 3/a, 5, 1926, November 11, 1926. The number of places allocated decreased year on year from 1923 onward. Alajos Kovács's article is quoted in Haller, *Harc a numerus clausus körül*, 233. Minister of Religion and Public Education István Haller complained in 1926 that non-Jewish Hungarians "even today are not in the right financial circumstances to be able to fill the quota allotted to them." Haller, *Harc a numerus clausus körül*, 144.

52 Haller, *Harc a numerus clausus körül*, 233.

the Christian professional class are not applying to university in greater numbers." The statistician Dezső Laky wrote that "the year 1924 already signaled that the almost abnormal rush of our country's youth to the universities has been reversed."[53]

The number of male Christian applicants to the Budapest Faculty of Medicine declined significantly. The number of places officially allocated for the first year at the school was 400. In 1923, there were 502 applicants for these places. The following year, however, instead of 400 applicants (376 of whom would had to have been Christian in order for the Jewish quota to be implementable), only 253 Christian students applied.[54] There were 280 Christian applicants for the 1925–26 academic year,[55] and 273 for 1926–27.[56] In 1927–28, there were 278 Christian applicants.[57] The Budapest Faculty of Medicine tried to rectify this situation by inviting first years to transfer from the universities of Pécs and Szeged; however, as a result of this, the composition of the year groups changed at those universities. In the end, the minister of education decreased the official allocation of places at the Budapest Faculty of Medicine to 240 from 400. Similar measures were necessary at other universities and faculties. At the University of Technology, for example, there were only 558 applicants for 670 places in 1925, of which only 472 could be admitted based on their academic results.[58]

The universities themselves sometimes asked the minister of education to reduce the official allocation of places. The Szeged Faculty of Medicine, for example, argued in 1927 that it was impossible to fill the allocated 150 places with Christian students. There was no prospect, the dean of the university wrote to the minister, that "150 Hungarian students would apply" for the first year. "Naturally," he continued, "this number would be achieved at once if we had to accept all the Jewish applicants as well, since we rejected 92 Jewish appli-

---

53 Quoted in Sándor Király, "Az egyetemi hallgatóság társadalmi arculata Magyarországon a két világháború között" (PhD dissertation, Debrecen, BTK, 2009), 16.

54 SOTE Archives, Minutes of the meetings of the Faculty of Medicine of the Royal Hungarian Pázmány Péter University of Budapest, First ordinary meeting, September 10, 1924.

55 SOTE Archives, Minutes of the meetings of the Faculty of Medicine of the Royal Hungarian Pázmány Péter University of Budapest, First ordinary meeting, September 10, 1925.

56 SOTE Archives, Minutes of the meetings of the Faculty of Medicine of the Royal Hungarian Pázmány Péter University of Budapest, First ordinary meeting, September 7, 1926.

57 SOTE Archives, Minutes of the meetings of the Faculty of Medicine of the Royal Hungarian Pázmány Péter University of Budapest, Third ordinary meeting, October 9, 1927.

58 BME Archives, Minutes of the University Council, 3/a, 5, 1926, November 11, 1926.

cants this year. If the official allocation of places were set at 70 or 80, this danger could be avoided."[59]

Intimidation of the universities of Pécs and Szeged

Despite the gradually increasing shortage of students, the admissions procedures at the universities of Pécs and Szeged were unacceptable for the race defenders. They were afraid that as Bethlen's postwar stabilization policies progressed, the strict application of the Jewish quota would be relaxed in the capital and would no longer apply, as was already the case in both the higher academic years and in Pécs and Szeged. Thus, they began a campaign against the two evacuated universities, which they accused of exploiting loopholes in the numerus clausus law. The campaign saw the return of the most influential proponent of the numerus clausus, Ottokár Prohászka. In January 1923, he made a speech addressed to "the Hungarian youth," entitled "To the Younger Generation." In it, he accused the leading politicians of Bethlen's government of having returned to "business as usual" despite the catastrophe befalling the country, and of wanting to "forget and make peace."[60] There was nothing to be done with "the greying generation led astray by the dubious charms of liberalism," he said. The race defenders could now count only on the younger generations to represent their beliefs.[61] The racialist university organizations managed to get the personal support of the regent, Miklós Horthy, as well. Horthy made a symbolic gesture of support to the race defenders when, in January 1923, he visited the Centrum publishing company, which had been indicted for anti-Semitic incitement.

The race defenders unleashed a series of scandals aimed at the universities of Pécs and Szeged. Starting in October 1922, racialist students carried out weekly beatings of Jewish students, in addition to attacking women, at the University of Pécs's chemistry practicum, until the rectorate was forced to cancel the practicums, which meant that the students in the entire year group had to forfeit the semester.[62] In the summer of 1923, the race defender students organized

59 Ladányi, "A numerus clausus-törvény 1928. évi módosításáról," 1135.

60 Ottokár Prohászka, "Az ifjú nemzedékhez," in *Iránytű*, 313–18. First published in *Cél*, November 1923.

61 Prohászka, "Az ifjú nemzedékhez."

62 Bethlen, *A magyar zsidóság almanachja*, 120.

Table 10. Number and proportion of Jewish students at the universities of Pécs and Szeged in the second semester of each academic year, 1920–1925

Academic year	University of Pécs		University of Szeged	
	number of	percentage of	number of	percentage of
1920/1921	407	31.5	370	57.3
1921/1922	240	24.7	835	56.0
1922/1923	2111	9.1	805	52.6
1923/1924	152	14.7	593	48.7
1924/1925	133	12.9	362	32.7
1925/1926	128	12.3	243	25.4

Source: Haller, *Harc a numerus clausus körül*, 137–43.

a protest because the "university council did not respect the numerus clausus law."[63] They attacked the rector of the University of Pécs, professor of philosophy József Halasy-Nagy, for his leadership style, which they called "liberal and Jew-friendly to the very core."[64] They addressed a memorandum to all the universities in the country demanding that Jewish students be prevented from sitting in the first row in classrooms, and that Jews be barred from being hired as assistant professors and teaching assistants. Even more ominous was their demand that every university review the status of their enrolled Jewish students and withdraw the right to study for those Jews among the student body who were in excess of the quota.[65] The race defender students also threatened the University of Pécs with a boycott.

By the autumn of 1923, the race defenders had got what they wanted. The University of Pécs promised that fees would be waived for every single Christian medical student at the university and that the university would be especially careful about enforcing the Jewish quota during the admissions process (see table 10). Following disturbances at the University of Szeged in 1923, Dezső Veszprémy, a professor of internal medicine noted for his racialist views, was appointed the new rector. Veszprémy left little doubt about his intentions in his inaugural speech. He declared that the regeneration of the Hungarian nation could only be expected from the success of "the flesh of the flesh of the Hungarian nation and the blood of its blood."[66] The proportion of Jews at both

63 N. Szegvári, *Numerus clausus rendelkezések*, 135.
64 N. Szegvári, *Numerus clausus rendelkezések*, 135.
65 N. Szegvári, *Numerus clausus rendelkezések*, 135.
66 N. Szegvári, *Numerus clausus rendelkezések*, 135.

universities took a nosedive. By 1926, there were a total of only 371 Jewish students at the two institutions combined, or about 400 fewer than had attended these universities in 1920.

Women

After the introduction of the numerus clausus law, it was not only Jews who had trouble getting into university, but women as well. Although the law did not contain any explicit restrictions on women, some faculties took it upon themselves to restrict the admission of female students.

The Faculty of Medicine of the University of Budapest, which was the first within the university to propose the idea of a numerus clausus in 1919, did not initially justify the introduction of a fixed number system by pointing to the high number of Jews. Instead, their argument was that during the war years—with the approval of the wartime governments—women had taken the places of male students who had been called up. Their proportion had risen from 5 percent in 1913 to 29 percent by 1917.[67] The Faculty of Medicine recommended introducing measures that would—with the help of the state—restore the proportion they considered desirable.[68] There was also an anti-Semitic edge to the antipathy towards women doctors, since more than half (62 percent) of the female medical students were Jewish.[69] Therefore, when the Faculty of Medicine took steps to exclude women, it was in fact looking to exclude a section of the student body that was mostly made up of Jews. This explains why the Faculty of Medicine already held the exclusion of female students to be necessary in 1919 "lest the Christian boys be forced out," the emphasis being placed on both "Christian" and "boys."[70]

Female students were not allowed to study law or technical subjects. In December 1918, the Károlyi government opened up these subjects too, but this measure ceased to apply after 1920. The Faculty of Medicine in Budapest did not take a single female student until 1925–26. The issue was reregulated

67 Andor Ladányi, "Két évforduló: A nők felsőfokú tanulmányainak száz éve," *Educatio* 5, no. 6 (1996): 378.
68 Women were mostly admitted as "special" students, and could only enroll as "ordinary" students if they completed their first-year exams satisfactorily. N. Szegvári, *Numerus clausus rendelkezések*, 107. Women could not attend the Technical University until the mid-1920s. N. Szegvári, *Numerus clausus rendelkezések*, 160–61.
69 Mária M. Kovács, "A magyar feminizmus korszakfordulója," *Café Bábel* 14, nos. 11–12 (1994): 179–83. In 1918, 48 percent of humanities students were Jewish.
70 N. Szegvári, *Numerus clausus rendelkezések*, 111.

in 1927. From then on, women could be admitted to study economics at the University of Technology, but were still barred from studying theology, law, and attending the College of Veterinary Medicine.

Selection, counter-selection, and selective dropout within the numerus clausus system

Because of the Jewish quota, a student's academic results were no longer the sole criterion for admission to higher education. Admissions boards still classed Jewish applicants by academic performance, but disregarded their rankings once the 6 percent quota was filled. As a result of the quota, students with good grades were excluded if they were Jewish while at the same time students with poorer results got in, provided they were Christian. Sometimes, the admissions boards' reports did not even show the grades of the Jewish students. This was the case, for example, with a report from the admissions board for the Faculty of Medicine in Budapest in 1921, which sorted the admitted students into the following categories:

Christians with excellent secondary school diplomas: 99
Christians with good secondary school diplomas: 116
Christians with secondary school diplomas (satisfactory or pass): 138
Born Jewish: 23[71]

The counter-selection system of the numerus clausus was applied in the first year at every higher education institution, but in the higher years there were significant differences between them. During the first five years of the law, students with poorer academic results at the Budapest University were in a two-thirds majority compared to their counterparts with stronger results. At the same time at the universities of Szeged and Pécs, where Jewish students who had been squeezed out of the capital were admitted to the higher years, students with good grades were in a majority and this was the same at the University of Debrecen (see table 11).[72]

71 N. Szegvári, *Numerus clausus rendelkezések*, 130.

72 Gyula Kornis, "Az egyetemi oktatás főbb kérdései," in *Magyar Felsőoktatás: Az 1936. év december hó 10-től december hó 16-ig tartott országos felsőoktatási kongresszus munkálatai*, vol. 3, ed. Károly Martonffy (Budapest: Királyi Magyar Egyetemi Nyomda, 1937), 10.

Table 11. Proportions of students with outstanding, excellent, and good secondary school diplomas among students in higher education in 1925 (in percentage)

University of Budapest	29
University of Pécs	60
University of Szeged	62
University of Debrecen	55

Source: N. Szegvári, *Numerus clausus rendelkezések*, 141.

The situation remained similar after the racial clause was amended in 1928. Jewish students with good grades were still rejected to a large degree, while a higher proportion of non-Jews with poorer grades were still admitted. The Faculty of Medicine in Budapest rejected a third of the applicants with excellent secondary school diplomas in September 1928, after the amendment of the racial clause. At the same time, they accepted almost twice as many applicants with satisfactory secondary school diplomas or applicants who had failed and then resat their exams than they did applicants with excellent secondary school diplomas (see table 12).[73]

Table 12. Applicants and admissions at the Faculty of Medicine at the Budapest University in 1928 according to secondary school diploma classifications

Diploma classification	Among all applicants	Among those admitted
Excellent	96	66
Good	114	66
Satisfactory	189	115

Source: Ladányi, "A numerus clausus-törvény 1928. évi módosításáról," 1134–35.

The situation was similar the next year. Bethlen's government was no longer willing to bear the international opprobrium that openly anti-Semitic discrimination had brought it. At the same time, in many institutions the leaders of the universities and the Ministry of Religion and Public Education continued the former practices behind closed doors, away from the public in an almost conspirational atmosphere. The dean of the Faculty of Medicine, Balázs Kenyeres, wrote a private memorandum in the autumn of 1929 to Zoltán Magyary, advisor to the minister of religion and education, to explain why it was impossible to make admissions decisions based on academic merit

73 Ladányi, "A numerus clausus-törvény 1928. évi módosításáról," 1134–35.

alone and therefore take all applicants with outstanding grades. The memo reflects well the situation that followed the amendment of the numerus clausus law in 1928.

"The report," wrote the dean, "contains only the bare facts because I don't know whose hands it might fall into during your absence."[74] He went on to explain why 30 of the outstanding applicants had to be rejected while the faculty took 115 satisfactory students. "The applicants were 66 percent Christian and 34 percent Jewish . . . if all the students with outstanding secondary school diplomas had been accepted, the intake would have been 43 percent Jews and 57 percent Christians. The proportions would have been roughly the same if all outstanding and excellent students had been accepted" (see table 13).[75]

Table 13. Applicants to the Faculty of Medicine at the Budapest University in 1929 according to secondary school diploma classifications

Diploma classification	Non-Jewish	Jewish
Excellent	54	41
Good	66	49
Satisfactory	106	40
Unsatisfactory	34	4

Source: N. Szegvári, *Numerus clausus rendelkezések*, 163.

The selectivity of the admissions process remained unfettered at many faculties even after the amendment of the law. No Christian applicants were turned down for the mathematics and pharmaceutical departments at the University of Szeged, the medical faculty in Pécs, or the Faculty of Law in Debrecen. At the same time, the proportion of Jewish students rejected from the medical faculties of all the universities was more than 80 percent. Similarly, almost all Christian applicants were accepted by the University of Technology, the pharmaceutical faculties of the universities of Budapest and Szeged, and the faculties of humanities in Debrecen and Pécs. Not counting the medical faculties, Jewish applicants were rejected to a very high degree—over 70 percent—by the law faculties of the universities of Pécs and Szeged and by the University of Technology.

74 N. Szegvári, *Numerus clausus rendelkezések*, 163.
75 N. Szegvári, *Numerus clausus rendelkezések*, 163.

Selective dropout

The repercussions of the counter-selection inherent in the admissions process were visible in the dropout rates as well. A serious situation developed at the Faculty of Medicine in Budapest, where the Jewish quota was enforced with great vigor. Balázs Kenyeres, a professor of medicine known for his anti-Semitic views who played a determining role in the admissions choices of the medical faculty, published some shocking data on the dropout rates. According to his figures, by 1930–31, 40 percent of the students accepted between 1920 and 1923 had failed to complete their degree.[76] Since hardly any Jews at all were accepted at the Faculty of Medicine in Budapest from 1920 onwards, most of the students failing to complete their studies were Christian.

Figure 15. The faculty of the Faculty of Medicine of the Royal Hungarian Pázmány Péter University (University of Budapest), with dean Balázs Kenyeres (sitting in the middle, with glasses). Source: Fortepan, 74470, Archives of Semmelweis University.

76 Baron Sándor Korányi's address at the June 24, 1933 session of the Upper House, in *Az 1931. évi július hó 18-ára hirdetett országgyűlés felsőházának naplója* (Budapest: Athenaeum Irodalmi és Nyomdai Részvénytársulat, 1934), vol. 2: 349. According to the figures from the Doctors' Union, until the end of the 1930–31 academic year, only 51.4 percent of students enrolled in 1920 had graduated. The figures for other years were 48.1 percent for 1921, 42.6 percent for 1922, and 39.8 percent for 1923. PTE Archives, Documents of the Faculty of Medicine and its Institutions, VIII. 105.b.

The dropout rates were high at all the law faculties. In 1929–30, the number of fourth-year law students was a mere 36 percent of first-years, unlike the humanities faculties, where the comparable figure was 72 percent.[77] According to estimates by contemporary statisticians, the number of students attending the four-year study programs at the universities of arts and sciences decreased by an average of 44.8 percent between the first and fourth years.[78] Although Jewish students dropped out too, more Christian students were affected in the predominantly Christian student body.

Minister of Religion and Public Education Klebelsberg mentioned the phenomenon in parliament. He explained the selective dropout rate by citing not the admissions procedure, but the poorer material circumstances of Christian families:

> My honorable friend [Gyula] Gömbös said that although the numerus clausus is set at 6 percent, more than 10 percent of university students are Jewish. Why is this? After all, admissions in the first year are in accordance with the numerus clausus (i.e., 6 percent). It is because there is another numerus clausus beyond the numerus clausus law. This is the numerus clausus of poverty which affects some Christian youth who often cannot finish their studies for financial reasons. I am thinking primarily of the University of Technology. For this reason, Christians drop out, and the proportion of Jews increases.[79]

But whatever the primary reason was for the selective dropout rate, the minister's statement that Christian students "dropped out," thereby "increasing the proportion of Jews" goes a long way towards explaining why the proportion of Jews decreased more slowly than might have been expected, given the 6 percent quota imposed on first-year admissions. It also answers the question of why in 1925–26, in the fifth year of the numerus clausus—when the Jewish students with "acquired rights" had already left the system—the proportion of Jews in higher education was still around 8.5 percent. Given that the effect of the selective dropout rate on the makeup of the student

77 Asztalos, *A magyar főiskolai hallgatók statisztikája az 1930/31 tanévben*, 37.

78 József Asztalos, *A magyar főiskolai hallgatók statisztikája az 1932/33-as tanévben* (Budapest: Magyar-Királyi Központi Statisztikai Hivatal, 1934), 31.

79 Minutes of the parliamentary session of February 23, 1928, in *Az 1927. évi január hó 25-ére hirdetett országgyűlés képviselőházának naplója*, vol. 9: 201.

body was cumulative, or in other words that first-year dropouts made their effect felt in all the years above, the proportion above accords with the minister's statement that the Jewish quota was largely enforced at 6 percent at all the universities.

According to data from the 1930 census, the exclusion of Jewish secondary school graduates from the country's universities led to dramatic changes in previous trends. The number of Jewish graduate professionals began to decrease. Due to the numerus clausus law, the majority of Jewish young people with secondary school diplomas no longer got into university. While before World War I, in 1910, 85 percent of Jewish youth with secondary school diplomas went on to higher education, by 1923 that proportion had decreased to 45 percent.[80] "The numerus clausus and associated measures (the removal of Jewish civil servants)," wrote Alajos Kovács, "have, to a certain degree, according to the census data, achieved their goal. Or rather, they have initiated a process that, if it were consistently maintained, would lead to that goal. The proportion of Jews among the professional class has markedly decreased and indeed their absolute numbers have also gone down."[81]

The impact of the Jewish quota in certain graduate professions

The decrease in the number of Jewish graduates was not, however, evenly spread among the various graduate professions. The number of Jews in civil service and in municipal and state teaching positions decreased significantly (by several thousand). In 1920, there were still 1,425 Jews employed in the civil service (4.4 percent), while by 1930 there were only 595 (1.7 percent). There were 3,560 Jews working in the education system in 1920 (9 percent), while in 1930 there were only 2,498 (6.2 percent).[82]

At the same time, for a small section of the graduate population, especially among doctors, lawyers, and other—smaller—liberal professions, the absolute number of Jews grew. The increase was slight—a few dozen people a year throughout the decade—but their overall proportion in these groups also decreased. This was thanks partly to Jews who had entered higher education

80 Karády, *Iskolarendszer és felekezeti egyenlőtlenségek*, 251.

81 Kovács, *A csonkamagyarországi zsidóság*, 20.

82 Kovács, *A csonkamagyarországi zsidóság*, 66.

before 1920 and who had studied abroad and thanks, in part, to law students accepted within the framework of the Jewish quota, since only a negligible number of law students actually went on to practice law. The number of Jewish doctors nationwide grew by 699 in the decade from 1920 (from 2,153 to 2,852); however, their proportion among doctors overall (since the number of doctors increased significantly) decreased from 46.3 percent to 34.4 percent. The number of Jewish lawyers grew by 387 (from 2,306 to 2,693) while their proportion among lawyers overall went from 50.5 percent to 49.2 percent.[83]

Hungarian Jewish students abroad

Some Jewish young people who could not go to university between 1920 and 1928 because of the racial clause never in fact went to university. Several thousand Jewish students, however, attended university abroad, many of whom never returned to Hungary.[84] Many of the Jewish youth who were excluded from Hungarian universities studied abroad in Vienna, Prague, Brno, Halle, Dresden, Leipzig, Rome, and Berlin. The fragmentary extant data indicates that in 1921, 1,100 Hungarian Jews were studying in Prague and 700 in Vienna.[85] The attraction of Italy grew after 1923, when foreign Jewish students could attend Italian universities without paying tuition or exam fees.[86] Many of the Jewish

83 Kovács, *A csonkamagyarországi zsidóság*, 66.

84 According to Alajos Kovács's calculations based on the census, in the decade beginning in 1920, a total of around 7,000 Jewish youths graduated from university. Approximately half of these, around 3,500, studied abroad. Alajos Kovács's figures are probably biased towards the lower end, however, because they do not include those Jewish graduates who did not return home after finishing university. Karády estimates the number of Hungarian Jews studying abroad at a few hundred lower, while Pál Bethlen puts it somewhat higher. See Karády, *Iskolarendszer és felekezeti egyenlőtlenségek*, 240; and Bethlen, *A magyar zsidóság almanachja*. According to Nathaniel Katzburg's data, there were 1,100 Jewish students studying in Prague in 1921 and 800 in Vienna in 1922. Katzburg, *Zsidópolitika Magyarországon*, 58. According to the data of the Central Committee of Jewish Students (run by the Hungarian Jewish organizations), of the people they supported up to 1928, 1,450 had graduated abroad. This figure, multiplied by five (for the five academic years), makes it likely that the overall number of those studying at university abroad was above five thousand. Until 1928, the Central Committee of Jewish Students kept track of 1,450 Hungarian Jewish students who had graduated abroad. MNL OL, K28, item 53. Lajos Szabolcsi's report on the workings of the Central Committee of Jewish Students. Report on the National Office of Hungarian Jews in 1929.

85 Michael L. Miller, "'A Numerus Clausus száműzöttjei' a berlini felsőoktatási intézetekben 1920 és 1933 között." *Múlt és Jövő* 17, no. 4 (2006): 84–91.

86 MNL OL, K28, item 53. Lajos Szabolcsi's report on March 13, 1929. The decree ordering Jewish students to be admitted was number 2102/5421. Mussolini issued the decree primarily because of the attacks on Jewish students at German universities in 1922. Jewish students from several European countries were admitted to university in Italy on this basis. Szabolcsi, *Két emberöltő*, 412.

students forced abroad by restrictive quotas and undignified circumstances, or in Victor Karady's words, "the numerus clausus exiles," never returned home after graduation. They made up that generation of emigrant Jewish intellectuals which went on to achieve outstanding successes in the fields of the arts and sciences abroad, and included: Ede (Edward) Teller, Jenő (Eugene) Wigner, Tódor Kármán, György (George) Hevesy, Leó Szilárd, János (John) Neumann, Károly (Karl) Mannheim, the Polányi brothers (Karl and Michael), György (George) Cukor, Jenő Ormándy, Antal Doráti, Robert Capa, Arnold Hauser, Sándor (Alexander) Korda, Marcell Breuer, László Moholy-Nagy, and Arthur Koestler. All of them emigrated due to the numerus clausus.[87]

The Jewish quota in everyday life

The Jewish quota was not applied uniformly against Jewish applicants by the various universities. At the Faculty of Medicine and the University of Technology in Budapest, the restrictions put in place were far more stringent than the quota required. Hardly any Jewish students were admitted in the capital: in the 1920s, there were an average of between 700 and 800 Jewish students in all the cohorts combined, as opposed to between 2,500 and 3,000 previously.

There were polytechnics which did not accept any Jewish students at all. For years, there were absolutely no Jewish students at the College of Mining, Engineering, and Forest Engineering in Sopron and at the schools of economics in Keszthely and Magyaróvár. The proportion of Jewish students lagged behind the national average at the College of Veterinary Medicine and the Academy of Economics in Debrecen.[88] But even in those institutions which strictly fol-

87 According to Alajos Kovács's estimate, their number was approximately 3,500 in a decade. There are no precise figures available to show the extent of the change in Jewish university graduates in the census data. We can get an approximate idea if we look at the overall figures of the "professional graduate class proper," since this social category was dominated by professions which required a university degree. In 1920, this class numbered 121,058 of whom 16,091 were Jewish. In 1930, these figures were 137,734 and 15,536 respectively. Kovács, *A csonkamagyarországi zsidóság*, 66. According to the census data for 1920 and 1930, the number of Jews in this class had decreased by 555 persons. This is fewer than the number of Jews excluded from university by the racial clause, since the census data only show the number of university graduates, not the number who obtained their degrees abroad. The proportion of Jews in the "professional graduate class proper" decreased from 13.3 to 11.3 percent in this decade, while the number of non-Jewish professional graduates grew by 17,231. If the approx. 5,000 Jewish students excluded by the racial clause had attended university, then by 1930, the proportion of Jews in the "professional graduate class proper" would have been 15 percent.

88 Ladányi, "A numerus clausus-törvény 1928. évi módosításáról," 1122.

lowed the letter of the law, and only accepted Jewish students up to the limit set by the quota, there was a constant debate over whether the anti-Jewish quota should be applied by the universities overall, or also by the individual faculties and departments. On this question, the 1920 law remained silent.

The numerus clausus law left the question of who should be considered Jewish for the purposes of university admissions vague, thereby providing constant ammunition for the anti-Semitic movements throughout the 1920s. At certain universities, such as Pécs and Szeged, they initially applied the quota only to those of the Jewish religion. By contrast, the council of the University of Budapest decided that Jews who had converted "are also classed as belonging to the Jewish nationality, or race."[89] Elsewhere, they marked the application files of converted Jews with the formula "born Jewish." Admissions panels sometimes reviewed the circumstances of someone's conversion specially to check whether the Jewish students had not converted to Christianity for "strategic" reasons, to make their admission to university easier. Kunó Klebelsberg made this test compulsory as well, in 1926, by ordering the faculties themselves to decide in each case whether the conversion took place "in fraudem legis," that is, in order to circumvent the law. It was at just such an examination that the race defender students on the admissions board beat the later world-famous physicist Leó Szilárd and shoved him down a marble staircase.[90]

The exclusion of Jews continued even in the postgraduate levels of higher education: Jewish students were not even admitted to unpaid intern positions in the Budapest Faculty of Medicine's postgraduate training course.[91]

Anti-Semitism at the universities was not confined to the students—it was significant among the professors as well. Most of the professors who had helped create the numerus clausus law continued to support the anti-Semitic students later on as well. Professors who were particularly well known for their anti-Semitism included Mihály Kmoskó (Theology), Károly Balás, Alfréd Doleschall, and Nándor Bernolák (all Law), Lajos Méhely (Zoology), Jenő Darkó (Classics/Philology) as well as János Bársony, Balázs Kenyeres, Károly Hoór, Zsigmond Ritoók, Lajos Bakay, and András Csilléry (Medicine). Lajos Méhely, who was dean of the Budapest Faculty of Humanities at the time of the numerus clau-

89 Quoted in Ladányi, "A numerus clausustól a numerus nullusig," 57.

90 Kati Marton, *Kilenc magyar, aki világgá ment és megváltoztatta a világot* (Budapest: Corvina, 2008), 43.

91 István Székács-Schönberger, *Egy zsidó polgár gyermekkora* (Budapest: Múlt és Jövő, 2007), 119–42.

sus amendment, stated at a faculty meeting that he supported the students organizing disruptive protests against the amendment and went on to defend the Jewish quota using brutal anti-Semitic rhetoric.[92] It was around this time that it was noted of Pál Teleki, who was working as a professor of geography, that when some anti-Semitic students tried to prevent their Jewish colleagues from getting into the examination hall by physical violence, he commented to journalists: "The noise doesn't bother me, because their exam is on the sea anyway, and the clamor is the equivalent of the noise of the sea."[93]

The series of scandals were brought to an end only by the intervention of the government. The medical faculties in Budapest and Szeged—following the German and Austrian example—debated in 1924 the idea of not taking any more Jewish students at all unless the Jewish community abrogated the Jewish religious ban on the dissection of corpses. Professor Hoór classed the ancient taboo on dissection as the "arrogant superciliousness of Judaism," which "deeply offends and humiliates the Hungarian race."[94] Hoór then went on to more or less legitimize the use of militant methods against Jews: "I personally have done whatever I could up to this point to keep the youth from any irresponsible actions, but from this point on, I cannot go on doing so."[95] At the Faculty of Medicine in Budapest in 1927, Professor János Bársony, in a distinctly anti-government vein, encouraged the race defender students not to let the government ease the racial paragraph. Pál Teleki did the same as a geography professor when he (in his own words) "convinced" the race defender students to submit a similar official petition.[96]

Several professors at the Faculty of Medicine in Budapest were no strangers to the symbolic humiliation of Jewish students. For instance, in the spring of 1928, when the minister of education instructed the universities by decree to admit Jewish students with outstanding secondary school diplomas, Lajos Bakay recommended that the members of the faculty should deny these stu-

92 ELTE Archives, d9212/1927-28, Meeting of the Faculty of Humanities of the Royal Hungarian Pázmány Péter University in Budapest, June 1, 1928.

93 Lead article in *Az Egyenlőség* (Equality), October 29, 1927, under the title "Kiverték őket" (They were beaten out). Quoted in Krisztián Ungváry, "Értelmiség és antiszemita közbeszéd," *Beszélő* 6, no. 6 (2001): 74–92. N. Szegvári, *Numerus clausus rendelkezések*, 99.

94 Hoór quoted by deputy István Lendvai in his contribution at the parliamentary session of June 4, 1924, in *Az 1922. évi junius hó 16-ára hirdetett nemzetgyűlés naplója*, vol. 24: 317.

95 *Az 1922. évi junius hó 16-ára hirdetett nemzetgyűlés naplója*, vol. 24: 317.

96 Teleki, *Válogatott politikai írások és beszédek*, 188.

dents "the act of welcome," which is to say, "the taking of the oath and the shaking of hands."[97]

Anti-Jewish violence at the universities

The exclusion of Jews was not limited to the admissions process but was part of the everyday life of the university as well. Anti-Semitic incidents occurred regularly at the universities in Budapest, both in the form of symbolic insults and in actual physical violence. The anti-Semitic student organizations, especially Hungária and the Turul Alliance, insulted and excluded the Jewish students, checked their papers, and forced them to sit in the back rows. They also told them to wear yellow stars and occasionally beat them.[98] In the spring of 1923, there were fights at all the universities, while in the capital the race defender students registered their demand that the ghetto and yellow badges be reinstated and that all Jewish students be excluded from higher education.[99] There were

Figure 16. Drawing by Mihály Bíró in protest against the numerus clausus, 1920. Source: MNM Levelezőlap Gyűjtemény.

97 SOTE Archives, Minutes of the meetings of the Faculty of Medicine of the Royal Hungarian Pázmány Péter University of Budapest, 179. Minutes of the extraordinary meeting, October 19, 1928.

98 Bethlen, *A magyar zsidóság almanachja*, 118–24.

99 Bethlen, *A magyar zsidóság almanachja*, 121.

also shameful incidents where students who were unable to prove their ethnicity with papers were examined—as the contemporary phrase went—"with a gross violation of their personal privacy."[100]

But Jews were not the only targets of violent anti-Semitism. The race defender students did not spare those professors who did not share their views either. On one occasion, Albert Szent-Györgyi upbraided the medical students at the University of Szeged for having failed en masse by telling them that the only "intelligent answer" had been from a Jewish student. The race defenders responded with a protest, as a result of which the police had to be called in to keep the peace at the university.[101]

With the spread of these violent incidents, the numerus clausus had a long-lasting and important political impact on the professional youth of the country. It accustomed race defender students to open violence against their colleagues while it made exclusion, stigmatization, and humiliation an everyday experience for the Jewish students.[102] The attacks also accustomed the young professional class to question the status of even those Jewish students who had been accepted legally—within the framework of the quota—and in this way to exercise pressure to eliminate their possible colleagues and competitors. The long-term effects of anti-Semitism in higher education, which Victor Karady categorized as "a fascist mentality of robbery," were well reflected in a 1943 publication of the Turul Alliance which, when recalling the 1920s, stated: "although we all knew that the Jewish question could not be solved by beatings, it is also certain that without those Jew beatings, we would never have gotten to the Jewish Laws."[103]

The quantitative measure of the numerus clausus among the non-Jewish professional class

In theory, the reduction in the number of Jewish students was not the sole purpose of the numerus clausus. In defense of the law, Kunó Klebelsberg and

100 Bethlen, *A magyar zsidóság almanachja*, 123.
101 *Délmagyarország*, November 14, 1930, 3.
102 János Pelle, "Egyetemi antiszemitizmus a két világháború között," *Hetek.hu*, December 19, 1998, http://www.hetek.hu/velemeny/199812/egyetemi_antiszemitizmus_a_ket_vilaghaboru_kozott (accessed April 8, 2010).
103 Róbert Kerepeszki, "A Turul Szövetség országos és debreceni szervezete (1919–1945)" (PhD diss. Debrecen, 2009); and Karády, *Iskolarendszer és felekezeti egyenlőtlenségek*, 243.

Figure 17. Rezső Rupert around 1928.
Source: MNM Történeti Fényképtár.

others frequently noted that the measure was also intended to prevent the formation of an "intellectual proletariat," and thus the number of Christian students also had to be kept in check. This idea was, however, unrealistic for a number of reasons.

First of all, a reduction in the number of Christian students was a political impossibility in the early 1920s. It was unimaginable for the government to limit university places in such a way that non-Jewish students returning from the war would be excluded from higher education in large numbers. As Rezső Rupert stated in parliament: "University-age Christians will in no way tolerate Christian youths being excluded. Thus, in effect, there will be no numerus clausus. The path to university is still open to the greater Christian masses, and we have done nothing towards blocking an educated proletariat. And if we have, if we have acted in a way that means that the poorer sort among university-age Christians is missing out, then we have committed a great crime."[104]

Rezső Rupert's prediction turned out to be correct. In 1922–23, the third year following the introduction of the numerus clausus, the number of university students climbed to a record high of 16,829 (20,240 when including polytechnic students). There was only one previous year in which the number of students had been this high, namely, 1917. By 1923–24, however, after the backlog of wartime year groups had left university, the overall number of students returned to roughly its prewar levels. The 13,000 university students that year were similar in number to the prewar student population of between 15,000 and 16,000 (when including polytechnic students). Given that before the war, there were between 3000 and 4000, or sometimes more, Jewish university students per year, with their numbers decreasing below 1500 after 1920, the post-

104 Minutes of the parliamentary session of September 20, 1920, in *Az 1920. évi február hó 16-ára összehívott nemzetgyűlés naplója*, vol. 5: 423.

1920 numbers for non-Jewish students showed an increase of approximately 15 percent compared to their prewar levels.[105]

To summarize: at the start of the 1920s, when student numbers grew to unprecedented levels because of the backlog from the war years, the numerus clausus law did not prevent this growth. The minister of education set the official allocations of places very high. But by the second half of the 1920s, a number of universities were no longer struggling with the problem of too many applicants, but rather the opposite, which is to say that they could not fill the allocated places because of a lack of Christian applicants.

In the end, then, the numerus clausus law did not constitute a serious restriction on Christian students. Although it was the state that decided on the number of students who could be admitted after 1920, it regularly allocated so many places that few Christian students were excluded from higher education. There was only one year, 1928, when the number of applicants significantly exceeded the official allocation of places, but there was a particular reason for this. Kunó Klebelsberg, by his own admission, decided to deliver an "object lesson" in a deliberate political maneuver. This meant that he allocated fewer than the usual number of university places to show that if the government allocated so few places that Christian students would also be excluded from higher education, a political scandal would erupt. The maneuver was necessary because the race defender opposition to the amendment of the numerus clausus law argued that a relaxation of the law would lead to the growth of the "intellectual proletariat." It was in response to this that Klebelsberg determined that "the situation has to be taken *ad absurdum* so that I can demonstrate its [that is, the low number of places allocated] unsustainability. They've whined so much to me about the rampant professional proletariat that in the end I had to show them the impossibility of these demands."[106] There was indeed no lack of uproar from Christian middle class families and, as Klebelsberg remarked, "the path indicated by the cacophony of assertions proved to be impracticable." The official allocation of places had to be increased.[107] This is how the situation became

105 Haller, *Harc a numerus clausus körül*, 132–46; and Kovács, *A csonkamagyarországi zsidóság*, 73.

106 Ladányi, "A numerus clausus-törvény 1928. évi módosításáról," 1135. Klebelsberg had reduced the official allocations the year before. At the Faculty of Law, the number of places decreased from 550 to 320, at the Faculty of Medicine from 300 to 180, while at the Faculty of Humanities, they went from 450 to 210. Klebelsberg raised the allocations after the scandal was over to 552 at the Faculty of Law, 240 at the Faculty of Medicine, and 410 at the Faculty of Humanities.

107 Ladányi, "A numerus clausus-törvény 1928. évi módosításáról," 1135.

possible whereby several universities (the Faculty of Medicine in Pécs, the faculties of mathematics and natural sciences in Szeged, as well as the pharmaceutical class in Szeged and the Faculty of Law in Debrecen) admitted 100 percent of their Christian applicants, which is to say that every single Christian applicant got into university, as if there was no numerus clausus at all.[108]

The numerus clausus system therefore did not bring serious restrictions for Christian male students, while the educational possibilities of Christian women began to open up from the start of the 1930s.

The overall number of students in higher education in Hungary in the 1930s was roughly on the same level as the prewar period. This meant that Hungary belonged to those European countries—Switzerland, Austria, Germany, and Belgium—where the numbers in higher education stagnated or experienced only slight growth after 1920.[109] A significant change was brought about only after the First and Second Vienna Awards (1938, 1940), which restored to Hungary some of the territories that were lost at Trianon. In 1942–43, the number of students grew to over 20,000.[110]

108 Ladányi, "A numerus clausus-törvény 1928. évi módosításáról," 1136.

109 Walter Maria Kotschnig, *Unemployment in the Learned Professions: An International Study of Occupational and Educational Planning* (London: Oxford University Press, 1937), 13.

110 Gyáni and Kövér, *Magyarország társadalomtörténete*, 279. The First Vienna Award (signed on November 2, 1938, with the assistance of Nazi Germany and Fascist Italy) resulted in the return of former Hungarian territories from Czechoslovakia, while the Second Vienna Award (signed on August 30, 1940) achieved the same with respect to territories in Northern Transylvania.

Chapter Three

The Amendment of the Numerus Clausus Law and the Restoration of the Explicit Jewish Quota

"The secret disapproval of many"

The proponents of the numerus clausus law often said that the law was created by the will of a majority in parliament. This was true in that the majority of those present for the parliamentary vote did indeed vote in the affirmative. However, very few of the 219 deputies were present at the vote—a mere 64 in fact—of whom 59 (which is to say only 26 percent of the total number of deputies) voted for the law. The Smallholder deputies left the chamber before the vote because, although their party opposed the law, their members could not—as part of the governing coalition—vote against it.[1] As the Smallholder György Vasadi Balogh said, the law was passed "to the secret disapproval of many" even if only very few people dared "openly oppose" it.[2] István Bethlen did not even go to parliament on the day of the vote, and although Kunó Klebelsberg was present at the reading of the law, he left the chamber before the vote because, as he later said, he did not agree with its wording.[3] The majority of the government ministers also did not attend the vote.

1 Bethlen, *A magyar zsidóság almanachja*, 60. Later, however, in the spring of 1923, at a vote for the repeal of the law, some of the Smallholder deputies also voted in favor of the law.

2 Bethlen, *A magyar zsidóság almanachja*, 70–71.

3 Klebelsberg agreed with the requirement of proving patriotic behavior. He was signatory to the "Combined report of the parliamentary committees on financial and education affairs," which did not yet contain the nationalities quota.

But if Bethlen and Klebelsberg did not vote for the law, they also did not support its repeal in the early 1920s. It was not for lack of bills aimed at repealing it in parliament, however. Between 1922 and 1924, there were eight such bills which failed to pass. István Bethlen openly opposed the calls for repeal.[4] And Klebelsberg—just as he had when the law was being passed—spent the votes themselves in the corridor outside the chamber.

Nonetheless, the camp openly opposing the law had started to grow by the mid-1920s, while from the government's side, Pál Pesthy—the Minister of Justice—said in November 1925 that the law was a temporary measure that should be repealed.[5] That same year, Pál Bethlen published a collection of essays in which he asked prominent members of public life to take a stand against the law.[6] Twenty-four deputies from the governing party lent their names to the volume.[7] Among them were three former ministers of the interior (László Grecsák, Gábor Ugron, and Vince Nagy), László Almásy (Executive Vice-President of the Unity Party), Hümér Hültl (head of the Hungarian National Medical Association), György Lukács (one of the leaders of the Revisionist League), and Baron József Szterényi (who had taken an active role in the legal return of Hungarian estates in Transylvania at the request of István Bethlen). The law also had influential ecclesiastical opponents, among them Dezső Baltazár (Protestant Bishop of Debrecen), Cardinal János Csernoch (Primate of All Hungary), and Canon Sándor Giesswein (also a parliamentary deputy). A good number of prominent conservative politicians and public figures had been against the law from the start. They included three former ministers of religion and education—Baron Gyula Wlassics (minister 1895–1903), Count Albert Apponyi (minister, June 1917—May 1918, and head of the Hungarian delegation at the League of Nations 1923–1933) and Albert Berzeviczy (minister 1903–1905, and President of the Hungarian Academy of Sciences 1905–1936). Also against the law were the Minister of Finance, Lóránt Hegedűs, and former Minister of Finance Tibor Kállay. Among the more prominent opponents of the law were Count Miksa Hoyos (Chairman of the National

4 Bethlen, *A magyar zsidóság almanachja*, 117; and minutes of the parliamentary session of July 31, 1922, in *Az 1922. évi junius hó 16-ára hirdetett nemzetgyűlés naplója*, vol. 3: 152.

5 Szabolcsi, *Két emberöltő*, 372.

6 Pál Bethlen, an opponent of the numerus clausus, was member of the Upper House of the National Assembly from 1922 to 1944.

7 Bethlen, *A magyar zsidóság almanachja*.

Chamber of Agriculture), Miksa Fenyő (Director of the National Association of Industrialists), Jenő Rákosi, István Dénes (President of the National Agrarian Laborers Party), Benő Haypál (noted Protestant priest), Gyula Szávay (Secretary of the Budapest Chamber of Commerce and Industry), István Strauss (Catholic politician), József Pap (Chairman of the Chamber of Lawyers), Elemér Simonsits (Vice-President of the Red Cross), István Bezerédj, Count János Hadik, and Vilmos Vázsonyi (Chairman of the Democratic Party). Also against the law were a number of Smallholder deputies and Liberal, Christian Socialist, and Social Democrat politicians. They included: Pál Hegymeghy-Kiss, Győző Drózdy, Gaszton Gaál, Gyula Berki, György Vasadi Balogh, and Rezső Rupert, Sándor Giesswein, Károly Rassay, Zéno Bessenyei, Imre Dréhr, Lajos Erdőhegyi, Kálmán Éhn, Miklós Forgács, István Görgey, Kálmán Hajós, Sándor Kovács Nagy, Lajos Könyves Tóth, Andor Nánássy, György Perlaky, István Rubinek, Zoltán Szabó, Sándor Szabó, Bálint Szijj, János Tankovics, József Pakots, Pál Sándor, Ernő Bródy, Károly Peyer, István Farkas, Imre Györki, Emil Pikler, Anna Kéthly, and Sándor Pető. Lajos Szabolcsi, the editor of the periodical *Egyenlőség* founded an association to help Jewish students forced to study abroad by the numerus clausus.

The university elite were divided over the law, although the proponents of the law were far more outspoken than its opponents. Nonetheless, there were a good number of respected professors who publicly opposed the Jewish quota. The prorector of the evacuated University of Kolozsvár, István Schneller, resigned his post in 1921 in protest over this very issue. Among the more well-known university professors opposed to the law were Albert Szent-Györgyi, Pál Angyal, Ernő Fináczy, Győző Concha, and Béla Issekutz. But even the united strength of the domestic opponents of the Jewish quota would not have been enough to force its amendment in 1928 without the external pressure of the League of Nations.

But the League of Nations itself was initially slow to react in the case of the Hungarian Jews. The Hungarian anti-Semitic commonplace of the League as "the philo-Semitic foreigners" was nothing more than the product of the provincial imagination. In reality, the League of Nations did not have a unified policy on the Jewish question. On issues affecting the Jews, such as the British Mandate in Palestine, Britain and France could only agree at the price of heavy compromises. There was also no agreement as to whether the League should sanction those countries which refused to accord citizenship to the hundreds of thousands of Jews within their new borders, having labelled them "a nomadic people." The members of the League were also divided over to what extent it was wise to intervene from outside in the domestic matters of European countries slowly consolidating after the war.[8] In the early 1920s, the League was therefore extremely cautious in taking a stand on the question of the injustices committed against the Jews of Hungary. It took years of hard work and the perseverance and realism of Lucien Wolf, almost the sole proponent of European Jewish diplomacy, to get the League of Nations to conform to its own principles and take appropriate action in the face of the anti-Jewish discrimination.

This was despite the fact that three European Jewish organizations, the Board of Deputies of British Jews, the Anglo-Jewish Association, and the Alliance Israélite Universelle, protested to the League as early as November 1921. The Council of the League put the issue on the agenda a year later, in September 1922. But this was more of a cautious warning. The Council did not formulate any kind of criticism of the Hungarian government at that time.

Geneva, 1922

On September 30, 1922, Foreign Minister Miklós Bánffy responded on behalf of the Hungarian government to the petitions presented to the League of Nations. Bánffy's response presented both the law and the situation that had arisen from its implementation with a cold cynicism. According to the foreign minister, the Jewish quota was not a restriction on the rights of Jews, but just the opposite—it was created with an "intention to protect." It was, according to him, meant to ensure that all minorities—including the Jews—would be guaranteed their places within higher education according to their percentage within the population overall. He denied what was common knowledge in Hungary itself, that in the case of the Jews, the law represented a serious restriction. He provided data denying that Jews were discriminated against. This data had been manipulatively put together with this goal in mind as it covered only the universities of Pécs and Szeged. At these universities, among the higher years, the proportion of Jewish students was indeed high, but the two universities comprised a mere 15 percent of the country's overall student population. Even the data from these universities had been manipulated because it did not show the pro-

8 Carole Fink, *Defending the Right of Others: The Great Powers, the Jews, and International Minority Protection, 1878–1938* (Cambridge: Cambridge University Press, 2004).

portion of Jewish students in the first year only, though the numerus clausus applied only to first-year admissions. The minister did not mention that both universities more or less conformed to the Jewish quota in their first years. His response did not contain data from the University of Budapest at all and was also silent about those roughly 3,000 higher-year Jewish students who did not come under the aegis of the law, but whose enrollment was nonetheless denied. Some 2,000 of these students ended up being excluded from higher education for good—in Hungary, at any rate.

The League of Nations greeted Bánffy's response with polite temporizing. It did request further information from the minister on admissions procedures, but it nonetheless acknowledged his response.[9] The League appointed a three-member panel to examine the data it had asked for, which consisted of the Belgian foreign minister, a Spanish minister, and a Chinese diplomat. On the basis of the data submitted by the Hungarian government in January 1923, which contained numbers only for the universities of Pécs and Szeged and not Budapest, the panel produced a negative report on the law.

The investigation into the numerus clausus did not, however, have any negative repercussions for Hungary at this moment. The League accepted Hungary as a member in the autumn of 1922 without Hungary having repealed the Jewish quota. The hope among the Octobrist émigrés (those who emigrated because of their role in the 1918 October Revolution) and domestic liberals that the League would make the international loan to Hungary in 1924 expressly conditional on the repeal of the numerus clausus, among other things, also proved illusory.[10]

Lucien Wolf and the League of Nations

It is also true, however, that the Western Powers were seriously uneasy about the pogroms and other anti-Jewish measures in Eastern Europe. They knew that the persecution of the Jews could not only lead to mass emigration, but also to the spread of political anti-Semitism from East to West. It was this concern that was exploited by the influential Anglo-Jewish politician Lucien Wolf, who between 1920 and 1928 undertook with patience and unbroken calm what

9 Thomas Spira "Hungary's Numerus Clausus, the Jewish Minority and the League of Nations," *Ungarn Jahrbuch* 4 (1972): 120.

10 Romsics, *Bethlen István*, 154.

was essentially a single-handed campaign against the Hungarian Jewish quota. Wolf was a foreign correspondent for the *Times*, as well as an editor and historian who had an important role in international campaigns against anti-Semitism. He was involved, for example, in proving that the anti-Semitic *Protocols of the Elders of Zion*, then doing the rounds of Europe, was nothing more than a downright forgery. He was the foreign policy representative of the most significant Anglo-Jewish organization, the Board of Deputies of British Jews, and had excellent connections in British government circles. He was known for his discretion, obstinacy, and sense of humor. The sixty-something year old politician had established a position of some significance for himself at the League of Nations. He was part of the British delegation at the Versailles peace talks, and went on to be a founder and member of the advisory committee to the League of Nations' High Commission for Refugees. Together with the Norwegian Fridtjof Nansen, he persistently fought against the practice of the successor states of the Austro-Hungarian Monarchy (principally Austria and Poland) of denying Jews citizenship. In his campaign against the Hungarian Jewish quota, Wolf employed both the instruments of international law and the application of political pressure.

Wolf fought for years to get the Hungarian Jewish quota declared contrary to the international law then in force. In his 1921 submission to the League of Nations, he explained that the Hungarian numerus clausus was contrary to Articles 56, 57, and 58 of the Treaty of Trianon.

Article 58 specified that "all Hungarian nationals shall be equal before the law and shall enjoy the same civil and political rights without distinction as to race, language or religion."[11] The Hungarian government, however, denied that there had been an infraction of the law in the case of the Jews, rejected the reference to equal rights for all citizens, and said that the nationalities quota of the numerus clausus law ensured equal treatment as far all the nationali-

11 "Treaty of Peace between the Allied and Associated Powers and Hungary and Protocol and Declaration, Signed at Trianon, June 4, 1920," *The World War I Document Archive, Brigham Young University Library*, https://wwi.lib.byu.edu/index.php/Treaty_of_Trianon. A longer excerpt of article 58 reads: "All Hungarian nationals shall be equal before the law and shall enjoy the same civil and political rights without distinction as to race, language or religion. Difference of religion, creed or confession shall not prejudice any Hungarian national in matters relating to the enjoyment of civil or political rights, as for instance admission to public employments, functions and honours, or the exercise of professions and industries.... Hungarian nationals who belong to racial, religious or linguistic minorities shall enjoy the same treatment and security in law and in fact as the other Hungarian nationals." On the submission, see Spira "Hungary's Numerus Clausus."

ties named therein were concerned. After three years of trying, Wolf got the Secretary General of the League of Nations to ask for a professional legal opinion from the Cambridge professor of law, Hugh H. L. Bellot. As soon as Bellot's negative opinion was complete, it became certain that if it came to legal proceedings, the International Court in The Hague would rule the law unlawful. It was also certain that, under the terms of Article 60 of the Treaty of Trianon, there could be no appeal against a negative ruling by the court.

Armed with this legal opinion, Wolf prepared a new petition. But then, in December 1924, Count Albert Apponyi, Hungary's representative at the League of Nations, met with Lucien Wolf at the request of Bethlen to discuss the fate of the numerus clausus.[12] No records remain of the meeting. The two parties, however, clearly did not reach an agreement, for Wolf turned to the League of Nations for a second time on January 1, 1925, and asked the organization to refer the matter to the International Court in The Hague. In addition to demonstrating that the law was against international law, Wolf's petition argued that if the League, or rather The Hague Court, did not take a stand against the Hungarian Jewish quota, other countries could follow its example and introduce similar quotas themselves. The League decided not to refer Wolf's petition to the Court in The Hague, but to the League's Council instead.

Wolf's petition came at a bad time for the Hungarian government. It is true that by the time of its submission, the government had finished its talks with the League of Nations about a loan.[13] Bankers in London had in fact asked Lucien Wolf for his opinion on the loans to the Hungarian government, and Wolf had been distinctly in favor. "Lucien Wolf, the old diplomat," wrote Lajos Szabolcsi, "was not the kind of lawyer who wanted to ruin his enemy, but the kind to negotiate."[14] It was Wolf's opinion that supporting Bethlen's plans for political and economic stabilization was just as much in the interests of Hungarian Jews as it was of the country as a whole.[15]

But the Hungarian government had other important diplomatic projects besides the loan negotiations. They had submitted dozens of objections to the League of Nations in the previous few years about the fate of the Hungarian

---

12 Szabolcsi, *Két emberöltő*, 356; and Béla Fábián's address at the parliamentary session of December 17, 1925, in *Az 1922. évi junius hó 16-ára hirdetett nemzetgyűlés naplója*, vol. 38: 232.

13 Szabolcsi, *Két emberöltő*, 356.

14 Szabolcsi, *Két emberöltő*, 356.

15 Szabolcsi, *Két emberöltő*, 356.

minorities that had ended up in the successor states to the Austro-Hungarian Monarchy. The Hungarian government did everything it could to direct the international community's attention to the bitter conflict then raging between Hungary and Romania on the issue of the "optants."

The optants issue and the Treaty of Trianon

The legal proceedings for the optants were begun on behalf of those landowners who had estates in the successor states of the Monarchy.[16] Under the terms of the peace treaty, the landowners' legal rights to their properties continued to be valid even if they decided (or "opted") to remain Hungarian citizens, or in other words, did not adopt the nationality of the successor state in which their estates were now located.[17]

But the successor states—Romania, Yugoslavia, and Czechoslovakia—did not keep to the terms of the peace treaty in this regard. From 1921 onwards, Romania, operating within the framework of a land reform, began redistributing the estates of those Transylvanian landowners who had chosen to keep their Hungarian citizenship and did so without providing them reasonable compensation. To a smaller extent, Czechoslovakia and Yugoslavia also made use of the estates of optant landowners for the purpose of land reform.[18] Among

16 The Romanian land reform in the newly acquired parts of the country was made possible by the new Romanian land law of July 30, 1921. "The land reform's anti-Hungarian edge was practically palpable [in this law], for the law included a provision for absentee landlords. This stated that the Romanian state could, without any compensation, expropriate all property and real estate in Romania of anyone who had been absent from the country for non-official purposes from December 1, 1918, until the passing of the law (July 30, 1921). 'Non-official purposes' referred mainly to those Hungarian citizens who did not wish to stay under Romanian rule and had left their homes." Gábor Aradi, "A San Remo-i tárgyalások magyarországi előkészülete." *Levéltári Szemle* 52, no. 3 (2002): 25. The optants cases in Romania affected nearly 850,000 acres (600,000 *holds*) of land, whose commercial value was in the region of 165–220 million *pengős*. The Hungarian government put the matter to the Council of the League of Nations twice, in 1923 and in 1927. The Council, however, recommended bilateral Hungarian-Romanian talks. Finally, in January 1930, a solution was found which linked the optants case to Hungary's war reparations. Under this decision, the compensation for the optants would have come from a separate fund to which Hungary would have had to contribute a sum equal to 13.5 million gold crowns a year for 23 years after the expiration of reparations payments in 1943. Had international debts not been cancelled in 1932 because of the world financial crisis, this solution to the optants case would have placed a heavy financial burden on the country.

17 The basis for this was articles 63, 232, and 250 of the peace treaty. The League of Nations did not treat the optants cases as a minorities issue.

18 The Hungarian government submitted its first petition to the League of Nations on March 15, 1923. See Francis Deák, *The Hungarian-Rumanian Land Dispute: A Study of Hungarian Property Rights in Transylvania under the Treaty of Trianon* (New York: Columbia University Press, 1928); and Denys

others in the Hungarian political elite, Pál Teleki, Miklós Bánffy (the Foreign Minister), and István Bethlen himself had estates in Transylvania. The compensation requested for the expropriated estates ran to 150–200 million gold crowns, which was roughly equal in size to the League of Nations loan.[19] There were altogether about eight hundred legal claims.[20] Prime Minister Bethlen himself claimed 2.5–3 million gold crowns in compensation for 14 thousand acres of land (or ten thousand *holds* in the traditional Hungarian unit of land measurement).[21] Bethlen took on significant personal debt in the 1920s in the hope of eventual compensation—by 1931, his debts stood at approximately 200–250,000 *pengős*.[22]

Others in the government were also involved in claims for compensation—directly or indirectly. Fülöp Weiss, president of the Magyar Kereskedelmi Bank (Hungarian Commercial Bank) and father-in-law of Foreign Minister Lajos Walkó, was reported at the time to have advanced Bethlen a 750,000 *pengő* loan—in the hope of future compensation.[23] The Weiss-Walkó family naturally tried to ensure that compensation would be forthcoming and that the bank would therefore have its loan repaid.

Bethlen's personal involvement placed the Hungarian government's diplomatic efforts in an unfavorable light—so much so that in the summer of 1927, Hungary's representative to the League of Nations advised Bethlen to withdraw his personal claim.[24] "It would be a wonderful moral stand," the representative wrote, "which would make Your Excellency irreproachable. Either we will eventually win the case, in which case the country would no doubt express its gratitude to Your Excellency, or we will lose it—in which case Your Excellency will only have renounced something that you would never have gotten anyway."[25] Bethlen did not take this advice. He did, however, consider resigning his posi-

Peter Myers, *A Handbook of the League of Nations: A Comprehensive Account of Its Structure, Operation and Activities* (Boston: World Peace Foundation, 1935).

19 Romsics, *Bethlen István*, 186. The loan amount was for 250 million gold crowns.

20 István Bekény et al., eds., *Magyarország a XX. században*, vol. 1 (Szekszárd: Babits, 1996), 67, http://mek.niif.hu/02100/02185/html/10.html.

21 The claim for compensation also included Bethlen's wife's estates.

22 Romsics, *Bethlen István*, 218. One gold crown was worth 1.16 *pengős*.

23 MTI Házi tájékoztató [Internal information], January 14, 1932, no. 13, 1.

24 Romsics, *Bethlen István*, 186. Romsics notes concerning Bethlen that Bethlen stolidly refused the compromise solution regarding compensation for the lost estates worked out by the Great Powers, and that his own interests played a role in this decision. Romsics, *Bethlen István*, 188.

25 The letter was dated July 12, 1927. Romsics, *Bethlen István*, 186.

tion while the claims of the optants were being settled.[26] Baron József Szterényi, who was asked by the government to work out the Hungarian strategy for the negotiations, accepted at a cabinet meeting on October 15, 1928, that the Hungarian position was vulnerable "because the prime minister also happens to be involved in the matter." However, he opposed Bethlen drawing any far-reaching conclusions from this.[27]

In the matter of the optants, Bethlen could rely on—among others—Pál Teleki, who was the president of the optants' association and who was similarly personally affected due to the loss of his Transylvanian estates. Together with Bethlen, he organized the diplomatic preparations for the 1927 discussion at the League of Nations on the optants case.[28]

The Bethlen government had already complained to the League of Nations about a Transylvanian estate in July 1922, but it could initially count on very little sympathy. The Secretary General, the British Eric Drummond, acknowledged in a confidential letter sent to the British delegation that "Hungarians are discriminated against unfairly by the agrarian law, inasmuch as the law is applied in a more severe form in Transylvania than in Old Romania," but he added that although Romania must be made to respect international law, "we do not wish to appear as protagonists on behalf of big Magyar landlords."[29] The League of Nations therefore chose a middle path. Following the Hungarian petition submitted on March 15, 1923, it decided that the Hungarian complaints should be examined by a mixed Hungarian-Romanian executive committee. However, the Romanians sabotaged the endeavor by playing for time and roundly rejecting the international lawyers proposed by the Hungarians. It seemed that the Hungarian government was left with few options, and it was even mooted that Hungary should leave the League of Nations in protest.[30] Finally, under pressure from the Great Powers, Romania agreed to the forma-

---

26 Romsics, *Bethlen István*, 188.

27 MNL OL, K27, Minutes of the Council of Ministers, October 15, 1928, 22–25.

28 MTI News Release, June 26, 1927. See also the correspondence between Bethlen and Teleki on the optants case, in particular Teleki's letter to Bethlen of January 23, 1927 and Bethlen's letter to Teleki of January 31, 1927. MNL OL, K468-1927-1931-B/17. The optants' association functioned within the framework of the formidable OMGE (Hungarian National Economic Association), which represented agricultural producers.

29 Cameron J. Watson, "Ethnic Conflict and the League of Nations: the Case of Transylvania, 1918–1940," *Hungarian Studies* 9, nos. 1–2 (1994): 173–80.

30 Watson, "Ethnic Conflict and the League of Nations."

tion of the executive committee in late 1924/early 1925. This raised the hope that there would finally be meaningful negotiations in the case of the landowners.[31]

However, in the next two years, the mood in Geneva worsened over the Hungarian-Romanian conflict. Romania threatened to leave the League of Nations if it was forced to pay large-scale reparations. Hungarian diplomacy, however, maintained its position that Romania must be made to recognize that international law was above the law of individual states. In the context of international law, the Hungarian landowners had to be compensated even if the confiscation of the Hungarian estates had been otherwise "lawful" under the terms of the Romanian land reform law.[32] The Hungarian position acknowledging the superiority of international law meant, however, that the Hungarian government could not then reject the judgement of the international community in the matter of the numerus clausus.

Hungarian diplomacy and its liabilities

It was at this time, concurrently with the hopeful news about the optants issue, that it became known that Lucien Wolf had submitted another petition to the League of Nations in the matter of the numerus clausus, in January 1925. It could be foreseen that if the Council of the League were to put the issue of the numerus clausus back on the agenda, the outcome for the Bethlen government would not be positive, since Hugh Bellot's negative opinion as well as the Tripartite Commission's negative opinion were by now both complete. There was the danger, then, that this could impact badly on the judgement of the other griev-

31 On September 5, 1925, the Council of the League of Nations placed the complaints concerning the optants case on its agenda. The Romanian party offered a sum in compensation which, although it was nowhere near the value of the estates, served to acknowledge that Romania did owe compensation. MTI News Release, September 16, 1925, 16.

32 In the end, the optants were awarded compensation by The Hague in January and April 1930 according to Bethlen's wishes. This, however, came at the price of the Hungarian government being obliged to pay 13.5 million gold crowns a year from 1943 to 1966 into a special fund which would be primarily intended to compensate the expropriated landowners. See Anikó Kovács, "Adalékok a magyar revíziós mozgalom történetéhez," *Regio: Kisebbség, politika, társadalom* 5, no. 3 (1994): 70–94. The burden of extra compensation was a diplomatic defeat. Ignác Romsics says that Bethlen's opposition, among them Rassay and the Social Democrats, "were entirely justified in pointing out that Bethlen was making post-Trianon Hungary pay for the landowners who had lost their estates in the dissolution of historic Hungary. The sad moral implications of this are not changed by the fact that following the collapse of the international financial system, the Great Powers cancelled all outstanding debts in 1932 and therefore the compensation for the Hungarian optants also did not come to pass." Romsics, *Bethlen István*, 188.

ances—among them the optants issue—that the Hungarian government had submitted to the League of Nations. György Lukács, who was representing the optant landowners in Geneva, drew attention to this: "The international community does not view this restrictive law positively, rather, in fact it sees it as sinister reaction. . . . The numerus clausus law, about which the international community is very well informed, not only makes our own task more demanding, it often downright paralyses the effect that our efforts might otherwise achieve."[33]

Following up on Lucien Wolf's petition, the League of Nations placed the numerus clausus law on its agenda at the beginning of November 1925.[34] Bethlen, however, wanted to avoid at all costs having the Council of the League declare the law to be contrary to international law. He decided on a drastic step—he gave the Hungarian Jewish community the task of preventing the law from being placed on the League's agenda. He called on the Jewish community in Budapest to have the Jews of Hungary—the very people wronged by the law—protest against the League of Nations considering the matter. He expected the Hungarian Jewish protests to take the edge off international objections and help prevent the League of Nations coming to a negative resolution on the numerus clausus law. Bethlen himself drafted the text of the protest and sent it to the Jewish community on November 17, 1925. He wanted the community to endorse the following points: "The Hungarian Jewish community would like to state that they have not, and are not, turning to the League of Nations in the matter of the numerus clausus. Hungarian Jewry considers this to be an internal matter and reject all foreign intervention. The Hungarian Jewish community would like to make clear that it has not entrusted the representation of its interests to anyone in Geneva, and denies the merit of the petition submitted there."[35]

"Our nation's grief cannot be the fountainhead of our law"

The Jewish community was sharply divided over Bethlen's draft. The majority leaned towards working with the prime minister, but Vilmos Vázsonyi, the doyen of Jewish politicians, was opposed. He was opposed primarily because he did not wish to discredit Lucien Wolf's five-year struggle. But Vázsonyi even-

---

33 Bethlen, *A magyar zsidóság almanachja*, 65.

34 MTI News Release, November 3, 1925, 5.

35 Szabolcsi, *Két emberöltő*, 364.

tually relented, on the condition that he himself would redraft Bethlen's text. This was the birth of that famous declaration which historiography has ever since held to be the patriotic creed of Hungarian Jewry, without properly taking into account the circumstances under which it was drafted.

This forced protest changed significantly under Vázsonyi's hand. Not only was the language embellished, but the text also contained new ideas. It ran:

> The equality before the law of our religion is part of the Hungarian constitution. Our civil and political rights were accorded by the free Hungarian legislature, and it was that same legislature that inscribed us on the roll of recognized religions. For this reason, we will rely in our fight against the institution of the numerus clausus solely on the Hungarian constitution and do not wish to invoke, nor will we invoke, the article of the Peace Treaty concerning religious equality. We are Hungarian, we believe ourselves to be part of the Hungarian people and the Peace Treaty, which is our nation's grief, cannot be the fountainhead of our law. . . . We want to settle the matter of the numerus clausus at home, with our own government and our own legislature. Therefore, we have sought out no international body and will seek out no international body for help, and even if [such help] would come out of good intentions, we will reject it of our own accord.[36]

The declaration, as redrafted by Vázsonyi, was intended to serve as the basis, in principle, for cooperation between the Jewish community and the government. The Hungarian Jews agreed not to turn to the minority protection system of the League of Nations.

In itself this statement of principle very much conformed to Vázsonyi's conservative liberal ideals, since he was skeptical of international minority protection anyway. He believed that the Hungarian Jews would be wrong to rely on international minority rights protection agreements in their fight for their rights. By doing so, they would effectively be admitting to a view they wished to deny: that the Jews were a minority, separate from the body of the Hungarian nation. This—in Vázsonyi's opinion—would have been a step back towards the pre-emancipation state of affairs, when the legal status of Jews was governed by special laws. An end to discrimination, therefore, had to be achieved not on the

36 Szabolcsi, *Két emberöltő*, 366.

basis of minority rights, but on the basis of the constitutional right to equality for all citizens. It was not a case of looking for new laws, but of reinstating the equality before the law that was guaranteed by emancipation. Vázsonyi believed that it was up to Hungarian society to neutralize the devotees of the numerus clausus from within, in such a way as to demonstrate the strength of political will behind the repeal of the discriminatory law. He believed that the Bethlen government had to make a public break with the race defenders.[37]

Figure 18. Vilmos Vázsonyi.
Source: Wikimedia Commons.

Vázsonyi's declaration was at the same time a stand against the Treaty of Trianon. Since the Jews were part of a common Hungarian nation, they could have no interests that diverged from the interests of the "Hungarian nation." The Jews, therefore, could have no recourse to foreign protection based on the Treaty of Trianon. They could have no recourse to the protection offered by that same League of Nations that had forced the unjust peace treaty on the country. If the entire nation was suffering, then no individual group within the nation could consider the Treaty of Trianon a legitimate basis of law. They could not seek legal remedies on its basis, because the equal rights of Jews could not derive from the "diktat" of Trianon, since "whatever does not come voluntarily can have no value."[38]

This element of Vázsonyi's declaration was aimed not only at the Entente powers and Western countries but—in an indirect way—at the Bethlen government itself. Vázsonyi was well aware that at the time of the Jewish community's declaration, Hungary was seeking legal redress for grievances in several cases at the League of Nations, primarily in the case of the optants and the Hungarian minorities living in the successor states. The demand that the Jews should reject the "intervention" of the League of Nations was at odds with the

37 Vilmos Vázsonyi's speech in parliament, December 17, 1925, in *Vázsonyi Vilmos beszédei és írásai*, vol. 2 (Budapest: Országos Vázsonyi-Emlékbizottság, 1927), 450–51.

38 "The numerus clausus is not merely a matter for the Jews, but for the nation and democracy," in Vázsonyi, *Vázsonyi Vilmos beszédei és írásai*, 446.

standpoint of the Hungarian government in the optants case and the grievances of the Hungarian minorities, where Hungarian diplomatic efforts were focused precisely on achieving effective intervention by the League. In the optants case, the government expected the League to force Romania to pay compensation for the Hungarian estates in Transylvania they had redistributed. The legal basis for this was none other than the Treaty of Trianon. Ultimately, then, Bethlen expected the Hungarian Jews to acknowledge the Hungarian government's monopoly on political relations with the League of Nations and recourse to the Treaty of Trianon as a source of international law.

Bethlen's foreign policy strategy, even independently of the numerus clausus issue, was heavily attacked domestically. The radical right did not like it that Bethlen acknowledged the Treaty of Trianon as a legitimate legal source and thus accepted the legitimacy of the new borders too. They accused him of subordinating the country's foreign policy—which in their opinion should have been working towards the revision of the borders—to particular group or private interests. By doing so, they felt, he had lost sight of the primary goal, which was the revision of the borders. When, therefore, the government relied on the Treaty of Trianon in the optants case, it was short-changing the country by giving up the necessary fight for the revision of the borders. "I personally do not know and will not accept an optants case or any foreign policy goal," Károly Wolff, representative of the Christian Economic and Social Party, said in parliament, "for which Hungarian society should renounce its right always and in every circumstance to raise its voice in protest against the Treaty of Trianon."[39] More cutting even than Wolff was the correspondent of the Kolozsvár-based periodical *Korunk* (Our Times), who said that the government's every step was guided by the progress of the optants case, because the Hungarian Foreign Ministry had "turned into the lawyers' office for the optant landowners."[40]

Geneva, 1925: The Hungarian government makes a promise

In the end, the Jewish community's declaration, which aimed at preventing the League of Nations putting the numerus clausus on its agenda, not only failed to

39 Minutes of the parliamentary session of December 6, 1927, in *Az 1927. évi január hó 25-ére hirdetett országgyűlés képviselőházának naplója*, vol. 7: 240.

40 Miklós Horner, "Az utolsó tíz év magyar külpolitikája," *Korunk* 5, no. 10 (October 1931): 731–35.

do so, it did not even delay the move. The League did not accept the Hungarian government's position that the Hungarian Jewish community's declaration removed all cause for the petition. The Council of the League considered the matter on December 10, 1925. Bethlen did not wish to be present at the meeting. Although he had been in Geneva up to the day before, only Minister of Religion and Public Education Kunó Klebelsberg represented Hungary at the meeting.

Klebelsberg delivered a lengthy address which, though full of apologetic evasion, nevertheless struck a conciliatory tone. He declared that since the Hungarian Jewish community had protested against the discussion of the matter, the petition should not even have been considered. Nonetheless, concerning the law he declared that "in the view of the Hungarian government . . . this is not a permanent legal institution, but a temporary legal measure derived from our post-Trianon situation, and which is open to change once our social and economic life regains its former stability."[41] In his address, Klebelsberg interchanged terms freely, using "numerus clausus" to refer to the official allocation of places in higher education, but also to refer to the nationalities quota, or to the Jewish quota. Which of these he promised to amend and the deadline to which the government intended to keep itself in this respect, he left vague. Nonetheless, the Council, taking into account that the government was prepared to modify the law, accepted the response and urged the government to change the law as soon as possible.[42]

Lucien Wolf considered the League's decision promising. Klebelsberg's draft resolution which aimed to change the law when Hungary's economic and social life "had regained its former stability" was modified by the Council to read that the law had to be changed "in the near future." Wolf also found it positive that the Council of the League clarified that they did not expect Hungary to change the whole numerus clausus law, but merely repeal the discriminatory quota in its third clause. With this—almost five years after the birth of the law—the Council of the League put an end to the Hungarian government's tactical antics, whereby it responded to protests about the Jewish quota not by arguing for its legitimacy, but by arguing for the legitimacy of creating a state numerus clausus system to restrict the number of students overall.[43]

---

41 MTI News Release, December 10, 1925, 1.

42 Ladányi, "A numerus clausus-törvény 1928. évi módosításáról," 1123.

43 "Lucien Wolf Regards the League Decision in Hungarian Numerus Clausus Question Favorable to Jews," *Jewish Telegraphic Agency, Daily News Letter*, February 2, 1926.

Klebelsberg never shied away from adapting his words to please his audience. It was nonetheless surprising that the minister, who had been so ready to compromise in Geneva, should return home and strike a decidedly anti-Semitic tone in parliament, since he had not previously been known for making such remarks in public. In his speech reporting on the meeting in Geneva, however, he called Lucien Wolf "that foreign Jew," while digging up the idea of the collective guilt of Hungarian Jews for the revolutions, saying that the supporters of the numerus clausus had nothing to fear, since "we've learned from the past and I can reassure everyone in this country that we will never again be forced to eat squash and barley [like the population had to during the food shortage after World War I]."[44]

Klebelsberg's anti-Semitic tone was very surprising to the authors of Vázsonyi's declaration on behalf of the Jewish community, published barely a month before. Vázsonyi himself gave vent to his anger in parliament:

> When we made this declaration . . . we were aware of the risk that it would serve to reinforce the government's position when the numerus clausus issue was discussed in Geneva, that it would rely upon it, and in this we were not disappointed. . . . But I could hardly have expected that the Honorable Minister of Education, who made the most of this declaration in Geneva, who made use of it, would strike a tone of hatred and mockery the second he was back on home territory . . . and would prove disloyal to those whose declaration he made such use of in Geneva.[45]

Vázsonyi also made it felt that he saw a contradiction between Prime Minister Bethlen's conciliatory tone and Minister of Education Klebelsberg's anti-Semitic statements. But he rejected the idea that the Hungarian Jews had to be partners in this "game." "I cannot distinguish between the Prime Minister and the Minister of Education as long as the latter is a member, nay the pride of his cabinet . . . Politics must be played out in public and one cannot be the secret intimate counsel of the liberals while the other is the secret intimate counsel

---

44 Minutes of the parliamentary session of December 16, 1925, in *Az 1922. évi junius hó 16-ára hirdetett nemzetgyűlés naplója*, vol. 38: 193–94.

45 Vilmos Vázsonyi's speech in parliament, December 17, 1925. In Vázsonyi, *Vázsonyi Vilmos beszédei és írásai*, 446–47.

of racial defense. . . . We have to know once and for all the direction this government is taking."[46] This, however, as it turned out, was not yet in the cards.

During the course of the following year, the government eased the implementation of the Jewish quota in minor matters. Klebelsberg instructed the universities by telephone not to include converted Jews within the framework of the Jewish quota.[47] He then—still by telephone—instructed that the 6 percent quota of Jews should be calculated based not on the number of students actually enrolled but on the original official allocation of places.[48] By doing so, he increased the number of Jews who could be admitted, since numerous university faculties were unable to fill their official allocation of spaces with Christian students, and the number of students actually enrolled was therefore lower than the official allocation of places as made public.

There were also changes in the tone of the political elite itself. In November 1926, Bethlen was already saying that the equality of the Jews "must not in any way be impaired."[49] The numerus clausus law had to be modified because, as he said, no one will be able to dispel "with any kind of dialectic or formula" the feeling of injustice felt by the Jews on account of the numerus clausus.[50] But with the passage of time it also became obvious that in 1926 the government would not commit itself to the repeal of the Jewish quota or the amendment of the law.

It was now Lucien Wolf's turn once again. In October 1926, he told Lóránt Hegedűs, who had been minister of finance in the early 1920s, that the White Paper on the discriminative practices of the numerus clausus that he was editing was now ready. If the Hungarian government did not change the law, Wolf wrote to Hegedűs, he would present the White Paper to the League of Nations in December.[51] Hegedűs passed all this on to Bethlen, stating: "I would find the most fitting and most European solution to be if the Hungarian government repealed this unfortunate and unchristian law of its own accord before then." He added that as a "liberal Christian," he would be willing to contact the "leaders of Hungarian Jewry" and ask them to work together to persuade Lucien Wolf to put off a renewed approach to the League of Nations. For this, of course, he

46 Vázsonyi, *Vázsonyi Vilmos beszédei és írásai*, 450–51.
47 Ladányi, "A numerus clausustól a numerus nullusig," 57.
48 Ladányi, "A numerus clausus-törvény 1928. évi módosításáról," 1124.
49 Ladányi, "A numerus clausus-törvény 1928. évi módosításáról," 1124–25.
50 Ladányi, "A numerus clausus-törvény 1928. évi módosításáról," 1125.
51 Lóránt Hegedűs was minister of finance from December 1920 to September 1921 initially under the first Teleki government and subsequently under the Bethlen government.

wrote, it would be necessary for Klebelsberg to apologize to Wolf, who had been "cut to the quick" after Klebelsberg called him "that French Jew" in parliament.[52]

Bethlen was not averse to Hegedűs's suggestion, but Klebelsberg did not want to take the path he suggested because, as he wrote to Bethlen on November 3, "it would be an unnecessary luxury to be indebted to Lucien Wolff [sic] and domestic Jewry." Klebelsberg went on to point out that the Hungarian government could hardly change the international interpretation of the law anyway, since its third clause really did "run counter to the clauses on minority protection and will not be permanently sustainable in its current form." If Wolf took the case to the International Court in The Hague, the Hungarian government could not hope to win. "The law will therefore have to be revised," Klebelsberg concluded—the only question was when. He suggested a date after the elections in December 1926, to prevent the amendment becoming a campaign issue. He was certain that Lucien Wolf would have no objection to this date and would agree to delay the submission of the White Paper to the League of Nations until after December 1926.[53] In his letter, Klebelsberg also wrote that as a result of the amendment, the situation must not be allowed to arise where "we unleash thousands of Jewish university students on the nation." He indicated that he would recommend several new ways of curtailing the enrollment of Jewish students. As an example, he mentioned merely that in future, greater emphasis must be placed on grades for physical education and comportment during the admissions process.[54]

The amendment

But Bethlen did not want to wait any longer. Following this correspondence, he announced publicly in November 1926 that the law would be modified.[55] A government deputy, Baron József Szterényi, suggested convening a conference of

52 Loránt Hegedűs's letter to Count István Bethlen, October 22, 1926, in Szinai and Szűcs, *Bethlen István titkos iratai*, 255–56. Klebelsberg, in fact, called Wolf a "foreign" and not a "French" Jew.

53 Count Kunó Klebelsberg's letter to Count István Bethlen, November 3, 1926, in Szinai and Szűcs, *Bethlen István titkos iratai*, 256–57.

54 Szinai and Szűcs, *Bethlen István titkos iratai*, 256–57.

55 István Bethlen's campaign speech at the Vigadó, November 16, 1926. In his speech, Bethlen referred to a promise to amend the law made by Klebelsberg at the meeting of the Council of the League of Nations a year before. Bethlen's speech is recorded by Ladányi, "A numerus clausus-törvény 1928. évi módosításáról," 1125. See also N. Szegvári, *Numerus clausus rendelkezések*, 173. Bethlen's position was described in more detail in articles published on November 1 and 20, 1927 in the paper *Pes-*

the governing party in December 1926, where he would introduce a motion to solve the question once and for all and pull the "poisoned tooth" of the numerus clausus.[56] But nothing happened. When five months after Bethlen's announcement, on May 13, 1927, deputy Béla Fábián introduced another motion to modify the numerus clausus in parliament, the motion was defeated just as it had been so many times before.

With the autumn admissions cycle for the 1927 academic year, the Jewish quota entered the seventh year of its enforcement. At the same time, the optants case entered its fifth year, with Romania—despite a warning from the League of Nations—continuing successfully to sabotage a solution. The Bethlen government decided at the beginning of 1927 to report Romania at the League of Nations. On September 2, the Council of the League announced that it had placed the Hungarian-Romanian dispute on its agenda.[57]

Lucien Wolf was not idle. Two days after the optants case was placed on the agenda, on September 4, he approached the Secretary General of the League of Nations with a submission from the Alliance Israélite Universelle, in which he pointed out that the Hungarian government—despite its earlier promise in 1925—had still not modified the numerus clausus law. Lucien Wolf also sent the Secretary General a personal letter on September 14 and on October 7 lodged a formal protest with the League.[58] In accordance with its rules, the Council

---

ter Lloyd. On the Unity Party's meeting of October 19, 1927, at which Bethlen announced his intention to amend the law, see MTI Press Survey, October 20, 1927, 9–10.

56 MTI Weekly Release, December 7, 1926, 2.

57 The Council of the League of Nations discussed the optants case on September 17 and 18, 1927. MTI Press Survey, September 19, 1927, 2. The Hungarian delegation wanted the League to nominate a judge in place of the judge recalled by Romania, because the executive committee could not function without him. The League's position was that Romania's recall of the judge was not without basis, because the bilateral committee had overstepped its mandate. In response to this, Albert Apponyi recommended that the legal case around the mandate be referred to the International Court in The Hague. The Council of the League once more called upon the two parties to agree among themselves. On September 18, they adjourned the discussions for another two months, until December. Although there were several speeches about the Hungarian-Romanian conflict in November in the British parliament, which were supportive of Hungary's position, and the idea that Romania's behavior was too rigid in the matter was gaining ground elsewhere in Europe too, Bethlen and his colleagues could not count on the unequivocal support of any of the Great Powers. At their meeting in December, the Council of the League delayed the matter once more, but by then a solution acceptable to the European Powers had taken shape. This was that the Hungarian state should compensate the optants itself, in lieu of some of its reparations payments. Bethlen at that time found this solution unacceptable, since the compensation would thus come from the coffers of the Hungarian state. Romsics quotes Bethlen as saying: "Under no circumstances would I be willing to burden Hungary with a sum of which any part would end up in my pocket." Romsics, *Bethlen István*, 187.

58 Ladányi, "A numerus clausus-törvény 1928. évi módosításáról," 1126.

of the League was obliged, in response to this petition, to place another discussion of the issue on the agenda for its next meeting, in December 1927.

Lucien Wolf's timing was spot on. There was already one Hungarian item on the agenda for the December meeting, since the League had delayed discussion of the optants case until this same Council meeting.[59]

Thus, by September 1927, an unusual foreign policy situation had developed. The League of Nations had put both Hungarian issues on the agenda for its next Council meeting in December. Thus, the agenda included both the issue of the Jews affected by the numerus clausus and the issue of the Hungarians affected by the actions of Romania. In the former, the Hungarian government was the defendant, in the latter—the plaintiff. The Bethlen government was now faced with a dilemma. If it wanted favorable progress in its compensation case, it could not allow itself to be censured at the very same meeting by the League.

Bethlen made a decision. At a meeting of the Unity Party on October 19, 1927, he announced that the government would remove the restrictions on Jews from the numerus clausus law in order to put an end to "the measures that have caused a significant amount of distaste and opprobrium to a part of the citizens of Hungary."[60] The universities received instructions to take half a percent more Jewish students than they had been doing up to that point.[61] A few weeks later, Bethlen gave a report on the law's expected amendment and the reasons behind it at a meeting of the Christian Economic and Social Party. In it, he stated: "The government wishes to avoid having the Hungarian delegates at the December meetings of the Council of the League of Nations being put into a potentially embarrassing situation by the issue of the numerus clausus."[62]

The far right greeted this decision with fury. Gyula Gömbös stated in so many words that the "reference to the international scene" was unacceptable: "The international community should first resolve the issue of the Hungarian optants and ensure the rights of the Hungarian minorities. Then we can talk

59 The Hungarian government, with the knowledge that justice was on its side, tried to ensure that the case be referred to the Hague Court at the December meeting of the Council of the League of Nations. MTI Press Survey, September 23, 1927, 40. The Romanian position was that the optants cases were private property suits over which the bilateral executive committee approved by the League of Nations had no jurisdiction. The Hungarian position was that the League should have compelled the Romanians to cooperate with the bilateral executive committee, or else refer the case to the International Court in The Hague. MTI Press Survey, September 21, 1927, 52.

60 MTI Press Survey, October 20, 1927, 9.

61 *Magyarság* [The Hungarian People], October 20, 1927, 2.

62 MTI Press Survey, November 17, 1927, 12.

about whether the League of Nations has any right whatsoever to interfere in domestic Hungarian politics."[63]

Klebelsberg was no stranger to the idea. The minister of education therefore repeated Bethlen's action of two years earlier: he called on Sándor Lederer, the head of the Jewish religious community, for the Hungarian Jews to again publicly protest against the "intervention" of the League of Nations in the matters of the numerus clausus. However, the stormy discussion led to Lederer's collapse and death.

But Bethlen would not be turned. The text of the amendment was ready by November 1927, and Bethlen took it to the League's Council meeting in Geneva himself. The first part of his campaign worked—he managed to get the discussion of the numerus clausus removed from the Council meeting's agenda.

The second part of the campaign, the issue of Romanian compensation, dragged on for another three years before the League decided in favor of it. During this time, the Hungarian government took careful pains that there should be at least enough improvement in the situation of Jewish applicants that it could present an overwhelming case in the event of diplomatic enquiries. The admissions issue was treated by the government as one of special diplomatic importance. The government ordered that the Foreign Ministry—that is, not the Ministry of Religion and Public Education—should be notified by telegram of the admissions decisions from all the universities in Hungary on the day that they were made. Needless to say, they were required to include breakdowns by religion.

In the weeks following the announcement of the amendment, Bethlen and Klebelsberg held a series of talks with influential opponents of the amendment, Gyula Gömbös and Pál Teleki among them. The minutes of the meetings are not known, but we can assume that at these discussions Bethlen and his colleagues explained the plan for the amendment. According to the plan, they would replace the Jewish quota with a professional quota that would continue to permit the implementation of anti-Jewish restrictions. It is to this that Gömbös was referring when, speaking to the press after the meetings, he said that "the Jews will long to have the current form of the numerus clausus back."[64]

---

63 *Magyarság*, October 21, 1927, 2.

64 MTI Press Survey, November 18, 1927, 13.

The eradication of the "yellow badge"

Bethlen was keen to cool the expectations associated with the amendment not only in private, but in public too. The prime minister would "not play a double game," as the press quoted him saying during his speech to the conference of the Unity Party.

> As to the question of what the practical effects of the amendment of the law will be, he replied that . . . the hopes attached by certain liberal circles to the amendment will in practice be somewhat disappointed. The Hungarian Jewish community should for the moment content itself with the thought that those measures which have been harmful to them, that they have felt to be a yellow badge, will be removed by the government. For this much, the government will publicly take responsibility—as for the rest, they should leave that to the future.[65]

Bethlen generally avoided criticizing the soon-to-be repealed Jewish quota itself on a moral basis. His public speeches do not say that the repeal of the Jewish quota was motivated by a restitution of the equality before the law that had heretofore been impaired, and that this was something he himself considered important. He did acknowledge the importance of the amendment from the point of view of the Hungarian Jews, but on a purely pragmatic (and not a moral) basis, saying that "the Jewish community needs to be reassured, so that they don't feel humiliated."[66] In the end, he presented the amendment as an enforced measure imposed on the country from outside, not born of the inner convictions of the country's leaders. It is difficult to decide with the numerus clausus issue whether Bethlen truly did not see, think, or believe that the principle of equality before the law had really been impaired by the Jewish quota, or whether he was merely silent on the question for tactical reasons. In any case, it is a fact that a decade later, in the spring of 1937, when he condemned the draft of the First Jewish Law in parliament, the jumping off point for his argument was that "equality before the law is an absolute requirement" and that the tensions around the "Jewish question" can only be addressed in "sober, intel-

65 The meeting took place on November 17. MTI Press Survey, November 18, 1927, 13.
66 MTI Press Survey, November 17, 1927, 13.

ligent, considered [ways], that do not infringe on the right to equality before the law."[67] Whether he considered the numerus clausus such a "sober, intelligent" measure, he did not say.

Like Bethlen, Regent Miklós Horthy presented the amendment of the numerus clausus as a foreign policy necessity. There are no extant records of a direct discussion between Horthy and Bethlen, but Horthy's speech recorded in the press on December 5, 1927, does remain. While the draft of the proposed amendment submitted by Bethlen was being studied in Geneva, a group of students led by Pál Teleki went up to Buda Castle to celebrate the regent's name day. "In possession of the trust that the youth has so many times . . . expressed to me," said Horthy to the students, "I can expect them to trust in the direction of their future, placed in the hands of the men I have selected to govern the country. The years of youth are years of learning. All your energy should be directed towards learning. Do not let matters whose connection to our country's important interests you cannot be aware of disturb you in your work."[68] Horthy's intended meaning was clear. The amendment of the "measure," that is the Jewish quota, was happening not because the quota itself was not right but because it was necessary for reasons of foreign policy.

Like Bethlen, Klebelsberg was also concerned to present the future impact of the amendment as negligible. He made a public promise, which was to come true, that "the law will mean a change in the racial proportions of barely a few tenths of a percent."[69] In this respect, the prognosis from Klebelsberg, who was for the repeal of the Jewish quota, was not much different from that of Pál Teleki, a staunch opponent of its repeal. According to the Budapest correspondent of the Viennese *Arbeiter Zeitung*, Teleki said at a meeting of race defender university students that "although the numerus clausus law will be changed in form, the restrictions it imposes will nonetheless remain."[70]

There were nonetheless serious tactical differences in the positions of Bethlen, Klebelsberg, and Pál Teleki. Bethlen and Klebelsberg were looking for compromise in both domestic and international politics, while Teleki was utterly

67 Minutes of the parliamentary session of May 11, 1937, in *Az 1935. évi április hó 27-ére hirdetett országgyűlés képviselőházának naplója*, vol. 13: 64.

68 MTI News Release, December 5, 1927.

69 Klebelsberg's statement was made in the corridors of parliament. *Ujság*, November 24, 1927, 5. Quoted by Anna Kéthly in her parliamentary speech on February 10, 1928, in *Az 1927. évi január hó 25-ére hirdetett országgyűlés képviselőházának naplója*, vol. 9: 15.

70 MTI Press Survey, October 31, 1927, 12.

determined. Bethlen and his colleagues could not calm his objections even during the confidential talks. Even arguments failed to convince him of the necessity of keeping on good terms with the League of Nations, although Teleki was heavily involved with the concerns of the Hungarian minorities in the lost territories and was Bethlen's close ally in developing the diplomatic strategy for the case of the optants. Teleki was accused in parliament of inciting the university students against the government, of giving his signature to the students' poster they had put up opposing the amendment, and of not calming the university unrest unleashed by the right-wing fraternities in November, which saw Jewish students beaten, having their documents checked, and being prevented from entering the universities.[71]

Figure 19. Lajos Méhely. Source: Wikimedia Commons.

Teleki was joined by numerous professors who also openly opposed the amendment. Lajos Méhely, the dean of the Faculty of Humanities, encouraged the students at the Turul Alliance's general meeting on October 24 "not to yield an inch" in the numerus clausus affair, saying that "as long as the university has an official council, and as long as that council is led by the people who lead it now, you will never be left to yourselves in this fight. We, too, will be sure to do our Hungarian and our Christian duty."[72] Many of the professors, however, took Bethlen's side. While the dean of the Faculty of Humanities organized resistance to the amendment, the rector of the university, Ernő Fináczy, stood up to the anti-Semitic students forcefully, and threatened "withdrawal from their studies" for those breaching the peace. In Debrecen, Protestant bishop Dezső Baltazár threatened to terminate accommodation in the Protestant halls of residence for those who caused

71 On the issue of the posters, see Ablonczy, *Teleki Pál*, 280; and *Ujság*, November 25, 1927, 6.
72 *Magyarság*, October 25, 1927, 1.

trouble.[73] The professors who took part in the leadership of the far-right fraternities, and who by doing so encouraged the organizers of the disturbances, were also condemned by Kunó Klebelsberg (although anonymously). He asked "those leading the youth from outside the student framework" to refrain from "firing up" the students."[74]

But none of that moved Teleki. In the parliamentary debate on the amendment in the spring of 1928, he sharply rejected the proposal. In his speech to the upper house, he presented an argument based on racial theory that would brook no compromise. In it, he put himself openly at odds with the conservative viewpoint concerning the maintenance of constitutionality. He denied that legality must be observed at all costs, since the law, in his words, was a "crutch," a "fence," but never a "real force of life." If the law and "reality" end up at odds with one another, then the law can no longer "be brought up as a proof of a universal reality, or a denial of it." In other words, the law dictating the equality of all people was for Teleki not "all-powerful." He branded arguments based on universal equality before the law "impossible," since "the races have different characteristics" and "despite all external changes, the original spirit of a race remains indestructible." Society had no need of superfluous "forms of politeness" which merely serve to mask the "racial struggle" that was raging in reality. For this reason, he considered the amendment of the numerus clausus law to be a mistake based on the "conventional lies of the cultured" and, as he put it, "there can be no compromise on this basis."[75]

Teleki could only enforce his views a decade later, with the so-called Second Jewish Law in 1939. For the moment, it was Bethlen's position that triumphed and the government sought a pragmatic compromise both with the League of Nations and the Hungarian Jews. The disturbances caused by the amendment of the numerus clausus were quelled by the Bethlen government within a few weeks, although they broke out every subsequent autumn during the admissions process. The minister of education told the rectors of the universities that if the disturbances continued, he would close the universities. The dean of the

73 *Magyarság*, October 27, 1927, 7.

74 Minutes of the parliamentary session of November 23, 1927, in *Az 1927. évi január hó 25-ére hirdetett országgyűlés képviselőházának naplója*, vol. 7: 29.

75 Minutes of the March 13, 1928 session of the Upper House, in *Az 1927. évi január hó 25-ére hirdetett országgyűlés felsőházának naplója* (Budapest: Athenaeum Irodalmi és Nyomdai Részvénytársulat, 1927), vol. 2: 105–10.

Budapest Faculty of Humanities, Lajos Méhely, who openly supported the actions of the right-wing fraternities, was reprimanded by Kunó Klebelsberg.[76] The scandals slowly subsided, but the government decided to delay the amendment itself to the spring of 1928 because of the disturbances. It was no longer urgent, in any case, since Bethlen had achieved his original foreign policy goal. On December 2, 1927, he took the draft of the amendment with him to Geneva and thus managed to get the discussion of the law removed from the agenda for the December meeting of the League of Nations. Bethlen promised in Geneva that the amendment would be passed in the spring. He was true to his promise: on February 9, 1928, he made it clear at a meeting of the governing Unity Party that he expected the members of the party to vote for the amendment, or else he would resign his position. The die was cast.

The professional quota: "A legerdemain, a risky game"

The amendment was debated in the lower house in February 1928 and in the upper house in March. Twenty-five deputies made speeches during the debate, and only five of them supported the motion. Six of them, including Gyula Gömbös, attacked the draft with well-worn arguments of racial defense. More interesting were the fourteen Liberal and Social Democratic contributions, which made it clear that the introduction of the professional quota could lead to further discrimination.

The amendment repealed clause three of the law, which contained the quota for nationalities and races. It replaced this with another quota, which limited the number of students who could be admitted according to the profession of the applicant's father.[77] The numbers behind the professional quota were estab-

76 ELTE Archives, d9212/1927–28, meeting of the Faculty of Humanities of the Royal Hungarian Pázmány Péter University, June 1, 1928.

77 "When granting admission, in addition to the requirements of loyalty to the nation and moral reliability, consideration shall be given, on the one hand, to the previous academic results and intellectual abilities of the applicant, and, on the other, to the requirement that primarily war orphans and the children of those who have completed combat duty, in addition to the children of public employees and those of the various professions (agriculture, industry, trade, liberal professions, etc.) in accordance with the number and importance of those belonging to these professions, should be admitted to institutions of higher education and that the number of those admitted should be fairly distributed among the various municipalities." In *Az 1927. évi január hó 25-ére összehívott országgyűlés felsőházának irományai*, vol. 4: 434. In his justification for the law, Klebelsberg expanded on the preference granted to public employees and agrarian workers: "We must also ensure that primarily the children of war widows and those who have undertaken combat duty and furthermore

lished in such a way as to ensure that the proportion of Jews could not significantly rise under the new system either. Under the new quota system, the children who benefited were those whose fathers were employed in professions which had a low proportion of Jews to begin with (for example, civil servants and agrarian workers). As the Social Democrat Dániel Várnai said, the introduction of the professional quota was a "risky game" since it openly stated that "one profession has more right to education than another."[78]

That restrictions on the Jews would remain even after the law was modified was something the government was—for understandable reasons—unwilling to talk about in public in 1928. The very reason behind the amendment was so that Hungary could no longer be censured by the League of Nations for discriminating against the Jews. Ten years later, however, when Hungarian diplomacy was less sensitive to the feelings of the Western Powers, the president of the Central Statistical Office, Alajos Kovács, described in detail the inner logic and mechanism of the professional quota created in 1928. According to this description,

> the milder form of the numerus clausus initiated by the late Count Klebelsberg, minister of religion and public education, fundamentally served the same purpose . . . though it did not explicitly say that each race was to be admitted to university according to its proportion within the population overall. . . . Since in the first [professional] category, which accounts for about half the students, there are hardly any Jews, while in the other half of places . . . it would have been the children of the agrarian workers who were in a majority . . . in the end, the proportion of Jews in the student body would have been roughly equal to their proportion within the population overall.[79]

---

those of public employees whose families have habitually pursued professions should be admitted in appropriate numbers to higher education. We must give each professional field its fair share of the opportunity to attend university. And we should look not only at their proportion but also, it goes without saying, at their importance. Thus, agriculture, which plays such an important role in our society as the country's chief producer, must be given its due respect." "Explanatory memorandum to the 'Draft Amendment to Law No. XXV of 1920 on the regulation of enrollment at the universities of arts and sciences, the University of Technology, the Faculty of Economics of the University of Budapest, and law academies,'" *Az 1927. évi január hó 25-ére összehívott országgyűlés felsőházának irományai*, vol. 4: 435–37.

78 Minutes of the parliamentary session of February 10, 1928, in *Az 1927. évi január hó 25-ére hirdetett országgyűlés képviselőházának naplója*, vol. 9: 4.

79 Kovács, *A csonkamagyarországi zsidóság*, 39.

The logic behind the professional quota did not escape Lucien Wolf's attention either. "We cannot say that we are totally satisfied with this draft," Wolf wrote about the amendment, "but it does remove all reference to differentiation by nationality or religion from the law . . . and this is what we asked for. The new categories included in the law seem to be superfluous . . . and the possibility exists that they could be used for anti-Semitic purposes. At the moment, however, we are not trying to criticize this." The point of departure had to be that the Hungarian government had acted "in good faith."[80] The League of Nations therefore did not pay any further attention to the intentions behind the new—professional—quota. It was merely content that the Jewish quota had been removed from the law.

The government, then, did not openly declare the logic behind the professional quota in 1928—as summarized by Alajos Kovács. But liberal and left-wing critics saw the situation plainly. Their opponents did so too, like the anti-Semitic rector of the University of Technology, Kálmán Szily. Szily argued for the necessity of introducing the professional quota by saying that without it "the proportion of Jews would once again without doubt reach 30 percent, as it did before the war, for there is no reason why it should not. The proportion of Jews and Christians in secondary education is exactly the same to this day."[81] Szily was right. On the basis of the sociological reality in Hungary and the educational habits of Jews, the conclusion really was that if there were no restrictions, a quarter to a third of university students would once again be drawn from among the Jews. The minor relaxation in the first three years of the professional quota should be measured against the reality sketched out by Szily.

The liberal critique

The Liberal critique of the introduction of the professional quota was best summarized in parliament by the Democratic Party's Marcell Baracs.[82] His considered statement was a significant rhetorical achievement, accompanied by shouts of "bravo" from the Liberal and Social Democratic aisles. For the later

80 Ladányi, "A numerus clausus-törvény 1928. évi módosításáról," 1130–31.

81 Minutes of the March 13, 1928 session of the Upper House, in *Az 1927. évi január hó 25-ére hirdetett országgyűlés felsőházának naplója*, vol. 2: 118.

82 As a well-known lawyer of Jewish origin, Marcell Baracs was representative of the Independent National Democratic Party from 1927 to 1933.

reader, it is simply astonishing how Baracs's predictions proved to be justified in almost every respect. The amendment, Baracs said,

> is pure illusion, a distraction, a *legerdemain*. The title will change but the *machtpolitik* will remain, the collar is different but the hound is the same.... The only difference will be in the justification. They won't take a single Israelite youth more at the universities than they did before, but while this was justified up to now with reference to the proportions of the religions—or rather, more precisely, the races and nationalities, to quote the language of the law—from now on, it will be the factors of the quota in the new law that will achieve the same goal. The offence remains, only the formula changes. The government wants to get rid of a formula that is causing it legal difficulties, in order nevertheless to maintain the effectively harmful, illegal, and unlawful measure.[83]

Even if Baracs's prognosis about there not being "a single Israelite youth more" was not correct, since the number of Jewish students increased somewhat after the amendment, he was correct in that Jewish students could still not expect to be judged on their academic results. He was also right in predicting that thousands of Jewish students would continue to be excluded from admissions.

Baracs also foresaw that whatever was to happen in the future, it would be more and more difficult to stand up to anti-Jewish discrimination, because after the amendment, discrimination would come in a more indirect, hidden way. As he put it, "what was illegal up to now will be cloaked in a greater appearance of legality."[84] He was also right in that the fragile coalition that had held together the Hungarian Jewish politicians and organizations for the last eight years in the common fight against the Jewish quota would break apart. "There will be a whole lot of Jews—perhaps even official Jewish bodies—who will believe the government, just as there is always a gentleman who believes that the handsome stranger hiding in his bedroom closet is indeed 'just waiting for the

83 Minutes of the parliamentary session of February 10, 1928, in *Az 1927. évi január hó 25-ére hirdetett országgyűlés képviselőházának naplója*, vol. 9: 6.

84 Minutes of the parliamentary session of February 10, 1928, in *Az 1927. évi január hó 25-ére hirdetett országgyűlés képviselőházának naplója*, vol. 9: 6. Although Baracs did not go into it, his argument was further supported by the fact that the most recent data available for the detailed numbers of the professional quota were from the 1920 census, and the law made no provision for the solution of this issue.

bus.' Everyone will believe who burns with the desire to believe, everyone will believe who has grown tired in the struggle for belief and for whom any excuse is enough to give up the fight."[85] The Hungarian Jews would lose the support of the League of Nations too, since "the yellow badge" had been removed from the law, and therefore the discrimination had seemingly been halted.

Baracs's critique was complemented in one important point by the Social Democrat Anna Kéthly.[86] She found it unacceptable that the law still made reference to the "loyalty to the nation" as a prerequisite for admission. With that, the universities maintained the opportunity created in 1920 to deny someone entry whose politics was not to their liking. Kéthly calculated that the young people applying in the autumn of 1928 were eight or nine years old in 1919, and that therefore probing into their political behavior at the time was absurd. But it was just as unacceptable that young people be potentially punished for the sins of their fathers. With the passing of the years—Kéthly said—people would soon be able to judge the "loyalty to the nation" of people who had been babes in arms in 1919.[87]

The parliamentary debate on the amendment had no real stakes. Since Bethlen had enjoined the Unity Party to vote, parliament finally accepted the amendment on February 24, 1928, by 139 votes to 34, with the governing party voting unanimously in favor. The sole Jewish member of the Unity Party, Géza Dési, left the chamber at the start of the vote, because he could not allow himself to vote for a law that continued the numerus clausus. Although the Jewish members of the upper house, Immánuel Löw and Samu Glückstahl, voted against the amendment, a majority of the upper house also passed it.[88]

Jewish popular opinion greeted the amendment with disappointment. They made their feelings felt by inflicting a humiliating defeat on Géza Dési, who was running for the presidency of the Budapest Jewish Community at the time with Bethlen's backing, by a margin of 6,669 votes to 338.[89] This was the

85 Minutes of the parliamentary session of February 10, 1928, in *Az 1927. évi január hó 25-ére hirdetett országgyűlés képviselőházának naplója*, vol. 9: 9.

86 Elected in 1922 as the second female member of the National Assembly, Anna Kéthly was one of the most prominent politicians of the Social Democratic Party during the interwar era.

87 Minutes of the parliamentary session of February 10, 1928, in *Az 1927. évi január hó 25-ére hirdetett országgyűlés képviselőházának naplója*, vol. 9: 16–17.

88 MTI Press Survey, February 25, 1928, 11.

89 Szabolcsi, *Két emberöltő*, 402–3; and Lajos Szilágyi's address at the parliamentary session of February 28, 1928, in *Az 1927. évi január hó 25-ére hirdetett országgyűlés képviselőházának naplója*, vol. 9: 228.

Jewish community's commentary on Bethlen's position that the Jews should content themselves with the fact that the government had removed the "yellow badge" from the law and should "leave the rest to the future."[90] The 1928 election within the Jewish community suggested that the Jews did not place much faith in the future that Bethlen promised.

The League of Nations and the amendment

The international Jewish organizations shared their Hungarian coreligionists' concerns. In March 1928, they submitted a new petition to the League of Nations in which they drew attention to the possibilities for discrimination hidden within the amendment. But the League was no longer willing to engage with the issue; they considered the matter of the Hungarian numerus clausus closed and consigned it to the archives.[91] The League considered the repeal of the Jewish quota a symbolic victory and had not expected much more.[92] Rusztem Vámbéry characterized the Hungarian government's tactics in his bitter article "Numerus Clausus Country" in *Népszava* by saying that the leaders of Hungary base their thinking on the idea that "with their cunning little brains, they'll outwit the silly English and the retarded French who will doubtless buy that a hierarchical ranking of your father's profession guarantees equality before the law and freedom to study. . . . Clearly, there is some deeper Christian truth hidden in the idea of the son of a registrar getting more easily into university than a smallholder's or a shopkeeper's. . . . It is inconceivable that the League of Nations, which is after all a union of predominantly Christian peoples, should not understand this."[93] The "silly English" and "retarded French" did not accept all this without difficulties, but the amendment undoubtedly gave them an opportunity to be rid of the problem of the numerus clausus—at least for the moment.

Lucien Wolf lived for only another two years after these events, and he was therefore not forced to witness the destructive twists in the fate of European Jews that were soon to come.

---

90 MTI Press Survey, November 18, 1927, 13.

91 MTI Press Survey, March 20, 1928, 27.

92 MTI News Release, March 19, 1928, 17–18.

93 *Népszava*, November 20, 1927, 3.

Discrimination after the amendment of 1928

The government was trying, for the moment, to keep both the domestic and the international scenes happy. After 1928, in line with the expectations of the League of Nations, they increased somewhat the number of Jews allowed in higher education, but only to an extent that would not put them into sharp opposition with the race defenders at home. In the next four years, the number of Jewish students admitted rose by around 250 people a year, from 8.8 percent in 1928–29 to 9.6 percent in 1930, 10.5 percent in 1931, 12.3 percent in 1932, and 12.5 percent in 1933. The reports of the admissions boards, which contained the breakdowns of the Jewish/non-Jewish student numbers, had to be sent by telegram to the foreign ministry, almost like dispatches from the front line.

None of this, however, meant in any way that Jewish students had actually obtained a level playing field with their non-Jewish colleagues. After 1928,

Figure 20. Lecture at the Royal Hungarian Pázmány Péter University (University of Budapest) by professor of geography Jenő Cholnoky in 1930. The photo was taken during a period of temporary relaxation of numerus clausus, which might explain the great number of female students, sitting in the front rows. Source: Fortepan, 29869, Tamás Cholnoky.

around two thirds (70 percent) of Jewish applicants were rejected by the universities, while the same figure was 10–15 percent for the Christian students. The majority of Jews with secondary school diplomas still did not have opportunities for higher education.

Thus, despite the Bethlen government's apologetic arguments for foreign consumption pointing out that the proportion of Jewish students had risen above the previous quota, there was no mention of the fact that fully two thirds of the Jewish applicants wishing to pursue further studies could not get into university even now. A cynical propaganda war was fought with the numbers and percentages, because while the proportion of Jewish students at 10–12 percent really was higher than the 6 percent mandated by the former Jewish quota, these percentages revealed nothing about how many Jewish students were excluded during the admissions process and on what basis. They also did not shed any light on whether the 10–12 percent proportion came about as a result of admissions decisions or because during the great depression the number of Christian students dropping out was even greater than before without increasing the number and proportion of Jews admitted during the first-year admissions process. In the end, despite the populist propaganda of the percentage proportions, thousands of Jews who wanted to pursue further study ended up outside the universities.

The fight for—and against—outstanding students

Because of the academic counter-selection created by the Jewish quota, there were a large number of Jewish students after 1920 who were not admitted to university, despite having completed their secondary school studies with excellent grades. It is telling that while the universities in general had quite a high proportion of students admitted with weak secondary school diplomas, the decree implementing the amended law nonetheless had to specify that "those with excellent grades for their secondary school diplomas should be admitted, if possible, to university."[94]

Many outstanding Jewish students, however, were still denied entry. Certain universities, like the Faculty of Medicine in Budapest, simply ignored

94 ELTE Archives, Documents of the Rector's Office, 3110/1928/29, ministerial letter no. 76.687/1928 by Kunó Klebelsberg, October 15, 1928. Decree 53 000/1928 is quoted in Ladányi, "A numerus clausus-törvény 1928. évi módosításáról," 1134.

Table 14. Proportion of admitted and rejected applicants (Jewish/non-Jewish) for the 1928-29 academic year

Faculty	Admitted Christian applicants (%)	Rejected Christian applicants (%)	Admitted Jewish applicants (%)	Rejected Jewish applicants (%)	Total number of students in 1926 (for comparison)
University of Budapest					
Faculty of Law and Political Science	46.8	53.2	38.1	69.1	2,222
Faculty of Medicine	81.5	18.5	15.5	84.5	1,729
Faculty of Humanities	81.2	18.8	43.0	57.0	1,065
Department of Pharmaceutics	97.5	2.5	44.4	55.6	216
University of Debrecen					
Faculty of Law and Political Science	100.0	0.0	36.6	63.4	314
Faculty of Medicine	83.1	16.9	18.6	81.6	356
Faculty of Humanities	98.6	1.4	57.0	43.0	113
University of Pécs					
Faculty of Law and Political Science	76.9	23.1	18.2	81.8	369
Faculty of Medicine	100.0	0.0	4.8	95.2	309
Faculty of Humanities	97.7	2.3	70.0	30.0	82
University of Szeged					
Faculty of Law and Political Science	83.3	16.7	28.4	71.6	502
Faculty of Medicine	93.3	6.7	13.8	86.2	361
Faculty of Humanities	88.3	11.7	50.5	50.0	138
Faculty of Mathematics and Natural Sciences	100.0	0.0	66.7	33.3	n.d.
Department of Pharmaceutics	100.0	0.0	53.3	46.7	42
University of Technology					
Faculties of engineering and architecture	98.0	2.0	28.3	71.7	2,068
Faculty of Economics	74.5	25.5	57.0	43.0	56

Source: MNL OL, K.636 1928-23-69628

Klebelsberg's instructions. They continued to favor Christians with weaker results from secondary schools over Jews with excellent results. In 1928–29, the Faculty of Medicine in Budapest rejected 30 applicants with excellent results (presumably Jews) while it accepted 189 people with satisfactory results and 115 who had either failed or retaken their exams. There were similar incidents at other faculties, too. No Christian applicants were rejected at the pharma-

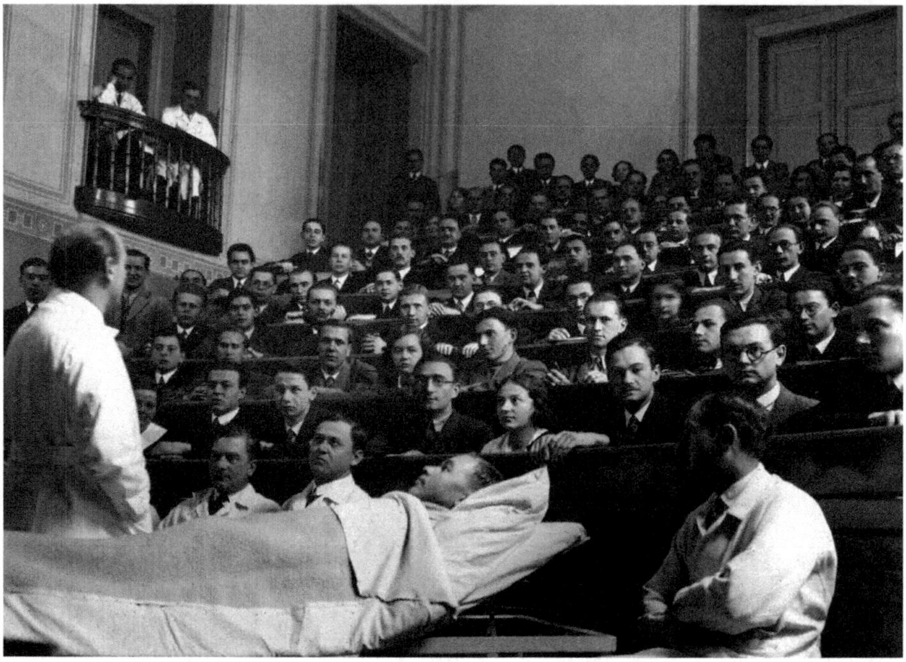

Figure 21. The lecture hall of the clinic of the Royal Hungarian Elizabeth University (University of Pécs) in 1928. Source: Fortepan, 130210, Pécs University of Medicine.

ceutical and mathematics faculties of the University of Szeged or at the Faculty of Medicine in Pécs and the Faculty of Law in Debrecen. At the same time, the proportion of Jews rejected from the medical faculties of all three universities exceeded 80 percent. Almost all Christian applicants were accepted at the University of Technology, the pharmaceutical faculties of the universities of Budapest and Szeged, and the faculties of humanities at the universities of Debrecen and Pécs. Jewish applicants were rejected in high numbers—above 70 percent—at the law faculties of the universities of Pécs and Szeged and at the University of Technology. There were courses, for example, the mathematics or pharmaceutical sciences at Szeged, where—once all the Christian applicants had been accepted—they also accepted 50–70 percent of the Jewish applicants, though these were smaller courses.

The government seemed incapable of getting the universities to cooperate in meeting the obligations it had undertaken towards the League of Nations. There was the threat of a diplomatic scandal, since theoretically there was no Jewish quota in this admissions cycle, yet the results testified to the continuation of a seriously discriminative practice. Eight years of the implementation of the numerus clausus could not be brought to an end overnight with a half-hearted and ambivalent amendment.

This was despite Klebelsberg's efforts by this time to improve the proportion of Jews admitted to university. He warned the rector of the University of Budapest, Alajos Wolkenberg, by means of a highly confidential letter delivered by one of his subordinates that it was not desirable "for [reasons of] international and domestic politics" that the "rejection of Jews with excellent secondary school diplomas" become an issue.[95] He even increased the official allocation of places so that those Jews with excellent secondary school diplomas would find a space. His efforts were nonetheless in vain. The Faculty of Medicine was subsequently only willing to take three out of ten Jews with excellent results, while the Faculty of Humanities took none.[96] Following this, Klebelsberg instructed the universities in a ministerial rescript to accept fourteen Jewish students he indicated by name, publicly naming them in parliament as well. One of the fourteen, Pál Turán—later a world-famous mathematician—was still perplexed decades later that his place at university had to have been secured through parliament.[97] In the end, 88 more Jewish students went to university in 1928 than had been able to the year before, while the total number of students grew compared to the year before by 216 (to 15,675). Although the proportion of Jews among all university students grew, the increase was practically negligible, the proportion going from 8.3 percent to 8.8 percent (see table 15). But even the admission of these extra 88 students required Klebelsberg to go on the warpath. The day after the Jewish students were ordered to be admitted, bloody fights broke out at the universities and the universities in Budapest, Pécs, and Debrecen had to be closed for a few days.

The situation was similar in the following academic year, 1929–30. At numerous faculties, even the majority of Jews with better academic results were rejected. At the Faculty of Medicine in Budapest, of 58 applicants with excellent results, 30 were rejected; these were most likely Jews. At the Faculty of Medicine in Debrecen, 90.5 percent of Jewish applicants were rejected, while at Szeged the number was 87.8 percent. Among them were six applicants with excel-

95 Quoted in Ladányi, "A numerus clausus-törvény 1928. évi módosításáról," 1137.

96 Minutes of the parliamentary session of October 17, 1928, in *Az 1927. évi január hó 25-ére hirdetett országgyűlés képviselőházának naplója*, vol. 15: 239.

97 Information provided by Miklós Ajtai.

lent grades.[98] The head of the admissions board at the Faculty of Medicine in Budapest, Balázs Kenyeres, turned to Zoltán Magyary, advisor to the Ministry of Religion and Public Education, in a confidential memorandum, to explain why it was impossible to make the admissions decisions on a meritocratic basis and accept all applicants with excellent grades. The document captures the situation that came into being in the numerus clausus issue after the amendment of 1928, when the Bethlen government was no longer prepared to risk the international opprobrium of open discrimination against Jews. At the same time, the leaders of the universities and the Ministry of Religion and Public Education continued the old practices behind closed doors, out of the public eye and in an almost conspirational manner. The situation was clear: since an admissions system based on academic performance alone would not have produced the desired racial composition, the Faculty of Medicine kept to the old practice.

The fight for the admission of those with excellent grades went on. Klebelsberg went on the warpath once more. By raising the official allocation of places, by making it possible to transfer between universities, and by his letters to the rectors, he tried to ensure that Jewish students with excellent grades were not excluded from admissions. It was an almost daily struggle with some universities and faculties, and the final result was that 95 more Jewish students attended university that year than the year before. The acceptance of these students led to renewed protests and violence.

All this was unpleasant for the government on an international level, since it had committed itself since 1927 to ending the discrimination against Jewish youths. The cabinet itself discussed the renewed outbreaks of anti-Semitism at the universities in 1929. Foreign Minister Lajos Walkó complained that "from the point of view of a favorable outcome for us in the reparations case now being discussed . . . the country's prestige is markedly harmed by the constant protests and persecution of Jews at the polytechnics."[99] Bethlen called on Klebelsberg to put an end to these anti-Semitic incidents. Klebelsberg promised to do so, although he also felt strongly that the time had not yet come to remove the restrictions imposed by the numerus clausus.[100]

98 Ladányi, "A numerus clausus-törvény 1928. évi módosításáról," 1139.

99 MNL OL, K27 19291025, Minutes of the Council of Ministers, October 25, 1929, 42–43, https://www.eleveltar.hu/digitalis-tartalom?source=preservica&ref=f0881689-f03d-426a-b397-1838ae142dae.

100 MNL OL, K27 19291025, Minutes of the Council of Ministers, October 25, 1929, 42–43.

Table 15. Number and proportion of Jewish students among higher education students, 1927–1943

Academic year	Total number of students	Number of Jewish students	Percentage of Jewish students
1927/1928	15,459	1,290	8.3
1928/1929	15,675	1,378	8.8
1929/1930	15,497	1,473	9.5
1930/1931	16,053	1,689	10.5
1931/1932	16,002	1,967	12.3
1932/1933	15,766	1,965	12.5
1933/1934	15,694	1,816	11.6
1934/1935	15,088	1,465	9.7
1935/1936	14,216	1,175	8.3
1936/1937	13,821	1,017	7.4
1937/1938	13,228	820	6.2
1938/1939	13,219	510*	3.9
1939/1940	13,815	437*	3.2
1940/1941	17,161	52*	3.1
1941/1942	19,900	584*	2.9
1942/1943	21,732	580*	2.7

Source: Hungarian Statistical Yearbooks, 1910–1943; and Kovács, *A csonkamagyarországi zsidóság*, 73. For the data marked with *, see Ladányi, "A numerus clausustól a numerus nullusig," 68.

But Bethlen did not want any more conflict around the numerus clausus issue. On the occasion of his trip to London in 1930, he offered to meet with Lucien Wolf, with whom he had tea at the Hungarian Embassy on June 18. He told Wolf that "the unhealthy postwar mentality is happily in abeyance now in Hungary and the position of the Jews will now become completely normal."[101] Lucien Wolf found the meeting reassuring. There was "only one problem" with Bethlen, he told the editor of *Egyenlőség*, Lajos Szabolcsi, a few weeks later, when summarizing the meeting, "he doesn't want to keep his post. He's tired, and he's bored of office."[102] It was the end of an era. Wolf died that same year, at the age of 73, and Bethlen did indeed resign his post as prime minister the following year. Kunó Klebelsberg, the minister of education, departed with him. The global financial crisis affected Hungary too.

The easing of the numerus clausus lasted another two years, until the admissions cycle of the 1931–32 academic year. The proportion of Jews among the

101 Szabolcsi, *Két emberöltő*, 425.
102 Szabolcsi, *Két emberöltő*, 426.

first years had started to grow noticeably by 1931, while their numbers had gone up to almost 2,000 in the student body overall by 1931–32. It is true that the more than 12 percent proportion of Jews reached twice during the years of easing was nowhere near the 30 percent proportion that would have been reached had restrictions been completely removed, based on the realistic expectations of the university leaders of the day (given their reading of secondary school statistics and the contemporary sociological situation). The tendency, nonetheless, was towards improvement. The proportion of Jews in the first year at all the universities of arts and sciences, the University of Technology, the law schools, and the polytechnics rose from 9.5 percent in 1929–30 to 12.5 percent in 1932–33, before starting to dip once more (see table 15).

The universities did not abide by the proportions of the professional quota when making their admissions decisions even in the years of easing. Rather, they calculated the proportion of Jews in the academic year using the old methods and then applied a slightly more lenient quota than 6 percent in their admissions decisions. Klebelsberg's biographer, József Huszti, summarized this in the following way: "[the new (professional) quota] would have required such complicated statistical calculations for its strict implementation and was so vague (perhaps deliberately so), opaque, and open to abuse that it was basically unusable in practice. Thus, the practice remained more or less what it had been before the new law, especially since admissions were still managed by the old authorities at the universities and polytechnics."[103]

The strengthening of discrimination in higher education after 1934

Bethlen's direct successor, Count Gyula Károlyi, carried on his policy. On taking office, he declared that the country's political life could not return to its anti-Semitic focus even after Bethlen's departure. "It is also my personal conviction," he said in his introductory speech to parliament, "as it is the conviction of the whole government that we must not discriminate between the religions in any way in this country."[104] Klebelsberg's immediate successors, Sándor Ernszt (August–December 1931) and Jenő Karafiáth (December 1931–September

103 József Huszti, *Gróf Klebelsberg Kunó életműve* (Budapest: MTA, 1942), 197.

104 Minutes of the parliamentary session of August 27, 1931, in *Az 1931. évi július hó 18-ára hirdetett országgyűlés képviselőházának naplója*, vol. 1: 357.

Figure 22. Minister of Religion and Public Education Bálint Hóman (standing in the center, third from left) at the signing of the Hungarian-Finnish cultural agreement in 1937, with undersecretary Kálmán Szily (former rector of the University of Technology, on the far left). Source: Fortepan, 177050, Sándor Bojár.

1932) followed Károlyi's lead as ministers of education. The changes came with the formation of the Gömbös government (October 1932) and Bálint Hóman taking on the role of minister of religion and education, also in October 1932.

After the admissions cycle in the autumn of 1932, when the usual anti-Semitic student disruptions started again, Hóman and Gömbös were still using Bethlen's methods. Those universities, such as Debrecen, where Jewish students were abused, were threatened with closure, which had the desired effect of calming the disturbances.[105] But one could tell from Hóman's public statements right from the start that he did not share the basic principles of Bethlen's politics of compromise. Although he did not consider the repeal of the 1928 amendment of the numerus clausus law timely, he dropped a number of hints that as minister he would endeavor to ensure that the original 6 percent racial quota would be implemented. During the first autumn of his tenure as minister, he instructed the universities to be "rigorous" in their admissions process,

105 For a detailed description of the disturbances, see Ladányi, "A numerus clausustól a numerus nullusig," 59–60.

which led to a significant and immediate drop in the proportion of Jewish students. By the second autumn of his tenure, he was discussing plans for reforms in his speech to parliament that would affect secondary schools as well and which would allow the 6 percent quota to be implemented after all. "We must make absolutely sure," he said, "that there will be no difference in the ratio of Hungarian Christian youth to Jewish youth in university compared to the national ratio."[106]

Hitler's assumption of power galvanized the Hungarian anti-Semitic student organizations, which led to their actions becoming more violent in the autumn of 1933. The leadership of the universities used these student movements to protest the government's cutbacks more than once. When Bálint Hóman—responding to the financial crisis—announced in the autumn of 1933 a reduction in the higher education budget, reduced financial support for the provincial universities, and the closure of 25 faculties, the anti-Semitic disturbances that broke out at the University of Debrecen (most threatened by the cuts) were even more serious than usual.[107] The disturbances later spread to the capital, and the Budapest University and the University of Technology were both closed. Gömbös finally dealt with the anti-Semitic disturbances by promising the anti-Semitic student organizations that the universities would in practice implement the original 1920 Jewish quota, but added that his government was not considering repealing the 1928 amendment.[108]

A month later, in January 1934, Minister of the Interior Ferenc Keresztes-Fischer, announced to the cabinet that "in the coming year, the Jewish quota will be enforced."[109] According to the minutes, Keresztes-Fischer did not need to do any explaining. He did not need to clarify what "Jewish quota" he had in mind. He did not have to deal with the fact that in theory, such a "quota" did not exist in law following the amendment of 1928, since everyone present at the cabinet meeting knew exactly what the "quota" was that was going to be "enforced."

106 Bálint Hóman's address at the parliamentary session of November 29, 1933, in *Az 1931. évi július hó 18-ára hirdetett országgyűlés képviselőházának naplója*, vol. 18: 332.

107 MTI News Release, October 30, 1933, 11–12.

108 The journal of the Turul Alliance reported this in the following way: "It was Gyula Gömbös who ensured the enforcement of the numerus clausus in the future, which it was impossible to achieve for ten years under the Bethlen-Klebelsberg regime." Quoted in Ladányi, "A numerus clausustól a numerus nullusig," 63.

109 MNL OL K27, Minutes of the Council of Ministers, January 16, 1934, 5.

Table 16. Number and proportion of Jewish students in higher education institutions in all year groups and among first years, in the second semester of each academic year, 1931–1942

Academic year	Jewish students		First year Jewish students	
	number of	percentage of	number of	percentage of
1931/1932	1,967	12.3	672	14.1
1932/1933	1,965	2.5	547	11.6
1933/1934	1,816	11.6	387	8.4
1934/1935	1,465	9.7	228	5.5
1935/1936	1,175	8.3	230	5.8
1936/1937	1,017	7.4	248	6.1
1937/1938	820	6.2	188	4.6
1938/1939	510	3.9	109	2.4
1939/1940	437	3.2	n.d.	n.d.
1940/1941	532	3.1	n.d.	n.d.
1941/1942	574	2.9	203	2.6
1942/1943	580	2.7	188	2.3

Source: Ladányi, "A numerus clausustól a numerus nullusig," 68.

Following the minister of the interior's announcement, the proportion of Jewish students immediately began to decrease. By the next year, 1935, it reached the lowest proportion recorded in the 1920s (8.3 percent), while thousands of Jewish applicants were excluded from the higher education system. The process now became linear. The proportion of Jewish students decreased to 7.4 percent in 1936, 6.2 percent in 1937, 3.9 percent in 1938, 3.2 percent in 1939, 3.1 percent in 1940, 2.9 percent in 1941, and 2.7 percent in 1942. In the autumn of 1938, when the First Jewish Law was passed, the proportion of Jews allowed into the first year of higher education was a mere 2.4 percent, and this proportion decreased further in the following years.

Despite the drastic decrease in the proportion of Jewish students at university after 1934, disturbances broke out again and again during the autumn admissions cycles, as if to prove that the anti-Semitic movements could not be satisfied with the reduction in the proportion of Jewish students. By then, only a public and unequivocal stand by the country's leaders could have mitigated the anti-Jewish hatred and attacks, but no such stand was forthcoming. On the contrary, the education portfolio was in the hands of a politician—Bálint Hóman—who took an active part in drafting the Jewish Laws. The exclusion of Jewish students now proceeded undisturbed, their proportion among the overall student body shrinking to under 4 percent by the 1938–39 academic year. This, too, served to demonstrate that there was significantly stricter discrimination in the admissions process than the 6 percent quota. For this reason, there was in fact no practical significance to the fact that there was no explicit Jewish quota in higher education included in the First Jewish Law of 1938.

This was despite the fact that the First Jewish Law extended the thinking behind the 1920 numerus clausus to almost all fields of economic life and the liberal professions. It capped, with the aid of a quota, the maximum proportion of Jews among white-collar workers in businesses and other liberal professions (doctors, lawyers, engineers, etc.). The quota capped the participation of Jews at 20 percent and said that as long as the proportion of Jews is higher, Jews can only be hired for new positions up to a maximum of 5 percent. This First Jewish Law followed such a familiar pattern for Hungarian public opinion, accustomed over the last two decades to the numerus clausus, that the law was dubbed "the 20 percent numerus clausus" at the time.[110]

Minister of Religion and Public Education Bálint Hóman, who was responsible for the universities, played a serious role in expounding the ideology of the First Jewish Law. It was he who, before the introduction of the bill for the First Jewish Law in parliament, declared as the official position of the government, the day after Prime Minister Kálmán Darányi's speech in Győr, the anti-Semitic idea familiar from the early 1920s, that "the Jews are disproportionately represented in economic and cultural life." He also resurrected the accusation of Jewish collective responsibility for the "revolutionary movements." He presented the Jewish Law then being prepared—just as its proponents had the numerus clausus before it—as a tool that the government was intending to deploy in order to "defuse the anti-Semitic mood."[111] The editor of the far-right journal *Összetartás* (Unity) captured the significance of the changes heralded by Hóman when he wrote: "We are particularly pleased that a serving minister has come out and said that the Jews are an alien body in this country, and that an end must be put to this impossible and dangerous situation."[112] Hóman also reported on a meeting where Prime Minister Darányi tried to convince—without success—Minister of Justice Andor Lázár to cooperate in intro-

110 Claudia K. Farkas, *Jogok nélkül: A zsidó lét Magyarországon, 1920–1944* (Budapest: Napvilág Kiadó, 2010), 47.

111 Bálint Hóman's speech at the Csongrád county office meeting of the governing party in Szentes, MTI News Release, March 6, 1938, 6–10.

112 Quoted in Andor Ladányi, "Az első zsidótörvény megszületése," *Múlt és Jövő* 21, no. 2 (2010): 105.

ducing the First Jewish Law. Despite Hóman's active role in the creation of the First Jewish Law, this did not, after all, reinstate an explicit Jewish quota at the universities. The 6 percent university quota for Jews did not fit with the First Jewish Law—for this law established a higher Jewish quota of 20 percent in all the fields that came under its aegis. The Second Jewish Law, in 1939, brought this quota down to 6 percent in the graduate professions and thus it became possible to reinstate the original 6 percent quota from 1920 within this law.

The reinstatement of the Jewish quota for the universities: The Second Jewish Law

The explicit Jewish quota was in the end reinstated by the seventh clause of the Second Jewish Law in 1939.[113] As opposed to the original Jewish quota of 1920, which the first Teleki government hid within a general "nationalities" quota system out of concern for its international reception, the second Teleki government in 1939 had no such international qualms about anti-Semitic measures. The openly anti-Jewish quota was introduced within the framework of a general anti-Jewish law that impacted on all sections of the economy.[114]

The university quota itself changed little compared to its predecessor from nineteen years before. The 1939 law extended the quota to those polytechnics which had not come under the aegis of the 1920 law. This, however, had little practical impact, since there was already serious discrimination in place at all the higher education institutions. The goal of the measure was explained by

113 "§ 7. Jews may be admitted to the first year of university and college courses only in such proportions that the number of Jewish students (educatees) does not exceed six percent of the total number of students (educatees) admitted to the faculty (department) of the university or college in question, and twelve percent of the total number of students in the Department of Economics and Commerce of the Faculty of Economics of the Palatine Joseph University of Technology and Economics. This provision shall not apply to students (educatees) of the faculties of theology at universities and the colleges of theology." Zehery and Térfy, *A zsidók közéleti és gazdasági térfoglalásának korlátozásáról*, 110. According to the implementing decree—in contrast with the 1920 numerus clausus law—the Jewish quota was to be applied at the arts colleges as well, and the concept of "first-years" was expanded to include those higher-year students who were applying to a specific course or faculty for the first time.

114 Law No. IV of 1939 banned Jews from being employed by the state, from teaching and working in the press, as well as occupying "leading" positions in the theatre. Paragraph 9 established a 6 percent quota in the graduate professions. It called for a review of all official trade and industrial licenses and capped the proportion of Jews at 6 percent for industrial licenses. It also restricted Jews to a maximum of 6 percent of state tenders and ordered agricultural real estate in the hands of Jews to be handed over. Additionally, it capped the number of Jews in white collar positions in private firms at 12 percent.

Minister of Justice András Tasnádi Nagy: "The law should be explicit about the numerus clausus—which so far has only been enforced through practice—and it should be set at 6 percent."[115]

The new law put the quota at 6 percent once more, but by then the proportion of Jews studying at universities and polytechnics nationwide was already well under this figure, at 3.9 percent. There was only one course that was exempt from the 6 percent quota under the new law. The quota for the economics and trade course at the economics faculty of the Palatine Joseph University of Technology and Economics had a quota of 12 percent and not 6 percent, in order to comply with clause 17 of the Jewish Law, which capped the number of white-collar workers at privately-owned enterprises at 12 percent. A confidential directive issued at the time of the introduction of the Second Jewish Law by Department V/I of Hóman's ministry set a quota of 6 percent for admissions to the first year of secondary school as well, since, as the directive argued: "From the spirit of Law No. IV of 1939 it follows that Jewish pupils [in secondary schools] may be admitted only up to proportion of the Jewish population of the country in relation to the Christian population."[116] Numerous secondary schools created A and B classes, the Christian students being put in the A class and the Jews in the B class. Jewish children were banned from the Scouts and the cadet corps.

The general justification for the Second Jewish Law was put forward by Pál Teleki.[117] But it was Bálint Hóman who—a year later, in November 1940—gave a review of the entire twenty-year history of the numerus clausus in explaining the new law regulating the university admissions process.[118] Hóman's review agrees entirely with the picture that emerged from the sources reviewed during the writing of this book.

To begin with, Hóman stated that the purpose of the 1920 numerus clausus was "to ensure that the number of Jews flooding into the graduate professions to

---

115 The parliamentary committee meeting is quoted in Ladányi, "A numerus clausustól a numerus nullusig," 67.

116 K. Farkas, "Az elkülönítés látható falai," 86–87. For the directive, see MNL OL, VKM K 592-1940-3-54654.

117 Claudia K. Farkas, "Zsidótörvények—egy egyházi ember szemével," in *Fiatal egyháztörténészek írásai*, ed. Csaba Fazekas (Miskolc: Miskolci Egyetem BTK Újkori Magyar Történeti Tanszék, 1999), 194–23.

118 The law concerned the "regulation of university and polytechnic admissions" and repealed the numerus clausus law of 1920 as well as its 1928 amendment, since after the regulations introduced in the Second Jewish Law, there was no need for them.

an alarming degree is restricted on the benches of the universities and colleges to a level corresponding to the proportion of the Jews in the country overall." He then explained that the law had to be modified "in the face of the constantly growing economic pressure from abroad and the pressing force of an increasingly hostile international opinion," but that the new law of 1928 suspended the "restrictive measures applied to the Jews" only "formally." He described the 1928 professional quota as "an indirect tool" of restricting the Jews:

> These measures [i.e., the professional quota] represented an indirect emergency measure in circumstances where (because of the international situation outlined above) direct legislative action against the flood of Jews into the graduate professions was not advisable. This was why, instead of explicitly naming the Jews, it was necessary to give preferential treatment in university and polytechnic admissions to the children of those social classes most in need of protection from the spread of Jewry.

Hóman also explained that after 1928, the Ministry of Religion and Public Education implemented restrictions on Jews through the use of temporary measures: "In the implementation of Law No. XIV of 1928, my predecessors in office continued to maintain the restriction on the admission of Jews to universities and polytechnics by means of case-by-case measures until the issue was given new and more comprehensive legal regulation by the creation of Law No. IV of 1939."[119]

The introduction of the Second Jewish Law—true to Hóman's description—did not bring great changes, since by the time of its introduction in 1939, the proportion of Jews at the country's universities had fallen to well below the 6 percent quota, at approximately 3 percent. Nonetheless, the anti-Semitic student organizations and the politicians of the far-right demanded that the government go further down the road they had started on and exclude all Jews from the universities, imposing a numerus nullus. Hóman approved of this demand in parliament and did not in fact permit the admission of Jews to several faculties (medicine, humanities, mathematics, and natural sciences) at the

119 Explanatory memorandum to the draft law on the "regulation of university and polytechnic admissions," November 15, 1940, in *Az 1939. évi június hó 10-ére összehívott országgyűlés felsőházának irományai*, vol. 4: 187–88.

reorganized University of Kolozsvár after the reannexation of Transylvania following the Second Vienna Award in 1940.

The wartime governments, notwithstanding, did not legislate for a numerus nullus until 1944, though it is true that there were hardly more than a few dozen Jewish students at the universities anyway. The situation only changed following the German occupation of Hungary in March 1944, when Regent Miklós Horthy handed power to the government of Döme Sztójay. Although the Sztójay government suspended the academic year in April 1944 because of the military situation, it still took the trouble to order the introduction of the numerus nullus in the universities on May 20 (after the deportation of the Jews had started). This, however, no longer had any effect in practice. At the beginning of the autumn semester, in September 1944, the minister of education for the Lakatos government, István Rakovszky, banned the enrollment of Jewish students.[120] A few weeks later, the Arrow Cross took power; two weeks later, teaching was once more suspended.

As the frontline approached, the universities shut their doors, and thus the movement to exclude Jewish students, which had begun in 1920, was in the end fulfilled with a numerus nullus in institutions now devoid of students and teachers alike.

The Jewish quota of the numerus clausus—despite a slight and temporary easing—was in force throughout the Horthy era. For fourteen years out of this twenty-five year period, it was enshrined in law: from 1920 to 1928 and again from 1939 to 1945. It was implemented in a somewhat less stringent and hidden way within the framework of the professional quota between 1928 and 1933, and though it was not officially in force in the five years from 1934 to 1939, it was nonetheless enforced through ministerial directives even more stringently than it had been in the 1920s. The implementation of the law was therefore, in reality, essentially continuous throughout the period. Thus, the assertion that anti-Jewish discrimination disappeared from Hungarian institutions after the amendment of the numerus clausus in 1928 and that the Jewish quota in the universities was reintroduced a decade later under external pressure does not stand up.

120 Ladányi, "A numerus clausustól a numerus nullusig," 74.

Chronology

Timeline of the Numerus Clausus in Hungary:

January 16, 1907: In speeches made in parliament, Károly Hencz and Károly Kmety recommend the introduction of restrictions on the number of Jewish students in universities and secondary schools, respectively.

1918

May 26: In his article, "Pro Juventute Catholica" in the periodical *Alkotmány* (Constitution), Bishop Ottokár Prohászka demands that Christian university students be placed at an advantage over Jewish ones.

June 22: The periodical *Alkotmány* demands that the Jewish question be placed on the political agenda.

July 31: Bishop Ottokár Prohászka makes a speech in the upper house of parliament in which he says that the Hungarian people must be protected from the power of the Jews, a power rooted in their "excess of intelligence."

September 11: Bishop Ottokár Prohászka demands the limitation of opportunity for Jews in an article entitled "Have We Had Enough?" in the periodical *Alkotmány*.

1919

August 7: At the Plenary Session of the Faculty of Medicine, three professors recommend that the admission of women to the faculty be limited as strictly as possible.

Early August: Paramilitary university organizations form in the capital's higher education institutions in order to maintain order and to remove left-leaning and Jewish students.

August 6–10: Attacks on Jewish students in Budapest's universities begin.

August 10: The head of the universities office of the Ministry of Religion and Public Education warns the rector of the University of Technology that "the exclusion of Jewish students is completely unlawful."

August 10: The Ministry of Religion and Public Education issues Decree No. 4.507/1919, rescinding the educational and cultural policies of the Hungarian Soviet Republic.

August 14: A memorandum issued in the name of the "Hungarian Christian youth of the technical universities" demands the "the exclusion of all Jews and Bolsheviks" from the universities.

August 18: Formation of the Preparatory Council of the Turul Alliance of Hungarian National Universities and Polytechnics.

August 22: Prime Minister István Friedrich instructs Minister of Religion and Public Education Károly Huszár to prevent violent anti-Semitic movements at the universities. The ministry orders the universities closed until the end of September.

The Hungarian Zionist Organization petitions the government, assuring it of their financial support and cooperation, while at the same time calling on it to put a stop to anti-Semitic attacks and incitement.

The Council of the Faculty of Medicine at the University of Budapest recommends a "numerus clausus for students." The recommendation is recorded by professors Károly Hoór and János Bársony. They recommend the restriction of the participation of women in higher education, and the exclusion of anyone found to have participated in the revolutions.

August 27: The Council of the University of Budapest discusses the Faculty of Medicine's recommendation. This is the first appearance of a plan for a nationalities/racial quota: Mihály Kmoskó, dean of the Faculty of Theology, recommends that "each faculty should establish, based on religion, past behavior, and race, the proportion of students to be admitted." The Faculty of Theology suggests at the same meeting that the quota should be extended to include the various "national minorities" as well.

September 6: The Council of the University of Technology—at the behest of the Department of Chemical Engineering—decides upon the implementation of a numerus clausus, and asks the university's various departments to work out the details.

SEPTEMBER 17: The Faculty of Humanities at the University of Budapest accepts, by verbal majority, Professor Ernő Fináczy's motion, which declares the recommendations for ethnic and racial quotas to be illegal, since such quotas are in contravention of "those fundamental national laws that state that every citizen of the Hungarian state is equal before the law, regardless of religion or ethnicity."

SEPTEMBER 25: At a rector's meeting at the University of Budapest, a department head of the Ministry of Religion and Public Education is informed that "a large mass of the students have formed a strong union . . . to enforce their desire that . . . not a single Jew should be allowed to take exams or enroll."

SEPTEMBER 27: Right-wing students demand the closure of the universities, citing the "lack of coal and continuing tensions among the youth." Károly Huszár, minister of religion and education, orders the temporary closure of Budapest's two universities. Teaching resumes in the spring of 1920.

The Faculty of Law at the University of Budapest adopts by verbal majority the recommendation of the Faculty of Medicine and the Faculty of Theology. A numerus clausus is to be implemented by "respecting the proportionality of nationalities, religions, and races" in the admissions process.

NOVEMBER 12: The Union of Hungarian Jewish University and Polytechnic Students holds its first general meeting (it is superseded in 1927 by the National Union of Hungarian Israelite University and Polytechnic Students).

DECEMBER 4: In a decree, the Council of the University of Budapest comes down on the side of implementing a numerus clausus. The Council draws the attention of the Ministry of Religion and Public Education to the recommendation of the Faculty of Law and the Faculty of Theology that "in the case of a shift to the numerus clausus system, the admission of students belonging to religious . . . and racial minorities should only be in proportion to their proportion in the overall population of the country." Alfréd Doleschall, the dean of the Faculty of Law in Budapest, emphasizes in his summarizing statement that the numerus clausus is "directed against the plethora of Jews," and that the "basic interests of self-defense of society and state justify, nay demand, that destructive elements, whether they are so by nature of their nationality or their race, . . . should be forced into the background."

December 9: The Turul Alliance organizes a general meeting at the Budapest University to discuss the "Jewish question in the universities."

1920

January 2: Prime Ministerial Decree No. 272/1920 regarding the establishment of the Faculty of Economics in Budapest is announced. The faculty begins operating in the 1920–21 academic year.

January 28: The Council of the University of Budapest establishes in a resolution that "it is a veritable cultural scandal that our university has, to this very day, not been able to commence its lawful operation for the 1919–20 academic year." It calls for an immediate consultation on the issue of the numerus clausus.

February 7: István Haller, minister of religion and education, convenes a meeting with the participation of the rectors and deans of the universities. They are agreed on the limitation of the number of students and also that the mode of selection of the students should be left up to the individual departments. They agree that "in the selection process, they do not wish to apply either racial or religious criteria." The minister declares that parliament will decide on the matter. They also decide that teaching in the 1919–20 academic year will begin with a four-month supplementary term.

February 9: Formation of the National Union of Hungarian University and College Students (MEFHOSZ). The Turul Alliance leaves the organization a few months later and continues as a federation of right-wing fraternities.

February 11: Formation of the Hungária Association of Hungarian Technicians.

February 11: The Ministry of Religion and Public Education issues Decree No. 4.131/1920 which establishes a four-month "replacement course" for the academic year (which counts as two semesters). Exams begin on February 16, applications on March 1, and lectures on March 16.

February 27: The Ministry of Religion and Public Education issues Amendment No. 16990/1920 to its decree of February 11: for those applying for admission to the replacement course for the 1919–20 academic year, only those who "are able to vouch for their behavior during the so-called dictatorship of the proletariat" may be admitted and allowed to take examinations." Members of university-based paramilitary cells do not have to provide proof of their behavior.

MARCH 2: The rector of the University in Budapest orders admissions suspended and the university closed until the paramilitary organizations leave the university's buildings. On March 8, the paramilitary cell leaves the university.

MARCH 16: The Turul Alliance—in protest against the rector's actions—holds a meeting in the Domed Hall of the university, and submits its written demands to deputies. The signatories of the demands—the Turul Alliance, The National Presidential Conference of the Association of Awakening Hungarians, The United National Christian League, and the Central Secretariat of the National Christian Socialist Union—demand that parliament "urgently introduce a law that the Jewish race, regardless of the religion of its individual members, be allowed to participate in all higher educational establishments only in the same proportion as exists between the number of Jews living in Hungary and the overall population of Hungary."

MARCH 17: Prime Minister Sándor Simonyi-Semadam mentions in his speech outlining the government's legislative program that "the first task of the minister of education will be to implement the reform of education from a national and Christian standpoint."

Prime Minister Sándor Simonyi-Semadam reads in parliament a letter from Count Albert Apponyi in Paris, in which the head of the Hungarian delegation to the Peace Talks warns the government that the general conditions in Hungary and the reports of anarchy and anti-Semitic detachments reaching the West are having a significantly deleterious effect on the position of the delegation.

APRIL 26: István Haller, minister or religion and education, announces in a speech to parliament that the numerus clausus must be implemented and that the number of university students be regulated.

APRIL 28: Deputy Gyula Zákány, one of the vice-presidents of the Association of Awakening Hungarians, presents a motion to parliament incorporating the legal introduction of the numerus clausus in the universities, and its extension to secondary schools as well.

According to Károly Ereky, a deputy for the Christian National Party, the main goal of the introduction of the Jewish quota is to use the political power "to take away from the Jews their billions in income within the framework of the law."

May 8: Students of the University of Technology prepare a resolution demanding that parliament "within the very near future prepare a draft law to solve the Jewish question in the universities."

June 4: An assembly of three thousand students of the Budapest University and the University of Technology, having debated the numerus clausus question, issues a memorandum calling upon the government to "move toward an institutional politics that defends the nation," having previously dispatched a delegation to deputy Ottokár Prohászka to inform him that "the next academic year . . . can only begin if the numerus clausus is law by then." On the day of the signing of the Trianon Peace Treaty, an anti-Semitic rally is organized in Budapest and 85 Jews are injured.

June 10: The minister of religion and education—on the advice of the Council of the University of Budapest—bars 54 medical students from all domestic universities for their actions during the Hungarian Soviet Republic.

June 29: Members of the Turul Alliance hold a general meeting at the Budapest University. They issue a memorandum informing the Ministry of Religion and Public Education of their demands for the introduction of the numerus clausus. Their starting point is that "in a rump [post-Trianon] Hungary, only Hungarians have the right to live and support their existence and themselves." Formation of the Catholic student society Foederatio Emericana.

June: The Ministry of Religion and Public Education issues Decree No. 113.240/1920 concerning admissions exams to secondary schools (this so-called secondary school numerus clausus is abolished in 1924).

July 5: István Haller, minister of religion and education, presents to the government the first official draft of the proposed numerus clausus law, sending copies to the universities. There is no mention as yet of a nationalities quota in this draft.

July 21: The government debates the draft numerus clausus law.

July 22: Pál Teleki, in his prime minister's speech outlining the government's legislative program, promises "to defend the interests of Christian society institutionally."

Minister of Religion and Public Education István Haller submits to parliament the proposed legislation for controlling admission to the scientific and technical universities, the law schools, and the Faculty of Economics at the University of Budapest; this is the so-called numerus clausus legislation.

July 27: A group of members of the Association of Awakening Hungarians burst into a central Budapest cafe and beat the Jewish guests bloody, killing a bank manager and a Jewish lawyer.

July 28: Deputy László Budaváry, one of the leaders of the Association of Awakening Hungarians, calls for the formulation of an overarching "racial defense law" in parliament. He calls for the law not only to be active in the sphere of education but also to apply anti-Jewish legislation in every sphere of life.

August 5: MEFHOSZ, with the cooperation of deputies and right-wing youth organizations, organizes a forum on the draft numerus clausus legislation. Bishop Ottokár Prohászka, chairing the meeting, formulates his recommendation, which meets with general approbation, that "admissions should be proportionate to the overall proportion of races and nationalities."

August 9: The Treasury and Education Committee of parliament debates the numerus clausus draft law. In their joint report, they recommend that the following be inserted into the first paragraph of the draft: "only such persons may enroll [at the universities] who are absolutely reliable in terms of their loyalty to the nation and moral standing."

August 11: The governing Christian National Union Party—with Ottokár Prohászka chairing—debates the draft numerus clausus law. Deputy Nándor Bernolák, a professor of law in Debrecen, outlines the need to establish quotas on a nationality, race, and religious basis. (At the next debate, on August 24, Bernolák is tasked with submitting an individual amendment to make the numerus clausus "explicit.")

August 20: István Haller, minister of religion and education, issues a decree fixing the number of students to be admitted for the 1920–21 academic year.

September 1: The United National Christian League, the Turul Alliance, and the Association of Awakening Hungarians recommend, in their petition to parliament, that the Jewish quota be extended to secondary schools, as well as demanding that "in the fields where Jewry is excessively overrepresented, no Jews should be allowed to join until the proper proportion is restored."

September 2–21: Parliamentary debate on the numerus clausus law (September 2, 3, 16–18, 20–21). Twenty deputies speak at the debate; 13 for, 7 against. During the specific debate on September 21, Nándor Bernolák formally submits the amendment—already mentioned in the general debate on September 3—to create a quota for ethnicity. Out of a total of 219 deputies, only 64 are present at the final vote on the proposed legislation, of whom 57 vote yes.

September 21: Parliament rejects deputy Pál Sándor's motion that a Jewish university be established.

September 22: Károly Ereky attacks the government in parliament by saying that "nothing is being done to bring down the Jews."

September 26: Publication of Law No. XXV of 1920 on the regulation of enrollment at the universities of arts and sciences, the University of Technology, the Faculty of Economics of the University of Budapest, and law academies, the so-called numerus clausus.

September 27: Publication of Decree No. 123.033 of 1920 of the Ministry of Religion and Public Education regarding the implementation of Law No. XXV of 1920. Its appendix contains figures on the division of the population by mother tongue, with the comment that "Israelites are [to be] treated as a separate nationality." The decree confirms that the Jewish quota can only be applied to first-year admissions.[1]

October 11–31: Disturbances arise at the universities due to the perceived "inadequacies" of the numerus clausus law as enacted by parliament. Right-wing student organizations block the doors to the main building of the Budapest Scientific University and demand identification from anyone wishing to enter. Jewish students from higher years are beaten up; their papers are taken away and thrown out of the building. On October 14, the rector suspends admissions and teaching does not start. The attacks spread to the other universities and polytechnics.

October 13: The scandals at the universities are taken up at a cabinet meeting. The government decides that it will be as determined as possible in the matter of university admissions and the freedom to study.

October 14: Forty representatives of the Turul Alliance meet with István Haller, minister of religion and education. They present their demands verbally and in writing. They want "the extension of the numerus clausus to all institutions of higher education, the invalidity of acquired rights, and student representation on the admissions boards."

---

1 Although the published version of the decree is dated October 27, 1920, there seems to be a consensus in literature that the correct date was in fact September 27, one day after the publication of Law No. XXV of 1920. For the published version, see *Magyarországi rendeletek tára, 1920* (Budapest: Pesti Könyvnyomda Részvénytársaság, 1920), 1455–60.

On the same day, a deputation from MEFHOSZ also visits the minister. On the one hand, they sharply condemn the unlawful actions taking place in the universities, while on the other they support the Turul Alliance's demands.

OCTOBER 19: The Ministry of Religion and Public Education issues Decree No. 136.515/1920 amending the decree implementing the numerus clausus law. According to the amendment, in those faculties where the approval of candidates for admission has not yet finished, the admissions boards can be complemented with two deputed members from the right-wing student fraternities. The young delegates to these committees "can examine documents, but have only a consultative vote."

END OF OCTOBER: The admissions process restarts at the scientific universities and teaching begins.

NOVEMBER 11: The Faculty of Humanities at Budapest University decides that they will not, in future, authorize admission to members of the Galileo Circle.[2] After all the other faculties follow suit, the Council of the University introduces a similar resolution.

1921

MARCH 3: After a lengthy debate, the cabinet accepts the Ministry of Defense's motion, with an amendment by Treasury Secretary Lóránt Hegedüs, that the right-wing student detachments should be maintained until July 1921. The members of the detachments, which will cease to exist, will be "coopted" into the university sports societies and will function under the cover names "MAFC Student House" and the "University Dormitory." Then, from the autumn of 1921, they will comprise groups of the National Labor Protection organization (NMV) at the University of Technology and the universities of arts and sciences.

APRIL 11: The University in Debrecen takes the name "The Royal Hungarian István Tisza University of Debrecen."

2 Funded in 1908, the Galileo Circle was a leftwing atheist-materialist student organization, with a membership of around a thousand students and intellectuals (including, for example, the economic anthropologist Karl Polányi, the sociologist Karl Mannheim, and the philosopher Georg Lukács). A number of the circle's members actively participated in the 1918 October (Aster) Revolution and many even became functionaries during the Hungarian Soviet Republic.

June 16: Parliament accepts Law No. XXV of 1921 regarding the "temporary transfer of the Royal Hungarian universities of Kolozsvár and Pozsony." The two universities, the Franz Josef University of Kolozsvár and the Erzsébet University of Pozsony, which lost their homes in the Trianon Peace Treaty, are transferred to Szeged and Pécs respectively.

November: The Joint Foreign Committee of the Board of Deputies of British Jews and the Anglo-Jewish Association, and the Alliance Israélite Universelle present a joint petition to the League of Nations on the matter of the Hungarian numerus clausus. The British Jewish politician Lucien Wolf, foreign correspondent at the *Times*, outlines in his submission to the League of Nations that the Hungarian numerus clausus contravenes articles 56, 57, and 58 of the Trianon Peace Treaty. The Council of the League of Nations debates the issue, but does not come to a decision.

A confidential Ministry of Religion and Public Education decree, No. 91.487/1921, extends the effect of the numerus clausus law to those who wish to continue their education in Hungary, having begun it abroad.

1922

Motions to abolish the law come one after the other in parliament. Between 1922 and 1924, eight such motions fail when put to the vote. István Bethlen openly opposes the motions for abolition.

July 20: The bishops of the Hungarian churches in Transylvania ask the Hungarian government to abolish the numerus clausus law because this would help the situation of the Hungarians who now constitute an ethnic minority in Romania.

September 18: The General Assembly of the League of Nations unanimously accepts Hungary as a member.

September 30: The Council of the League of Nations asks the Hungarian government for detailed information on the implementation of the numerus clausus law. In his response, Foreign Minister Miklós Bánffy denies that the law represents a severe restriction in the case of the Jews. The League of Nations acknowledges the response, but asks for further data on admissions procedures.

October: At the University of Pécs, right-wing students beat their Jewish colleagues bloody during a chemistry practicum. The rector suspends practicums throughout the university and all the students in that academic year have to repeat the semester.

DECEMBER 16: In a speech to parliament, Gyula Gömbös, Vice-President of the Unity Party (Egységes Párt), demands the introduction of the numerus clausus to all fields of economic life.

1923

JANUARY: The Hungarian government submits the data requested regarding admissions processes to the League of Nations. The League appoints a three-member committee to examine the statistics. The committee's report—based on the data—is condemnatory of the numerus clausus law.

MARCH 15: University students in Budapest stage protests in favor of the anti-Semitic periodicals *Szózat* (Appeal) and *Nép* (People), and against *Est Lapok* (Evening Papers).

MARCH 16–17: Attacks on Jewish students begin at the College of Veterinary Medicine and the University of Economics. Teaching is temporarily suspended.

SUMMER: University students in Pécs threaten a boycott and organize a protest demanding that the university's council adhere to the numerus clausus. In a memorandum addressed to all the universities in the country, they demand that Jews not be allowed to be employed as assistant professors or teaching assistants, and that every university review the status of the Jews enrolled as students there.

1924

JANUARY 4: Deputy Pál Sándor, president of the Hungarian Jewish Educational Association (OMIKE), introduces a motion in parliament recommending the abolition of the numerus clausus law and the establishment of a Jewish University. The motion is rejected.

JUNE 4: Kunó Klebelsberg, minister of religion and education, declares in parliament that the fate of the numerus clausus law depends on what concessions the Great Powers are willing to make in the question of Hungary's borders.

SEPTEMBER 23: In a court case against an extreme right-wing journalist charged with incitement, the Royal Curia determines that "according to our laws, Hungarian Jewry represents neither a separate nationality nor a distinct social class."

1925

Beginning of January: The Joint Foreign Committee of the Board of Deputies of British Jews presents another petition on the subject of the numerus clausus to the League of Nations, where the matter of the classification of Jews as a race, nationality, or religion is raised.

January 1: Lucien Wolf turns to the League of Nations for a second time, requesting that the League refer the matter of the numerus clausus to the International Court in The Hague. The League refers the case not to the Hague Court but to the Council of the League of Nations.

May 19: The Hungarian government, in its note to the League of Nations, explains that the numerus clausus law "deliberately avoids any reference to religious minorities . . . since it is within the individual's power to change their religion at any time."

August 18: In response to a question from the delegation sent by the Council of the League of Nations seeking to know whether the government is planning to modify the numerus clausus law, Foreign Minister Lajos Walkó declares that the government sees no need to modify either the law or its method of application.

November 23: The Jewish community—at Prime Minister István Bethlen's behest and with the formulation worked out by deputy Vilmos Vázsonyi—accepts a unanimous declaration: "We are Hungarian, we believe ourselves to be part of the Hungarian people and the Peace Treaty, which is our nation's grief, cannot be the fountainhead of our law. . . . [W]e want to settle the matter of the numerus clausus at home, with our own government and our own legislature. Therefore, we have sought out no international body and will seek out no international body for help. If this is forthcoming we will, though it be well-intentioned, reject this of our own accord."

December 10: The Council of the League of Nations adds a detailed debate on the numerus clausus law to its agenda. The Council acknowledges the argument and promise of the Hungarian representative, Minister of Religion and Public Education Kunó Klebelsberg, that the law is an exceptional and a temporary measure and will be modified as soon as the social situation permits.

December 1–17: Debate between Klebelsberg and Vázsonyi in parliament.

December 17: Prime Minister István Bethlen, replying to Vilmos Vázsonyi's question in parliament as to whether the government considers Jewry a racial group or a religion, states that "the law establishing the numerus clausus declared the Jews to be a racial group or a nationality, respectively. . . . This, naturally, does not mean that this is the position of this government."

1926

SEPTEMBER 9: Kunó Klebelsberg, minister of religion and education, accepting the April petition of the Pest Israelite Community, orders that Jews who have converted and are applying to the universities and polytechnics are to be treated in the same way as Christian applicants.

EARLY OCTOBER: Lucien Wolf's letter to former Finance Minister Lóránt Hegedűs informing him that his White Paper on the discriminative practices of the numerus clausus law is ready and will be submitted to the League of Nations and the International Court in The Hague in December.

OCTOBER 22: Lóránt Hegedűs's letter to Prime Minister István Bethlen, in which he offers to act as an intermediary between Lucien Wolf and the Hungarian government. Bethlen forwards Hegedűs's letter to Klebelsberg for his opinion.

NOVEMBER 3: Klebelsberg's reply to Bethlen, in which he recommends rejecting Hegedűs's offer. In his letter, Klebelsberg declares that "we will have to revise the law," since it really does contravene international law, but that the change cannot lead to a situation where "we unleash thousands of Jewish university students on the nation."

NOVEMBER 16: Prime Minister István Bethlen, in a campaign speech at the Vigadó theatre, officially announces that the numerus clausus law will be modified.

1927

MAY 13: Béla Fábián's recommendation for the amendment of the numerus clausus is voted down in the parliament.

SEPTEMBER 2: The Council of the League of Nations announces that the League will discuss the Hungarian government's complaint against Romania in the case of the "optant" landowners.

SEPTEMBER 4: The Alliance Israélite Universelle and the Joint Foreign Committee (on September 14) approach the League of Nations again regarding the numerus clausus.

SEPTEMBER 14: Lucien Wolf writes personally to the Secretary General of the League of Nations in the matter of the numerus clausus.

September 17–18: The Council of the League—following a complaint from the Hungarian government—debates the Hungarian-Romanian optants issue. There is no decision, and the matter is deferred to their next meeting, in December.

October 7: Lucien Wolf again makes a formal complaint against the Hungarian government. Under the rules of the League of Nations, the matter of the numerus clausus is to be added to the agenda of its December session.

October 19: Prime Minister István Bethlen announces at a meeting of the Unity Party that the government will erase the restrictions on Jews from the numerus clausus law.

November 18: Kunó Klebelsberg, minister of religion and education, following cabinet approval on November 4, presents a motion to modify Law No. XXV of 1920.

November: The right-wing student fraternities make posters protesting against the planned changes to the numerus clausus law. They beat Jewish students, check their papers, and prevent them from entering the universities. Because of these disturbances, the government delays the changes to the law until the spring of 1928.

December 2: István Bethlen informs the League of Nations of the planned changes to the numerus clausus law. He also enters into discussions with international Jewish organizations through third parties.

1928

February 9: The debate on modifying Law No. XXV of 1920 begins in parliament. The changes are approved on February 24, with 139 voting for and 34 against. The upper house debates and accepts the changes in March.

February 13: University students organize protests and strikes against the softening of the numerus clausus law.

March: The international Jewish organizations submit another petition to the League of Nations regarding the potential for discrimination hidden in the amended law. The League of Nations does not consider the petition, and considers the matter of the Hungarian numerus clausus closed.

April 26: Publication of Law No. XIV of 1928 "concerning the amendment of Law No. XXV of 1920 regarding the regulation of enrollment at the universities of arts and sciences, the University of Technology, the Faculty of

Economics of the University of Budapest, and law academies." The amendment removes the restrictions according to "racial groups and ethnicities," but prescribes that the children of persons involved in "various" occupations should be admitted to the universities and polytechnics in the corresponding ratios.

October 15–25: Outbreak of university protests due to the softening of the numerus clausus law.

October 17: University admissions boards fail to comply with the instructions for the execution of Law No. XIV of 1928. As a result, Kunó Klebelsberg issues ministerial instructions for the admission of 14 Jewish students with exemplary secondary school diplomas. He mentions the Jewish students by name in parliament. The universities of Pécs, Debrecen, and Budapest are closed for several days following disorders and violence in the wake of his announcement.

1929

October 25: At a cabinet meeting, Foreign Minister Lajos Walkó declares that "the constant student protests and anti-Jewish attacks in our higher education institutions are indeed harming the country's standing." Prime Minister István Bethlen calls on Minister of Religion and Public Education Kunó Klebelsberg to stop these anti-Semitic incidents.

1931

August 27: Prime Minister Gyula Károlyi in his introductory speech to parliament highlights that "it is also my personal conviction, as it is the conviction of the entire government, that we must not discriminate between the religions in any way in this country."

1932

October: At a series of violent protests at the universities in Szeged and Budapest, demands are made that the admission of Jewish students be limited according to the original 1920 law.

November 14: Outbreak of attacks at the University of Debrecen. A memorandum written in the name of the "Christian Hungarian youth" demands that during the admissions process the "already very much expanded numerus reductus be applied as strictly as possible."

November 26: The National Union of Hungarian Students—the principle organization of radical right-wing Hungarian university students—issues a memorandum, asking Bálint Hóman, Minister of Religion and Public Education, to rescind the 1928 amendment of the law.

November 29: Minister of Religion and Public Education Bálint Hóman, in response to a question in parliament, declares that "I will use all means to ensure the freedom to study at the universities for every student, regardless of social or denominational belonging."

1933

November-December: There are a number of serious physical attacks on Jewish students at the University of Debrecen, and street protests against budget cuts caused by the recession. The disturbances then spread to the universities of Budapest, Pécs, and Szeged. The organizers demand the reinstatement of the original numerus clausus law. Teaching is suspended.

November 20: In a memorandum addressed to Minister of Religion and Education Bálint Hóman, the youth organizations at the University of Technology demand that "Jewish students not be admitted to the universities until the number of Jewish students already enrolled is reduced to the same proportion as represented by Jews in the overall population of the country."

November 29: Bálint Hóman, Minister of Religion and Education, having repeatedly condemned the physical attacks on Jews at the universities, explains in parliament that "we must strive towards the result that there should be no difference in the proportion of Hungarian Christian and Jewish youth at the universities compared to the proportion [of Christians and Jews] in the country as a whole."

December 7: Prime Minister Gyula Gömbös and Bálint Hóman, minister of religion and education, meet the leaders of university youth groups. The prime minister declares that although there is no question of amending Law No. XIV of 1928, the university admissions boards will in practice enforce the controls on admitting Jewish applicants in accordance with Law No. XXV of 1920.

1934

January 16: At a cabinet meeting, Ferenc Keresztes-Fischer, Minister of the Interior, announces that the "Jewish quota" will be enforced in the next academic year.

1935

NOVEMBER 20: The student society Foederatio Emericana organizes a demonstration against the Jewish students at the University of Szeged.

NOVEMBER 29: Between 60 and 80 students of the Law Faculty and the University of Technology in Budapest disrupt lectures, expelling the Jewish students from the lecture halls. Teaching is suspended for several days.

1936

DECEMBER 2: At the general assembly of the Turul Alliance, the representative of the Hungária Association demands that "Jewry be classified as a race and that the numerus clausus be applied accordingly."

1937

FEBRUARY 24: A group of students wearing hats of the Turul Alliance abuse Jewish students at the Faculty of Humanities at Budapest University. At the University of Pécs, Jewish students are prevented from taking part in lectures.

MAY 11: In a parliamentary speech, István Bethlen protests against the Jewish law under preparation. He finds it unconscionable that the equality of citizens before the law be prejudiced on the basis of religion or ethnicity.

SEPTEMBER 15: Bálint Hóman, minister of religion and education, announces at a meeting with the rectors of the universities that the "racial quota" of the numerus clausus "is being respected." He asks them to prevent renewed disturbances among the youth.

OCTOBER: At a demonstration in the Trefort Garden campus of Budapest University, right-wing youth groups demand a "numerus nullus." At the request of Elemér Császár, dean of the Faculty of Humanities, the police intervene and 19 students are placed in preliminary detention.

1938

APRIL 8: Prime Minister Kálmán Darányi introduces the so-called First Jewish Law in parliament.

APRIL 23–24: Foederatio Emericana, at its national diet in Pécs, issues a resolution demanding that stricter university admission limits be applied to Jews who have converted to Christianity.

MAY 5: 59 Hungarian writers, artists, and scientists protest against the proposed Jewish Law.

May 29: Publication of Law No. XV of 1938, "on the more efficient assurance of equilibrium in social and economic life" (the so-called First Jewish Law). The law makes explicit that Jews can only be admitted to the various professional associations if the percentage of Jewish members does not exceed 20 percent.

December 23: The government submits to parliament the draft of the proposed Second Jewish Law. The draft does not include arrangements regarding the numerus clausus.

1939

March 8: Prime Minister Pál Teleki meets with the leaders of youth groups about the proposed amendment to the Second Jewish Law regarding the numerus clausus.

March 11: Bálint Hóman, minister of religion and education, receives the leaders of the youth groups and promises that the numerus clausus for the universities will be applied in the form that they requested.

April 11: Hungary leaves the League of Nations.

May 5: Publication of Law No. IV of 1939 "on the restriction of the role of Jews in public and economic life" (the so-called Second Jewish Law). The law establishes the proportion of Jews in intellectual professions at 6 percent. Clause 7 states that "Jews may be admitted as students or undergraduates to the first year of universities and polytechnics only in such proportion that their numbers do not exceed six percent of all the students admitted to the university, or to the specific faculty (class); in the case of the Faculty of Economics and Trade of the Palatine Joseph University of Technology and Economics, this percentage is to be 12 percent."

July 25: Publication of Prime Ministerial Decree No. 7.300/1939 regarding the implementation of clause 7 of Law No. IV of 1939. Unlike the 1920 numerous clausus law, the decree implementing the 1939 law specifies that the Jewish quota is to be applied in the arts colleges, and that higher-year students who are applying for specific subjects or faculties for the first time are to be treated as first-year students.

Summer: Secret decree of the Ministry of Religion and Public Education concerning the introduction of a numerus clausus for secondary schools. The ministry's explanatory memorandum states that "from the spirit of Law No. IV of 1939 it follows that Jewish pupils [in secondary schools] may be admitted only up to proportion of the Jewish population of the country in relation to the Christian population."

1940

NOVEMBER 15: Bálint Hóman, minister of religion and education, provides an historical overview of the numerus clausus in his justification for Law No. XXXIX of 1940 on the regulation of admissions of university and polytechnic students.

1941

AUGUST 8: Law No. XV of 1941, on "the amendment and expansion of Law No. XXXI of 1894 on marriage and the concomitant necessary arrangements for the protection of racial purity" (the so-called Third Jewish Law) enters into force.

NOVEMBER 11: During a debate in parliament on the Ministry of Religion and Public Education's 1942 budget, Dénes Tömböly, a government deputy, declares in his speech presenting the budget that "we must fix as a principle that no Jew should be allowed to participate in Hungarian higher education," adding that "in the Jewish question at the universities, it is not the letter of the law that should be obeyed, but its spirit."

1942

NOVEMBER 18: Publication of Ministry of Defense Decree No. 69.056/1942, which obligates male Jews between the ages of 18 and 48 to labor service.

1944

MARCH 31: Publication of Government Order No. 1210/1944 ME, which ends the employment of Jews in the public sphere, as well as ending their public contracts and preventing their further employment as lawyers.

APRIL 13: The 1943–44 academic year is ended due to the state of the war.

APRIL 25: Publication of Statute No. 1540/1944 ME prohibiting the employment or activity of Jews in white-collar jobs.

APRIL 30: Publication of Statute No. 10.800/1944 ME on the protection of Hungarian intellectual life from the works of Jewish authors.

May 6: Publication of Decree No. 8.700/1944 of the Ministry of Religion and Public Education, which forbids Jewish students from wearing school uniforms.

May 12: Publication of Decree No. 8.960/1944 of the Ministry of Religion and Public Education, which withdraws existing authorization from Jews for the maintenance of schools, courses, or houses of learning.

May 20: István Antal, minister of justice as well as minister of religion and education, gives verbal instructions that in the draft law to be prepared on the exclusion of Jews from the public, cultural, and economic life of the country, there should also be a passage laying down a numerus nullus to be introduced in institutions of higher education. This however, does not come to pass.

June 24: Publication of Decree No. 11.300/1944 ME on removing the works of Jewish authors from public circulation.

December 5: Publication of Decree No. 960/1944 BM of the Ministry of the Interior on changing the names of streets, roads, and squares.

October 29: Teaching is suspended for the 1944–45 academic year, despite having never really started.

1945

January 19: Publication of Decree No. 444/1945 ME on erasing students of Jewish descent from student rosters of secondary and vocational schools.

March 17: Decree No. 200/1945 ME abolishes the Jewish Laws (the National Provisional Government establishes in paragraph 2 that these laws contravene the constitutional spirit of the Hungarian people and proudly declares the renewed equality of all citizens before the law).

1946

November 15: Publication of Law No. XXV of 1946 condemning the persecution of Hungarian Jewry and the mitigation of its consequences.

Appendixes

Appendix No. 1

Law No. XXV of 1920
on the regulation of enrollment at the universities of arts and sciences, the University of Technology, the Faculty of Economics of the University of Budapest, and law academies

1. § From the start of the 1920–21 academic year, only such persons may enroll at the universities of arts and sciences, the University of Technology, the Faculty of Economics of the University of Budapest, and the law academies, who are absolutely reliable in terms of their loyalty to the nation and moral standing and only in such numbers as to ensure that every student can be educated thoroughly.

The number of students who may be admitted to each faculty (department) shall be determined by the Minister of Religion and Public Education on the recommendation of the relevant faculty (or, in the case of the University of Technology, the Council).

Non-ordinary students may be admitted only if the number of students determined in accordance with the preceding paragraph have not been filled by regular students, and only within the established maximum number of places.

This provision shall not apply to students enrolled in the faculties of law and political science (law academies) for the purpose of studying public accounting, but the Minister of Religion and Public Education may, after consulting the competent faculties and in agreement with the Minister of Finance, determine the number of such non-ordinary students.

2. §. The provisions of § 1 shall not affect the right of further enrolment of regular students who have already been enrolled in previous academic years, nor of non-ordinary students who have been enrolled with a secondary school graduation certificate in the faculties of humanities (humanities, languages, history

and quantitative sciences) and medicine, provided that they are absolutely reliable in terms of their loyalty to the nation and moral standing.

3. §. A person seeking enrollment under the provisions of § 1 shall apply to the relevant faculty (or, in the case of the University of Technology, the Council) for permission to enroll.

The granting or refusal of permission to enroll within the limits for the number of students set in accordance with the provisions of § 1 shall be decided with binding force by a plenary session of the relevant faculty (or, in the case of the University of Technology, the Council).

When granting admission, in addition to the requirements of loyalty to the nation and moral reliability, on the one hand, consideration shall also be given to the intellectual ability of the applicant, on the other, and to the requirement that the proportion of young people belonging to a given racial group and nationality residing in the country shall preferably reach the national proportion of the racial group or nationality concerned, but shall at least be nine-tenths of the national proportion.

Likewise, those wishing to enroll under § 2 may do so only with the permission of the competent faculty (or, in the case of the University of Technology, the Council). The rules governing the enrollment of such persons shall be laid down by decree by the Minister of Religion and Public Education.

4. §. This Act, which shall enter into force on the day of its promulgation, shall be implemented by the Minister of Religion and Public Education.

Source: *Magyar Törvénytár: 1920. évi törvénycikkek*, annot. by Gyula Térfy (Budapest: Franklin-Társulat, 1921), 145. See also online version in *Ezer év törvényei*, https://net.jogtar.hu/ezer-ev-torveny?docid=92000025.TV&searchUrl=/ezer-ev-torvenyei?keyword%3D1920.%2520%25C3%25A9vi%2520XXV.

Appendix No. 2

Motion for the immediate institutional resolution of the Jewish question in Hungary

1. No Jew shall be allowed to buy or rent land in Hungary. Land owned by Jews is to be acquired by the state in the course of the present year, 1920, at the price that the owners originally paid for it. For land purchased after July 1, 1914, the price of acquisition will be the market price in the given region before July 1, 1914. The price of acquisition however shall in no case exceed 10 million crowns, even for the largest estates, which naturally is to include the acquisition price of agricultural chattels (buildings, machines, animals, etc.). The agricultural stock of Jewish estates acquired in this way may only be sold to the state. Rental contracts leasing land to Jews will cease to apply on October 1, 1920. The land thus falling vacant is to be urgently subdivided and distributed to Christian Hungarian smallholders, agricultural workers, employees, public employees, civil servants, and their widows and orphans, as well as war invalids, war widows, war orphans, industrial workers, and artisans at equitable prices (leased or owned). Also to be acquired are building plots owned by Jews. The acquisition and redistribution of land as necessary is primarily to be enforced on Jewish estates.

2. Jews may no longer continue to own more than one house. The rest are to be acquired by the state at the price current at the time of building and are to be rented out as flats to displaced persons, employees, workers, pensioners, etc. All large flats are to be reviewed and surplus space to be requisitioned. In future, the state in the first instance and the county in the second shall have preemptive rights on the sale of any property.

3. Jews shall no longer be given permission to settle in Hungary nor acquire citizenship. Those Jews who have immigrated since January 1, 1914, are to be deported without delay, any property acquired here is to pass into the hands of the state without compensation. Large fortunes acquired during the war (whether personal or corporate) from shipments to the military during the war or by profiting from the wartime situation are to be expropriated and used for the purposes of the state to aid war invalids, war widows, war orphans, and other Christians that have suffered from the war.

4. The numerus clausus is to be strictly introduced in all schools and offices, public institutions, factories, workshops, banks, etc., in Hungary. Jewish schools will no longer be permitted. Jews are not to be admitted to any teacher training courses. The schools in the capital are to be urgently nationalized. Private educational institutions are to be shut throughout the whole country, or to be reorganized into state-run institutions. Cabarets, music halls, and dance halls in Jewish hands are to be put under the strictest moral policing. No Jew may be head of a theatrical association. Cinemas are to be nationalized.

5. State-funded construction, transport, and other work may be undertaken only by Christian contractors, artisans, cooperatives, etc. Sixty percent of shares in factories are to be placed into the hands of their workers and other Christians with state support. Raw materials for industry are to be issued primarily to Christian small industry and factories. Christian tradesmen and cooperatives are to be entrusted with the distribution of official goods. All warehouses, cellars, etc., are to be searched immediately and raw materials and industrial goods stockpiled there in large amounts are to be confiscated. In workshops, shops, and factories, correct accounting must be used. Only trained craftsmen may open workshops. Jews cannot employ Christians for personal service (servant, cook, driver, butler, etc.).

6. The three principal responsible heads of journals (newspapers) and magazines (publisher, editor in chief, head of production, chief reporter) cannot be Jews or Freemasons. All journalists are to swear an oath that they will serve the Hungarian national spirit with all their writings, that they will endeavor for the reinstatement and maintenance of the territorial integrity of Hungary, will foster the bond between the sons of the Hungarian people, Christian morality, and the good name of Hungary in the international arena, and will never transgress against these, even in thought. Hebrew language newspapers or flyers may not be published or distributed in Hungary. Address plates, shopsigns, and other signs with Hebrew lettering are to be removed at once.

7. All state licenses (tobacco, stamps, alcohol, brewing, etc.), are to be reviewed. Applicants should primarily be Christian war invalids in need, war widows, war orphans, pensioned public employees, widows of public employees, and Christian traders who have held such licenses in the past.

8. Jews and Freemasons may not be ministers, deputy-ministers, heads of state offices, bureau chiefs, or members of the diplomatic corps of Hungary. They may no longer be judges, notaries, military officers, responsible for public safety, or holders of high office in a county, city, assize, or region. Jews in Hungary may not exercise political rights.

9. All internationally-based non-Christian political or social organizations or parties, and all Masonic organizations are to be disbanded immediately and permission for the formation of such organizations is to be withheld in the future.

10. All those who are guilty in the rise of Communism in Hungary, and thereby the ruin of our country, all those who agitate or incite here or abroad in word or in writing, openly or covertly, against the interests of the Hungarian state, Hungarian national unity, and Hungarian territorial integrity; those who fraternize with our enemies on occupied territory, and do any service for them to Hungary's detriment; and finally those who agitate in any way in the interests of Bolshevism, or mock or threaten any Hungarian citizen for their national or Christian feelings, or do them harm for the aforesaid, on being apprehended or found are to be punished by death under martial law.

Budapest, July 28, 1920.
Submitted by: László Budaváry, parliamentary deputy.

Source: *Az 1920. évi február hó 16-ára összehívott nemzetgyűlés irományai* [Documents of the National Assembly convened on February 16, 1920], vol. 3 (Budapest, Pesti Könyvnyomda Részvénytársaság, 1920), 338–39.

Bibliography

Primary Sources

Magyar Törvénytár [Hungarian Law Directory] (https://net.jogtar.hu/ezer-ev-torvenyei)

Magyarországi rendeletek tára, 1920 [Directory of Hungarian Decrees, 1920]. Budapest: Pesti Könyvnyomda Részvénytársaság, 1920.

Documents of the Hungarian National Assembly

Minutes of the House of Representatives

Az 1910. évi június hó 21-ére hirdetett országgyűlés képviselőházának naplója [Minutes of the House of Representatives of the National Assembly convened on June 21, 1910]. Vols. 1–41. Budapest: Athenaeum Irodalmi és Nyomdai Részvénytársulat, 1910–18.

Az 1920. évi február hó 16-ára összehívott nemzetgyűlés naplója [Minutes of the National Assembly convened on February 16, 1920]. Vols. 1–17. Budapest: Athenaeum Irodalmi és Nyomdai Részvénytársulat, 1920–22.

Az 1922. évi junius hó 16-ára hirdetett nemzetgyűlés naplója [Minutes of the National Assembly convened on June 16, 1922]. Vols. 1–46. Budapest: Athenaeum Irodalmi és Nyomdai Részvénytársulat, 1922–26.

Az 1927. évi január hó 25-ére hirdetett országgyűlés képviselőházának naplója [Minutes of the House of Representatives of the National Assembly convened on January 25, 1927]. Vols. 1–37. Budapest: Athenaeum Irodalmi és Nyomdai Részvénytársulat, 1927–31.

Az 1931. évi július hó 18-ára hirdetett országgyűlés képviselőházának naplója [Minutes of the House of Representatives of the National Assembly convened on July 18, 1931]. Vols. 1–24. Budapest: Athenaeum Irodalmi és Nyomdai Részvénytársulat, 1931–35.

Az 1935. évi április hó 27-ére hirdetett országgyűlés képviselőházának naplója [Minutes of the House of Representatives of the National Assembly convened on April 27, 1935]. Vols. 1–22. Budapest: Athenaeum Irodalmi és Nyomdai Részvénytársulat, 1935–39.

Minutes of the Upper House

Az 1927. évi január hó 25-ére hirdetett országgyűlés felsőházának naplója [Minutes of the Upper House of the National Assembly convened on January 25, 1927]. Vols. 1–6. Budapest: Athenaeum Irodalmi és Nyomdai Részvénytársulat, 1927–31.

Az 1931. évi július hó 18-ára hirdetett országgyűlés felsőházának naplója [Minutes of the Upper House of the National Assembly convened on July 18, 1931]. Vols. 1–3. Budapest: Athenaeum Irodalmi és Nyomdai Részvénytársulat, 1932–35.

Documents of the House of Representatives

Az 1920. évi február hó 16-ára összehívott nemzetgyűlés irományai [Documents of the National Assembly convened on February 16, 1920]. Vols. 1–13. Budapest: Pesti Könyvnyomda Részvénytársaság, 1920–22.

Az 1935. évi április hó 27-ére összehívott országgyűlés irományai [Documents of the National Assembly convened on April 27, 1935]. Vols. 1–13. Budapest: Athenaeum Irodalmi és Nyomdai Részvénytársulat, 1935–39.

Documents of the Upper House

Az 1927. évi január hó 25-ére összehívott országgyűlés felsőházának irományai [Documents of the Upper House of the National Assembly convened on January 25, 1927]. Vols. 1–14. Budapest: Athenaeum Irodalmi és Nyomdai Részvénytársulat, 1927–31.
Az 1939. évi június hó 10-ére összehívott országgyűlés felsőházának irományai [Documents of the Upper House of the National Assembly convened on June 10, 1939]. Vols. 1–5. Budapest: Athenaeum Irodalmi és Nyomdai Részvénytársulat, 1939–42.

Archival materials

Hungarian National Archives (MNL OL)

MNL OL K 636 Ministry of Religion and Public Education (VKM Töredék Iratok)
MNL OL K 592-1940-3-54654 Ministry of Religion and Public Education (VKM)
MNL OL K28 Department of Nationalities and Minorities (Nemzetiségi és Kisebbségi Osztály)
MNL OL P4 330 (Diary of Mrs. Gyuláné Andrássy)
MNL OL K27, Minisztertanácsi jegyzőkönyvek (Minutes of the Council of Ministers)
MNL OL K468-1927-1931-B/17 (letter of Pál Teleki, January 23, 1927; and letter of István Bethlen, January 31, 1927)

University archives

Budapesti Műszaki Egyetem (BME) Levéltára (Archives of the Budapest University of Technology), Egyetemi tanácsi jegyzőkönyvek (Minutes of the University Council)
Eötvös Loránd Tudományegyetem (ELTE) Levéltára (Eötvös Loránd University Archives), Rektori Hivatal, Egyetemi tanácsi jegyzőkönyvek (Rector's Office, Minutes of the University Council); Bölcsészeti Kar üléseinek jegyzőkönyve (Minutes of the meeting of the Faculty of Humanities)
Pécsi Tudományegyetem (PTE), Egyetemi Levéltár (University of Pécs, University Archives), Elnöki iratok (Chairman's Papers); Rektori hivatali iratok (Documents of the Rector's Office)
Semmelweis Orvostudományi Egyetem (SOTE) Levéltára (Archives of the Semmelweis University of Medicine), A budapesti kir. Magyar Pázmány Péter tudományegyetem orvoskari tanártestülete üléseinek jegyzőkönyvei (Minutes of the meetings of the Faculty of Medicine of the Royal Hungarian Pázmány Péter University of Budapest); Budapesti egyetem és a menekült egyetemek orvoskarainak összevont ülésének jegyzőkönyve, 1920. november 22. (Minutes of the combined meeting of the medical faculties of the Budapest University and the evacuated universities, November 22, 1920)
Szegedi Tudományegyetem Általános Orvostudományi Kar, Dékáni Hivatal Irattára (Szeged University Archives, Papers of the Faculty of Medicine, Archives of the Dean's Office)

Statistics

Magyar Statisztikai Évkönyv (Hungarian Statistical Yearbooks)
Magyar Statisztikai Közlemények (Hungarian Statistical Bulletins)

Hungarian Telegraph Agency (MTI)

MTI hírarchívum 1920-1945 (MTI news archive), https://archiv1920-1944.mti.hu/Pages/PDFSearch.aspx?Pmd=1
MTI Bizalmas Értesítések (Confidential Notifications)
MTI Házi Tájékoztató (Internal Information)
MTI Heti Kiadás (Weekly Release)
MTI Hírkiadás (News Release)
MTI Lapszemle (Press Survey)

Periodicals

A Nép (The People)
Alkotmány (Constitution)
Beszélő (Speaker)
Budapesti Hírlap (Budapest Newspaper)
Budapesti Negyed (Budapest Quarter)
Café Bábel
Délmagyarország (Southern Hungary)
Educatio
Egyenlőség (Equality)
Élet és Irodalom (Life and Literature)
Gyulai Hírlap (Gyula Newspaper)
Hetek (Weeks)
Hungarian Studies
Jewish Telegraphic Agency, Daily News Letter
Korunk (Our Times)
Magyarság (The Hungarian People)
MONE Orvostársadalmi Szemle (National Association of Hungarian Doctors, Medical Society Review)
Mozgó Világ (Moving World)
Múlt és jövő (Past and Future)
Múltunk (Our Past)
Népszabadság (People's Freedom)
Népszava (People's Voice)
Népújság (People's Paper)
Összetartás (Unity)
Pesti Élet (Life in Pest)
Pesti Napló (Pest Diary)
Regio: Kisebbség, politika, társadalom (Regio: Minority, Politics, Society)
Statisztikai Szemle (Statistical Review)
Századok (Centuries)
Társadalomtudomány (Social Science)
Ujság (Newspaper)
Ungarn Jahrbuch
Valóság (Reality)
Világosság (Light)

Secondary Literature

A zsidókérdés Magyarországon: A Huszadik Század körkérdése [The Jewish question in Hungary: A Survey of *Huszadik Század*]. Budapest: Társadalomtudományi Társaság, 1917. http://old.fszek.hu/mtda/_Zsidokerdes.pdf.

Ablonczy, Balázs. *Teleki Pál.* Budapest: Osiris, 2005.

———. "Teleki Pál és a zsidótörvények" [Pál Teleki and the anti-Jewish laws]. *Rubicon* 15, no 2 (2004): 62–64.

———. "Vázlat a magyar konzervativizmusról" [An outline of Hungarian conservatism]. *Confessio: A Magyarországi Református Egyház figyelője* 29, no. 4 (2005): 12–17.

Andorka, Rudolf. "Az egyetemi és főiskolai hallgatók társadalmi összetétele, 1898–1942" [The social composition of university and college students, 1898–1942]. *Statisztikai Szemle,* 57, no. 2 (1979): 176–98.

Aradi, Gábor (2002): "A San Remo-i tárgyalások magyarországi előkészülete" [The Hungarian preparations for the San Remo talks]. *Levéltári Szemle* 52, no. 3 (2002): 24–38.

Asztalos, József. *A magyar főiskolai hallgatók statisztikája az 1930/31 tanévben* [Statistics for Hungarian higher education students for 1930–31]. Budapest: Magyar Királyi Központi Statisztikai Hivatal, 1932.

———. *A magyar főiskolai hallgatók statisztikája az 1932/33-as tanévben* [Statistics for Hungarian higher education students for 1932–33]. Budapest: Magyar Királyi Központi Statisztikai Hivatal, 1934.

Bangha, Béla. *Magyarország újjáépítése és a kereszténység* [Christianity and the reconstruction of Hungary]. Budapest: Szent István Társulat, 1920.

Barta, Róbert. "A numerus clausus és a baloldali magyar zsidó politikai közvélemény" [The numerus clausus and left-wing Hungarian Jewish political opinion]. *Sic Itur ad Astra* 4, nos. 1–2 (1990): 8–32.

Békés, Márton. "Az ellenforradalom két arca Vas megyében" [Two faces of the counter-revolution in Vas County]. *Vasi Szemle* 62, no. 6 (2008): 693–702. http://www.vasiszemle.hu/2008/06/bekes.htm.

Bene, Lajos. *A mérnökök szociális és gazdasági viszonyai Budapesten* [Social and economic conditions of engineers in Budapest]. Statisztikai Közlemények 71/4. Budapest: Székesfőváros Statisztikai Hivatala, 1935.

Bethlen István emlékirata, 1944 [Memoirs of István Bethlen, 1944]. Edited by Ignác Romsics. Budapest: Zrínyi Kiadó, 1988.

Bethlen István gróf beszédei és írásai [Count István Bethlen's speeches and writings]. Budapest: Genius, 1933.

Bethlen, Pál, ed. *A magyar zsidóság almanachja: Numerus clausus* [The almanac of Hungarian Jewry]. Budapest: Franklin, 1925.

Bibó, István. "Zsidókérdés Magyarországon 1944 után." In *Zsidókérdés, asszimiláció, antiszemitizmus,* ed. Hanák Péter, 135–295. Budapest: Gondolat, 1984. First published in 1948.

Bihari, Péter. "Antiszemitizmus az első világháború Magyarországán" [Antisemitism in World War I Hungary]. *Beszélő* 13, no. 2 (2008): 66–83. http://beszelo.c3.hu/cikkek/antiszemitizmusaz-elso-vilaghaboru-magyarorszagan. Accessed September 24, 2009.

———. *Lövészárkok a hátországban: Középosztály, zsidókérdés, antiszemitizmus az első világháború Magyarországán* [Trenches in the Hinterland: Middle class, Jewish question, and anti-Semitism in World War I Hungary]. Budapest: Napvilág Kiadó, 2008.

Bodo, Bela. "Paramilitary Violence in Hungary after the First World War." *East European Quarterly* 38, no. 2 (2004): 129–73.

Bojtár, Endre. "A litvákok" [The Litvaks]. *Kétezer,* no. 12 (2009): 3–16.

Braham, Randolph L. *A népirtás politikája: a Holocaust Magyarországon* [The politics of genocide: the Holocaust in Hungary]. Budapest: Belvárosi Könyvkiadó, 1997.

———. "Gondolatok a magyarországi holokausztról hatvan év után" [Thoughts on the Holocaust in Hungary sixty years later]. In *A holokauszt Magyarországon európai perspektívában,* ed. Judit Molnár, 25–36. Budapest: Balassi Kiadó, 2005.

Cohen, Israel. *Jewish Life in Modern Times.* London: Methuen, 1914. http://www.ibiblio.org/yiddish/Book/Cohen/icohen.html.

Cole, Tim. "Hungary, the Holocaust, and Hungarians: Remembering Whose History?" In *Hungary and the Holocaust: Confrontation with the Past; Symposium* Proceedings, 3–20. Washington, DC: Center for Advanced Holocaust Studies, United States Holocaust Memorial Museum, 2001.

Deák, Francis. *The Hungarian-Rumanian Land Dispute: A Study of Hungarian Property Rights in Transylvania under the Treaty of Trianon.* New York: Columbia University Press, 1928.

Drewek, Peter. "Limits of Educational Internationalism: Foreign Students at German Universities Between 1890 and 1930." *Bulletin of the German Historical Institute,* no. 27 (Fall 2000): 39–64. https://www.ghi-dc.org/fileadmin/publications/Bulletin/bu27.pdf. Accessed December 6, 2022.

Eörsi, István. "Teleki szobra" [Teleki's statue]. *Magyar Hírlap,* February 16, 2004.

Erdész, Ádám. "A kolozsvári felekezetközi magyar egyetem, 1920–1921" [The Interdenominational Hungarian University of Cluj, 1920–1921]. *Történelmi Szemle* 40, nos. 3–4 (1998): 257–76.

Fazekas, Csaba. "Prohászka Ottokár és a numerus clausus" [Ottokár Prohászka and the numerus clausus]. In *Jogfosztás—90 éve: Tanulmányok a numerus claususról* [Deprivation of rights—90 years ago: Studies on the numerus clausus], edited by Molnár Judit, 78–105. Budapest: Nonprofit Társadalomkutató Egyesület, 2011.

———. "Prohászka Ottokár zsidóellenességéről" [About Ottokár Prohászka's anti-Semitism]. *Egyháztörténeti Szemle* 9, no. 4 (2008): 132–55.

Fejtő, Ferenc. *Magyarság, zsidóság* [Hungarians, Jews]. Budapest: Historia Könyvtár, 2000.

Fink, Carole. *Defending the Right of Others: The Great Powers, the Jews, and International Minority Protection, 1878–1938.* Cambridge: Cambridge University Press, 2004.

Gángó, Gábor. "Az 1868. évi nemzetiségi törvény és következményei" [The Nationalities Law of 1868 and its consequences]. *Korunk* 20, no. 5 (2009).

Gárdonyi, Máté. "Az antiszemitizmus funkciója Prohászka Ottokár és Bangha Béla társadalom- és egyházképében" [The function of anti-Semitism in the social and ecclesiastical policies of Ottokár Prohászka and Béla Bangha]. In *A Holokauszt Magyarországon európai perspektívában,* edited by Judit Molnár, 193–204. Budapest: Balassi Kiadó, 2005.

Gergely, Jenő. *A keresztényszocializmus Magyarországon, 1903–1923* [Christian socialism in Hungary, 1903–1923]. Budapest: Akadémiai Kiadó, 1977.

Gerlach, Christian, and Götz Aly. *Das letzte Kapitel: Realpolitik, Ideologie und der Mord an den ungarischen Juden 1944–1945.* Stuttgart: Deutsche Verlags-Anstalt, 2002.

Gerő, András. *A zsidó szempont* [The Jewish point of view]. Budapest: PolgART, 2005.

Götz, Aly. *Hitler's Beneficiaries: How the Nazis Bought the German People.* London: Verso, 2007.

Gratz, Gusztáv. *A forradalmak kora: Magyarország története, 1918–1920* [The age of revolutions, Hungary's history 1918–1920]. Budapest: Magyar Szemle Társaság, 1935.

Gyáni, Gábor and György Kövér. *Magyarország társadalomtörténete a reformkortól a második világháborúig* [Social history of Hungary from the reform period to the Second World War]. Budapest: Osiris, 2006.

Gyurgyák, János. *A zsidókérdés Magyarországon* [The Jewish question in Hungary]. Budapest: Osiris, 2001.

Hajdu, Tibor. "A diplomások létszámnövekedésének szerepe az antiszemitizmus alakulásában" [The role of the growth of the numbers of university graduate in the development of anti-Semitism]. In *A Holokauszt Magyarországon európai perspektívában*, ed. Judit Molnár, 54–66. Budapest: Balassi Kiadó, 2005.

———. "Kun Béla mint zsidó" [Béla Kun as a Jew]. *Élet és Irodalom* 54, no. 27 (July 9, 2010). https://www.es.hu/cikk/2010-07-11/hajdu-tibor/kun-bela-mint-zsido.html. Accessed December 15, 2022.

Haller, István. *Harc a numerus clausus körül* [Fight over the Numerus Clausus]. Budapest: n.d., 1926.

Hilberg, Raul. *Perpetrators, Victims, Bystanders: The Jewish Catastrophe, 1933–1945*. New York: Harper Collins, 1992.

Hoór, Károly. "A numerus clausus." *MONE Orvostársadalmi Szemle* 2, no. 4 (1925): 1–34.

———. *A numerus clausus a szegedi és a pécsi egyetemen* [Numerus clausus at the universities of Szeged and Pécs]. Budapest: Centrum, 1923.

Horner, Miklós. "Az utolsó tíz év magyar külpolitikája" [Hungarian foreign policy in the last decade]. *Korunk* 5, no. 10 (October 1931): 731–35. http://epa.uz.ua/00400/00458/00268/1931_010_5585.html. Accessed December 14, 2022.

Hubai, László. "A szociáldemokrata párt részvétele a választásokon, 1922–1947" [The participation of the Social Democratic Party at elections, 1922–1947]. *Múltunk* 42, no. 2 (1997): 119–45. https://web.archive.org/web/20060906001634/http://www.vokscentrum.hu/tanulm6.htm#. Accessed December 6, 2022.

Huszti, József. *Gróf Klebelsberg Kunó életműve* [The life's work of Count Kunó Klebelsberg]. Budapest: MTA, 1942.

Illyefalvi, I. Lajos. *Az ügyvédek, orvosok és mérnökök szociális és gazdasági viszonyai Budapesten 1940–43* [Social and economic conditions of lawyers, doctors and engineers in Budapest 1940–43]. Statisztikai Közlemények 83/1. Budapest: Székesfőváros Statisztikai Hivatala, 1939.

Jäckel, Eberhard. *Hitler in History*. Hanover, NH: University Press of New England, 1984.

Janik, Gyula. *A magyar főiskolai hallgatók statisztikája az 1931/32. tanévben* [Statistics of Hungarian higher education students in the 1931–32 academic year]. Budapest: Magyar Királyi Központi Statisztikai Hivatal, 1933.

Jarausch, Konrad H. "Removing the Nazi stain? The quarrel of the historians." *German Studies Review* 11, no. 2 (1988): 285–301.

K. Farkas, Claudia. "Az elkülönítés látható falai" [The visible walls of discrimination] *Kutatási füzetek* 11 (2005): 86–96.

———. *Jogok nélkül: A zsidó lét Magyarországon, 1920–1944* [Without rights: Jewish life in Hungary, 1920–1944]. Budapest: Napvilág Kiadó, 2010.

———. "Zsidótörvények—egy egyházi ember szemével" [Jewish laws viewed by a Churchman] In *Fiatal egyháztörténészek írásai*, edited by Csaba Fazekas, 194–23. Miskolc: Miskolci Egyetem BTK Újkori Magyar Történeti Tanszék, 1999. http://mek.oszk.hu/02000/02082/html/index.htm. Accessed August 31, 2012.

Kádár, Gábor and Zoltán Vági. "Rendszerváltások és pogromok" [Transitions and pogroms]. *Népszabadság*, June 20, 2008.

Karabel, Jerome. *The Chosen: The Hidden History of Admission and Exclusion at Harvard, Yale, and Princeton*. New York: Houghton Mifflin, 2005.

Karády, Viktor. "A numerus clausus és a zsidó értelmiség" [The numerus clausus and Jewish intellectuals]. In *Vázsonyi Vilmos emlékezete*, edited by Ferenc Kőszeg, 79–98. Budapest: Beszélő Kiadó, 1995.

———. *Iskolarendszer és felekezeti egyenlőtlenségek Magyarországon (1867–1945)* [School system and denominational inequalities in Hungary, 1867–1945]. Budapest: Replika, 1997.

———. "Zsidóság és modernizáció a történelmi Magyarországon" [Jews and modernization in Hungary]. In *Zsidóság és társadalmi egyenlőtlenségek (1867–1945): Történeti-szociológiai tanulmányok*, 7–40. Budapest: Replika Kör, 2000.

———. *Zsidóság Európában a modern korban* [Jews in Europe in the modern era]. Budapest: Új Mandátum Könyvkiadó, 2000.

Karsai, László. "Could the Jews of Hungary have survived the Holocaust? New Answers to an Old Question." In *Jewish Studies at the Central European University IV, 2003–2005*, edited by András Kovács and Michael L. Miller, 63–78. Budapest: Central European University, Jewish Studies Program, 2006.

———. "Magyarországi zsidótörvények és rendeletek, 1920–1944" [Anti-Jewish laws and decrees in Hungary, 1920–1944] *Századok* 138, no. 6 (2004): 1285–1304.

———. "Még egy szobrot Teleki Pálnak?" [Another statue for Pál Teleki?]. *Magyar Narancs*, April 14, 2004.

Katzburg, Nathaniel. *Hungary and the Jews: Policy and Legislation, 1920–1943*. Jerusalem: Bar-Ilan University Press, 1981.

———. *Zsidópolitika Magyarországon, 1919–1943* [Policy toward the Jews in Hungary, 1919–1943]. Budapest: Bábel Kiadó, 2002.

Kerepeszki, Róbert. "A Turul Szövetség országos és debreceni szervezete (1919–1945)" [The national and Debrecen organizations of the Turul Alliance 1919–1945] PhD dissertation, Debrecen, 2009. https://dea.lib.unideb.hu/server/api/core/bitstreams/c88020b5-5990-4fce-a3a6-a2e7c9ab97ef/content. Accessed December 16, 2022.

———. "A Turul Szövetség" [The Turul Alliance]. In *A magyar jobboldali hagyomány, 1900–1948*, ed. Ignác Romsics, 341–76. Budapest: Osiris, 2009.

Kershaw, Ian. "1933: Continuity or Break in German History." *History Today* 33. no. 1 (1982): 13–18.

Keynes, John Maynard. *The Economic Consequences of the Peace*. New York: Harper and Row, 1971.

Király, Sándor. "Az egyetemi hallgatóság társadalmi arculata Magyarországon a két világháború között" [The social composition of university students during the interwar era]. PhD dissertation, Debrecen, BTK, 2009.

Komoróczy, Géza. *A zsidók története Magyarországon* [The history of the Jews in Hungary]. 2 vols. Bratislava: Kalligram, 2012.

Kornis, Gyula. "Az egyetemi oktatás főbb kérdései" [The main questions of university education]. In *Magyar Felsőoktatás: Az 1936. év december hó 10-től december hó 16-ig tartott országos felsőoktatási kongresszus munkálatai*, vol. 3, ed. Károly Martonffy. 1–16. Budapest: Királyi Magyar Egyetemi Nyomda, 1937.

Kósa, Ferenc. "Diktatúra, vagy demokrácia? Harag és elfogultság nélkül a Horthy-korszakról" [Dictatorship or democracy? Looking at the Horthy period without anger or prejudice]. *Gyulai Hírlap*, October 29, 2009. https://www.gyulaihirlap.hu/936-diktatura-vagy-demokracia. Accessed December 23, 2022.

Kotschnig, Walter Maria. *Unemployment in the Learned Professions: An International Study of Occupational and Educational Planning*. London: Oxford University Press, 1937.

Kovács, Alajos. *A zsidóság térfoglalása Magyarországon* [The Jewish takeover of Hungary]. Budapest: n.d., 1922.

———. *A csonkamagyarországi zsidóság a statisztika tükrében* [The Jewish population of post-Trianon Hungary in the mirror of statistics]. Budapest: Egyesült Nemzeti Keresztény Liga, 1938.

———. "Értelmiségünk nemzeti jellegének biztosítása" [Ensuring the national character of our intelligentsia]. *Társadalomtudomány* 6, no. 4 (1926): 257–69.

Kovács, András, ed. *A modern antiszemitizmus* [Modern anti-Semitism]. Budapest: Új Mandátum Könyvkiadó, 1999.

Kovács, Anikó. "Adalékok a magyar revíziós mozgalom történetéhez" [Additions to the history of the Hungarian revisionist movement]. *Regio: Kisebbség, politika, társadalom* 5, no. 3 (1994): 70–94. http://epa.oszk.hu/00000/00036/00019/pdf/05.pdf. August 31, 2012.

Kovács, M. Mária. "A kisebbségek nemzetközi jogvédelmének csapdája: Vázsonyi Vilmos és a numerus clausus" [The trap of the international protection of minorities: Vilmos Vázsonyi and the numerus clausus]. *Beszélő* 5, no. 14 (1994): 28–30.

———. "A magyar feminizmus korszakfordulója" [The turning-point of Hungarian feminism]. *Café Bábel* 14, nos. 11–12 (1994): 179–84.

———. "A numerus clausus és a zsidótörvények összefüggéséről" [On the connection between the numerus clausus and the anti-Jewish laws]. In *A Holokauszt Magyarországon európai perspektívában*, edited by Judit Molnár, 128–39. Budapest: Balassi Kiadó, 2005.

———. "A numerus clausus és az orvosi antiszemitizmus a húszas években" [The numerus clausus and anti-Semitism in the medical profession in the 1920s]. *Budapesti Negyed* 8, no. 2 (1995): 137–58.

———. "Hungary." In *Women, Gender and Fascism in Europe, 1919–45*, ed. Kevin Passmore, 79–90. Manchester: Manchester University Press, 2003.

———. *Liberal Professions and Illiberal Politics: Hungary from the Habsburgs to the Holocaust.* London: Oxford University Press, 1994.

———. *Liberalizmus, radikalizmus, antiszemitizmus: A magyar orvosi, ügyvédi és mérnöki kar politikája 1867 és 1945 között* [Liberalism, radicalism, anti-Semitism: The politics of Hungarian doctors, lawyers and engineers from 1867 to 1945]. Budapest: Helikon, 2001.

———. "Luttes professionelles et antisemitisme: chronique de la montee du fascisme dans le corps medical hongrois 1920–1944." *Actes de la recherche en sciences sociales* 56 (1985): 31–44.

———. "Numerus clausus Magyarországon, 1919–1945" [Numerus clausus in Hungary, 1919–1945]. In *Jogfosztás—90 éve: Tanulmányok a numerus claususról*, edited by Judit Molnár, 29–59. Budapest: Nonprofit Társadalomkutató Egyesület, 2011.

———. "The Case of the Teleki Statue: New Debates on the History of the Numerus Clausus in Hungary." In *Jewish Studies at the Central European University IV, 2003–2005*, edited by András Kovács and Michael L. Miller, 191–208. Budapest: Central European University, Jewish Studies Program, 2006.

———. "The Problem of Continuity between the 1920 Numerus Clausus and Post-1938 Anti-Jewish Legislation in Hungary." *East European Jewish Affairs* 35, no. 1 (2005): 23–32.

Ladányi, Andor. *Az egyetemi ifjúság az ellenforradalom első éveiben* [University youth in the first years of the counter-revolution]. Budapest: Akadémiai Kiadó, 1979.

———. "A kisebbséggé nyilvánítás kérdéséhez: A történelmi előzmények" [A contribution to the question of registering as a minority: Historical antecedents]. *Múlt és Jövő* 17, no. 1 (2006): 99–106.

———. "A numerus clausus-törvény 1928. évi módosításáról" [On the amendment to the numerus clausus in 1928]. *Századok* 128, no. 6 (1994): 1117–48.

———. "A numerus clausustól a numerus nullusig" [From numerus clausus to numerus nullus]. *Múlt és Jövő* 16, no. 1 (2005): 56–74.

———. "Az első zsidótörvény megszületése" [The birth of the first anti-Jewish law] *Múlt és Jövő* 21, no. 2 (2010): 102–21.

———. "Két évforduló: A nők felsőfokú tanulmányainak száz éve" [Two anniversaries: one hundred years of women in higher education] *Educatio* 5, no. 6 (1996): 375–89.

Levene, Mark. *War, Jews and the New Europe: The Diplomacy of Lucien Wolf, 1914–19*. London: Oxford University Press, 1992.

Maier, Charles. *The Unmasterable Past: History, Holocaust and German National Identity*. Cambridge, MA, Harvard University Press, 1988.

Marton, Kati. *Kilenc magyar, aki világgá ment és megváltoztatta a világot* [Nine Hungarians who went out into the world and changed it]. Budapest: Corvina, 2008.

Méhely, Lajos. *A numerus clausus mérlege* [The balance of numerus clausus]. Budapest: Held, 1932.

Miller, Michael L. "'A Numerus Clausus száműzöttjei' a berlini felsőoktatási intézetekben 1920 és 1933 között" ["Exiles of the Numerus Clausus" in the higher education institutions of Berlin between 1920 and 1933]. *Múlt és Jövő* 17, no. 4 (2006): 84–91.

Mink, András. *Teleki jövője* [The future of Teleki]. *Beszélő* 9, no. 4 (2004). http://beszelo.c3.hu/cikkek/teleki-jovoje.

Monori, Áron. "A numerus clausus és a magyar katolikus sajtó 1919–1920" [The numerus clausus and the Hungarian Catholic press 1919–1920]. *Médiakutató*, no. 2 (Summer 2003): 48–52.

Myers, Denys Peter. *A Handbook of the League of Nations: A Comprehensive Account of Its Structure, Operation and Activities*. Boston: World Peace Foundation, 1935.

N. Szegvári, Katalin. *Numerus clausus rendelkezések az ellenforradalmi Magyarországon* [Numerus clausus provisions in counter-revolutionary Hungary]. Budapest: Akadémiai Kiadó, 1988.

Nagy, Péter Tibor. "A numerus clausus—hetvenöt év után" [The numerus clausus—after seventy-five years]. *Világosság* 36, no. 2 (1995): 72–80.

———. "Antiszemitizmus és felsőoktatáspolitika—a numerus clausus törvény jelentősége" [Anti-Semitism and higher education policy—the significance of the numerus clausus law]. *Neveléstörténeti Füzetek* 14 (1996): 81–94.

———. "Az állami befolyás növekedése a magyarországi oktatásban, 1867–1945" [The growth of state influence in Hungarian education, 1867–1945]. *Iskolakultúra* 15, nos. 6–7 (2005): 3–229.

———. "Keresztény konzervatív oktatáspolitikába rejtett szélsőjobboldali fordulat" [A far-right turn hidden in a Christian conservative education policy]. 2004. https://docplayer.hu/25464310-Kereszteny-konzervativ-oktataspolitikaba-rejtett-szelsojobboldali-fordulat.html.

Németh, András and Béla Pukánszky. *Neveléstörténet: Pedagógia, nevelés/Nevelés- és iskolatörténet* [Education history: Pedagogy, education/Education and school history]. Budapest: Nemzeti Tankönyvkiadó, 1996. https://mek.oszk.hu/01800/01893/html/.

Nyerges, András. "Kis Prohászka-breviárium—Szemelvények a püspök megnyilatkozásaiból" [A small Prohászka-breviary—Excerpts from the bishop's statements]. *Mozgó Világ* 35, no. 2 (2009): 49–54.

O'Boyle, Leonore. "The Problem of an Excess of Educated Men in Western Europe, 1800–1850." *Journal of Modern History* 42, no. 4 (1970): 471–95.

Oren, Dan A. *Joining the Club: A History of Jews and Yale*. New Haven: Yale University Press, 2001.

Pálfy, Zoltán. "Nemzetállam és felsőoktatási piac" [Nation state and the higher education market]. *Erdélyi Társadalom* 2, no. 2 (2004): 151–80. https://erdelyitarsadalom.ro/files/et04/et-bbu-04-07.pdf.

Paxton, Robert. *The Anatomy of Fascism*. London: Penguin, 2005.

Pelle, János. "Egyetemi antiszemitizmus a két világháború között" [Anti-Semitism at the universities between the wars]. *Hetek.hu*, December 19, 1998, https://www.hetek.hu/velemeny/199812/egyetemi_antiszemitizmus_a_ket_vilaghaboru_kozott. Accessed April 8, 2010.

Pók, Attila. "Bűnbakkeresés és holokauszt a rendszerváltás utáni Magyarországon" [Search for scapegoats and the Holocaust in Hungary after the democratic transition]. In *A Holokauszt Magyarországon európai perspektívában*, edited by Judit Molnár, 594–606. Budapest: Balassi Kiadó, 2005.

Prohászka, Ottokár. "A magyar keresztény irányzat a kereskedelemben" [The Christian Hungarian way in business]. In *Iránytű*, 297. First published in *Fejérmegyei Napló*, February, 21, 1922.

———. "Az ifjú nemzedékhez" [To the younger generation]. In *Iránytű*, 313–18. First published in *Cél*, November 1923.

———. "Elég volt-e?" [Have we had enough?]. In *Iránytű*, 189–90. First published in *Alkotmány*, September 11, 1918.

———. *Iránytű* [Compass]. Edited by Antal Schütz. Prohászka Ottokár összegyűjtött munkái [The collected works of Ottokár Prohászka], vol. 22. Budapest: Szent István Társulat, 1929. http://gondola.hu/media/prohaszka/Prohaszka22.pdf. Accessed December 12, 2022.

———. *The Jewish Question in Hungary*. The Hague, 1920.

———. "Pro Juventute catholica." In *Iránytű*, 184–86. First published in *Alkotmány*, May 26, 1918.

Romsics, Ignác, ed. *A magyar jobboldali hagyomány, 1900–1948* [The Hungarian right-wing tradition, 1900–1948]. Budapest: Osiris, 2009.

———. *Bethlen István: Politikai életrajz* [István Bethlen: Political biography]. Budapest: Magyarságkutató Intézet, 1991.

Romsics, Ignác. *Magyarország története a XX. században* [A history of Hungary in the twentieth century]. Budapest: Osiris, 1999. (3rd ed. 2005.)

———. "Telekiről—szakszerűen" [About Teleki—in a professional way]. *Élet és Irodalom* 49, no. 18 (2005).

———. "Tudomásul kell venni, de nem nyaldosni a sebeket—Romsics Ignáccal beszélget Várnai Pál" [We must acknowledge, but not lick the wounds—Pál Várnai talks to Ignác Romsics]. *Szombat*, September 22, 2008.

Rürup, Reinhard. "Die 'Judenfrage' der bürgerlichen Gesellschaft und die Entstehung des modernen Antisemitismus." In *Emanzipation und Antisemitismus: Studien zur "Judenfrage" der bürgerlichen Gesellschaft*, 74–94. Göttingen: Vandenhoeck und Ruprecht, 1975.

———. "Jewish Social History in the Nineteenth and Early Twentieth Centuries." UCLA Conference Papers. UCLA Center for European and Eurasian Studies, 2, 2004. https://escholarship.org/uc/item/7jn764jt.

Spira, Thomas. "Hungary's Numerus Clausus, the Jewish Minority and the League of Nations." *Ungarn Jahrbuch* 4 (1972): 115–28. http://epa.oszk.hu/01500/01536/00004/pdf/UJ_1972_115-128.pdf. Accessed December 14, 2022.

Synnot, Marcia Graham. "Anti-Semitism and American Universities: Did Quotas Follow the Jews?" In *Anti-Semitism in American History*, edited by David A. Gerber, 233–74. Urbana, IL: University of Illinois Press, 1986.

Szabó, Miklós. "A modernizáció kiválasztott népe" [The chosen people of modernization]. *Mozgó Világ* 26, no. 9 (2000): 106–9. https://epa.oszk.hu/01300/01326/00009/szep8.htm. Accessed August, 31, 2012.

———. *Az újkonzervativizmus és a jobboldali radikalizmus története 1867–1918* [The history of neoconservatism and right-wing radicalism, 1867–1918]. Budapest: Új Mandátum Könyvkiadó, 2003.

———. *Politikai kultúra Magyarországon 1896–1986* [Political culture in Hungary, 1896–1986]. Budapest: ELTE-MKKE, Medvetánc Könyvek, 1989.

Szabolcsi, Lajos. *Két emberöltő: Az Egyenlőség évtizedei* (1881–1931) [Two generations: The decades of Equality, 1881–1931]. Budapest: MTA, 1993.

Székács-Schönberger, István. *Egy zsidó polgár gyermekkora* [A bourgeois-Jewish childhood]. Budapest: Múlt és Jövő Könyvkiadó, 2007.

Szinai, Miklós and László Szűcs, eds. *Bethlen István titkos iratai* [The secret papers of István Bethlen]. Budapest: Kossuth Könyvkiadó, 1972.

———, eds. *Horthy Miklós titkos iratai* [The secret documents of Miklós Horthy]. Budapest: Kossuth Könyvkiadó, 1963.

Teleki, Pál. *Válogatott politikai írások és beszédek* [Selected political writings and speeches]. Edited by Balázs Ablonczy. Budapest: Osiris, 2000.

Udvarvölgyi, Zsolt. "Fejezetek a magyar szélsőjobboldal korai történetéből: fasiszták, kékingesek és a Meskó-párt" [Chapters from the early history of the Hungarian extreme right: fascists, blue shirts, and the Meskó party]. 2004. https://mek.oszk.hu/02100/02105/02105.pdf.

Újszászi, Ilona. "Időutazás a Délmagyarral: Perpatvar és numerus clausus" [Time Travel with the Délmagyar: fracas and numerus clausus]. *Délmagyar.hu*, October 17, 2008. https://www.delmagyar.hu/szeged-es-kornyeke/2008/10/idoutazas-a-delmagyarral-perpatvar-es-numerus-clausus.

Ujváry, Gábor. "Egyetemi ifjúság a 'neobarokk társadalomban': A bajtársi szövetségekről" [University Youth in the "neobaroque society": On the brotherhood associations]. *Valóság* 34, no. 5 (1991): 64–73.

Ungváry, Krisztián. "'Árjásítás' és 'modernizáció': Adalékok Imrédy Béla miniszterelnöki működéséhez és a zsidótörvények geneziséhez" ["Aryanization" and "modernization": Additions to Béla Imrédy's work as prime minister and the genesis of the Jewish laws]. *Századvég* 7, no. 26 (2002): 3–37.

———. "Értelmiség és antiszemita közbeszéd" [The intelligentsia and anti-Semitic public discourse]. *Beszélő* 6, no. 6 (2001): 74–92. http://beszelo.c3.hu/cikkek/ertelmiseg-es-antiszemita-kozbeszed. Accessed December 26, 2022.

———. "'Sacco di Budapest,' 1919: Gheorghe Mardarescu tábornok válasza Harry Hill Bandholtz vezérőrnagy nem diplomatikus naplójára" ["Sacco di Budapest," 1919: General Gheorghe Mardarescu's reply to Major General Harry Hill Bandholtz's non-diplomatic diary]. *Budapesti Negyed* 8, nos. 3–4 (29–30, 2000): 173–202. https://epa.oszk.hu/00000/00003/00023/ungvary.html. Accessed December 26, 2022.

———. "Szobrot Teleki Pálnak?" [A statue for Pál Teleki?]. *Népszabadság*, February 17, 2004.

Vázsonyi, Vilmos. *Vázsonyi Vilmos beszédei és írásai* [The speeches and writings of Vilmos Vázsonyi]. 2 vols. Budapest: Országos Vázsonyi-Emlékbizottság, 1927.

Vonyó, József. "Gömbös fajvédő csoportja és a numerus clausus" [Gömbös's race defense group and the numerus clausus]. In *Jogfosztás—90 éve: Tanulmányok a numerus claususról*, edited by Molnár Judit, 106–20. Budapest: Nonprofit Társadalomkutató Egyesület, 2011.

———. *Gömbös Gyula és a jobboldali radikalizmus* [Gyula Gömbös and right-wing radicalism]. Pécs, Pro Pannónia, 2001.

Watson, Cameron J. "Ethnic Conflict and the League of Nations: the Case of Transylvania, 1918–1940." *Hungarian Studies* 9, nos. 1–2 (1994): 173–80. http://epa.oszk.hu/01400/01462/00015/pdf/173-180.pdf. Accessed December 15, 2022.

Zehery, Lajos, and Térfy Béla. *A zsidók közéleti és gazdasági térfoglalásának korlátozásáról szóló 1939: IV. t.c. és annak végrehajtásáról szóló rendeletek* [Law IV of 1939 regarding the restriction of the extent of the presence of Jews in economic and public life and its implementation decrees]. Budapest: Grill, 1939.

Zeidler, Miklós. "A Nemzetek Szövetsége és a magyar kisebbségi petíciók" [The League of Nations and Hungarian minority petitions]. In *Etnopolitika: A közösségi, magán- és nemzetközi érdekek viszonyrendszere Közép-Európában* [Ethnopolitics: The relationship between community, private, and international interests in Central Europe], edited by Nándor Bárdi and Csilla Fedinec, 59–83. Budapest: Teleki László Alapítvány, 2003.

Zinner, Tibor. *Az ébredők fénykora, 1919–1933* [The heyday of the Awakening Hungarians, 1919–1933]. Budapest: Akadémiai Kiadó, 1989.

Index

For Product Safety Concerns and Information please contact our EU representative GPSR@taylorandfrancis.com Taylor & Francis Verlag GmbH, Kaufingerstraße 24, 80331 München, Germany

Batch number: 10703954

Printed by Printforce, the Netherlands